The Communicator's Commentary

1, 2 Corinthians

THE COMMUNICATOR'S COMMENTARY SERIES

Lloyd J. Ogilvie

General Editor

The Communicator's Commentary

1, 2 Corinthians

Kenneth L. Chafin

WORD BOOKS, PUBLISHER • WACO, TEXAS

Library of Congress Cataloging in Publication Data
Main entry under title:

The Communicator's commentary.

  Includes bibliographical references.
  Contents: v. 7. 1, 2 Corinthians/Kenneth L. Chafin
  1.   Bible, N.T.—Commentaries—Collected works.
I. Ogilvie, Lloyd John.   II.   Kenneth L. Chafin
BS2341.2.C65   225.7'7   81–71764
ISBN 0–8499–0347–5 (v. 7) (regular edition) AACR2
ISBN 0–8499–3807–4 (v. 7) (deluxe edition)

Printed in the United States of America

5 6 7 8 9 9 AGF 9 8

This commentary is lovingly dedicated to all
the members past and present of the
South Main Baptist Church of
Houston, Texas
with appreciation for the way they have
modeled what it means to be the
People of God
in an increasingly secular society

Contents

Editor's Preface

God has called all of His people to be communicators. Everyone who is in Christ is called into ministry. As ministers of "the manifold grace of God," all of us—clergy and laity—are commissioned with the challenge to communicate our faith to individuals and groups, classes and congregations.

The Bible, God's Word, is the objective basis of the truth of His love and power that we seek to communicate. In response to the urgent, expressed needs of pastors, teachers, Bible study leaders, church school teachers, small group enablers, and individual Christians, the Communicator's Commentary is offered as a penetrating search of the Scriptures of the New Testament to enable vital personal and practical communication of the abundant life.

Many current commentaries and Bible study guides provide only some aspects of a communicator's needs. Some offer in-depth scholarship but no application to daily life. Others are so popular in approach that biblical roots are left unexplained. Few offer impelling illustrations that open windows for the reader to see the exciting application for today's struggles. And most of all, seldom have the expositors given the valuable outlines of passages so needed to help the preacher or teacher in his or her busy life to prepare for communicating the Word to congregations or classes.

This Communicator's Commentary series brings all of these elements together. The authors are scholar-preachers and teachers outstanding in their ability to make the Scriptures come alive for individuals and groups. They are noted for bringing together excellence in biblical scholarship, knowledge of the original Greek and Hebrew, sensitivity to people's needs, vivid illustrative material from biblical, classical, and contemporary sources, and lucid communication by the use of clear outlines of thought. Each has been selected to contribute to this series because of his Spirit-empowered ability to help people live in the skins of biblical characters and provide a "you-are-there" intensity to the drama of events of the Bible which have so much to say about our relationships and responsibilities today.

The design for the Communicator's Commentary gives the reader an overall outline of each book of the New Testament. Following the introduction, which reveals the author's approach and salient background on the book, each chapter of the commentary provides the Scripture to be exposited. The New King James Bible has been chosen for the Communicator's Commentary because it combines with integrity the beauty of language, underlying Greek textual basis, and thought-flow of the 1611 King James Version, while replacing obsolete verb forms and other archaisms with their everyday contemporary counterparts for greater readability. Reverence for God is preserved in the capitalization of all pronouns referring to the Father, Son, or Holy Spirit. Readers who are more comfortable with another translation can readily find the parallel passage by means of the chapter and verse reference at the end of each passage being exposited. The paragraphs of exposition combine fresh insights to the Scripture, application, rich illustrative material, and innovative ways of utilizing the vibrant truth for his or her own life and for the challenge of communicating it with vigor and vitality.

It has been gratifying to me as Editor of this series to receive enthusiastic progress reports from each contributor. As they worked, all were gripped with new truths from the Scripture—God-given insights into passages, previously not written in the literature of biblical explanation. A prime objective of this series is for each user to find the same awareness: that God speaks with newness through the Scriptures when we approach them with a ready mind and a willingness to communicate what He has given; that God delights to give communicators of His Word "I-never-saw-that-in-that-verse-before" intellectual insights so that our listeners and readers can have "I-never-realized-all-that-was-in-that-verse" spiritual experiences.

The thrust of the commentary series unequivocally affirms that God speaks through the Scriptures today to engender faith, enable adventuresome living of the abundant life, and establish the basis of obedient discipleship. The Bible, the unique Word of God, is unlimited in its resource for Christians in communicating our hope to others.

It is our weapon in the battle for truth, the guide for ministry, and the irresistible force for introducing others to God. In the New Testament we meet the divine Lord and Savior whom we seek to communicate to others. What He said and did as God with us has been faithfully recorded under the inspiration of the Spirit of God. The cosmic implications of the Gospels are lived out in Acts and spelled out in the Epistles. They have stood the test of time because the eternal Communicator, God Himself, communicates through them to those who would be communicators of grace. His essential nature is exposed, the plan of salvation is explained, and the Gospel for all of life, now and for eternity, is proclaimed.

A biblically rooted communication of the Gospel holds in unity and oneness what divergent movements have wrought asunder. This commentary series courageously presents personal faith, caring for individuals, and social responsibility as essential, inseparable dimensions of biblical Christianity. It seeks to present the quadrilateral Gospel in its fullness which calls us to unreserved commitment to Christ, unrestricted self-esteem in His grace, unqualified love for others in personal evangelism, and undying efforts to work for justice and righteousness in a sick and suffering world.

A growing renaissance in the church today is being led by clergy and laity who are biblically rooted, Christ-centered, and Holy Spirit-empowered. They have dared to listen to people's most urgent questions and deepest needs and then to God as He speaks through the Bible. Biblical preaching is the secret of growing churches. Bible study classes and small groups are equipping the laity for ministry in the world. Dynamic Christians are finding that daily study of God's Word allows the Spirit to do in them what He wishes to communicate through them to others. These days are the most exciting time since Pentecost. The Communicator's Commentary is offered to be a primary resource of new life for this renaissance.

A primary aim of the Communicator's Commentary series is to exemplify how to preach and teach straight through a particular book of the Bible, to show how this can be done in a way that is faithful to the flow of thought of the biblical text and at the same time is relevant to today's problems. Listening to the expressed needs of our people will lead us to a particular book. Then verse-by-verse, paragraph-by-paragraph exposition provides us an excellent way to deal with contemporary needs, questions, and struggles with biblical authority. At the same time, such continuity helps us move on from favorite themes into passages we might be tempted to bypass. Challenging truth, neglected doctrine, and unpopular issues can be confronted in a natural way as we work through the progression of the exposition. Preachers and teachers who do this faithfully contribute immeasurably to the consistent biblical education, theological depth, and practical ethical training in discipleship of their listeners.

In our efforts to speak to the struggles of people today, one of the most helpful and urgently needed sections of Scripture is 1 and 2 Corinthians. The same problems, pressures, and perversities faced by the believers in the Corinthian church trouble us today. Our urgent questions and distressing difficulties are focused and dealt with in an incisive way. An exposition of the Corinthian letters provides us an excellent way to communicate the triumphant Christ for troubled times and to help people be faithful and obedient in the trials and temptations of living in a society not unlike ancient Corinth. And the great advantage is that Paul's teaching to the Corinthians comes burning and flaming out of the depth of his love for them. The revelation of truth is relationally communicated in response to their real needs.

Our listeners deserve nothing less. They long for an assurance of their eternal status as forgiven sinners. They need to understand the cross and the atonement. There is a desire for clear explanation of the crucial doctrine of righteousness, redemption, and sanctification— the central themes of these letters. At the same time, Christians today wrestle with their own frustrations and urgently want to discover the power of the Holy Spirit, the secret of dynamic love, the creative use of the gifts of the Spirit as equipment for ministry, and the freedom and joy of living at full potential. Questions persist. Can human nature be changed? Can we find unity in Christ in the midst of the power struggles in the church today? Can the church run with the Master on a two-legged gospel of personal faith and social responsibility? What does the gospel have to say about the moral illness of our time? And most of all—how can we live out our faith in a way that will make a difference in the lives of people around us who desperately need Christ?

All these questions, concerns, problems and aching human needs can be responded to with an inspired, imaginative and contemporary expositional preaching and teaching of the Corinthian letters. It's a demanding and rewarding challenge. To do that effectively we need a commentary which plumbs the depths of Paul's mind in the epistles, applies the truth incisively to our times, and gives us examples of how we can approach our own exposition with impelling freshness.

That's why I am so excited by this volume written by Dr. Kenneth Chafin, one of America's most gifted biblical expositors. A scholar-preacher who is fully immersed in authentic twentieth-century discipleship, he lives on the cutting edge of creative church renewal. His broad and extensive experience as a man in Christ, pastor, expositor, evangelist, professor, and distinguished church statesman has enabled him to write what, in my opinion, is a superb contemporary exposition of the Corinthian epistles—a blend of profound scholarship, helpful applications, and unforgettable illustrations. Here is a master expositor at his finest as he explains the text and spells out its meaning for Christians and the church today. This exposition is the fruit of years of working with people, leading pivotal churches, shaping contemporary theological thought and pioneering in innovative ways of bringing revival and renewal to the American church. And the secret of his effectiveness is unswerving commitment to Christ, his ability to relate Scripture to the deepest needs of people today and his dedication to the evangelistic mission of the church.

Dr. Chafin's outstanding ministry has impacted not only theological education, his Southern Baptist denomination, and the local churches he has served, but also the church at large. For some years he was professor of evangelism at the Southern Baptist Theological Seminary in Louisville, Kentucky. His writing and teaching at that time was strategic in the development of contemporary evangelism in America. A part of his concern for equipping pastors was expressed in his dynamic leadership of the Schools of Evangelism held in conjunction with the Billy Graham Crusades throughout the nation and the world. Pastors and church leaders from a broad spectrum of denominational backgrounds well remember the inspiration and vision of his development of these crucial events.

Following his teaching position at Southern Baptist Theological Seminary, Dr. Chafin returned to the parish to serve as pastor of the 7,000-member South Main Baptist Church in Houston, Texas. For twelve years his powerful expository sermons attracted large congregations. The example of scholarship, application, and vivid illustration you will enjoy in this commentary was the distinguishing quality of those years of preaching. But as with any great preaching ministry, the program of the local church must be congruent with the excellence of the pulpit. Under his leadership, South Main Church was a laboratory of new life in which people met Christ and were equipped for their ministry of evangelism, discipleship and service in the world.

Recently, Dr. Chafin returned to the Southern Baptist Theological Seminary to assume the Carl Bates chair of preaching. His commitment to preaching as a key element in the renewal of the church and the evangelization of society is now expressed in the training of pastors, utilizing his rich experience as a communicator. In addition to his teaching responsibilities, he continues to be a sought-after preacher for strategic speaking engagements.

When I drew up a list of the scholar-preachers to be enlisted to be contributors to this Communicator's Commentary series, I knew that 1 and 2 Corinthians would require the skills of someone who not only could do a superb job of expositing the text but also was able to speak to the issues of contemporary discipleship and church renewal. I was gratified when my friend Ken Chafin agreed to assume the challenge. The result, a stirring and moving exposition brimming over with insight and wisdom, awaits your own adventure of speaking to the problems and potentials of Christians today as you preach and teach through 1 and 2 Corinthians.

LLOYD OGILVIE

Introduction to 1 Corinthians

A study of Corinthians can be one of the most relevant studies the church today could make, for several reasons. *First, it was written to a church in an urban setting.* It is easy to see from the content of the book that it could have been written to a young, small, struggling congregation in New York, Los Angeles, Tokyo, Paris, Berlin, or Rio de Janeiro.

Twenty years ago as a young seminary evangelism professor, I became acutely aware of the need for a strategy for building churches and living the Christian life in an urban setting. My roots, like those of my denomination, were deeply embedded in rural America.

I was born in a farmhouse out from town in one of those typical agricultural counties of northeast Oklahoma. In this setting, the school and the church were the two key institutions, and the teacher and the preacher were the two most important persons in the community. A Christian ethic was assumed and reinforced to some degree by the whole community. While there were the usual exceptions in terms of behavior, these were always considered wrong and never enjoyed the approval of the community. This is the setting in which most of the denominations in our country developed.

As the people reared in these types of communities moved into the cities of America, they had a difficult time adjusting. The support system that the community had provided in the country wasn't there. Many people came to the conclusion that the cities were evil. They felt that while God had made the country, the city was probably bad because it was man's making.

But when we look at the New Testament we discover that the great cities of the world were the very places to which the early church carried the gospel. This is where people were converted and where churches were established. While the churches in the United States began in the country, the great churches of the first century were located in the great urban communities of the Roman Empire.

Second, the questions that were being asked and the problems that were being faced by the Corinthian church are the same as those for the churches today. On the surface a person might wrongly conclude that Paul's letters deal with a lot of "antique issues." But when we look at the underlying ethical and theological issues, they seem much more contemporary. The first problem that Paul addressed was division in the church, and one of the most persistent problems of the modern church is its difficulty in establishing real community. We act as though the sexual revolution our society is going through is an invention of the twentieth century, but one of the questions dealt with in Corinthians is how to be faithful to God in a totally permissive society.

While we don't have to deal with the problem of animals sacrificed to idols, we continue to have the problem of how involved we can be in a secular society without compromising ourselves or the gospel we preach. From my perspective, this is a critical question because I see many Christians and churches adopting secular definitions of success for God's work. While they wouldn't *think* of eating meat offered to idols, they often pattern their lives more after the chief executive officer of a corporation than after the simple Galilean. Another problem Christians have today is in finding their own uniqueness and worth in the church. No amount of bootstrap "help yourself" psychology could possibly help them as much as really understanding Paul's discussion of the spiritual gifts with which God has endowed each believer.

Third, Paul's style for dealing with the questions and problems makes Corinthians helpful for today. While he started with some everyday concern like, "What should you do if your spouse isn't a Christian?" he would usually probe to see if there were some theological understanding that could be reached. Only then would he apply the principle to the experience of the Christian. This approach may seem slow and often circuitous, but it gives us a better basis for decisions. While the problems we face are not identical to those faced in Corinth, often the underlying principle will serve us well for problems that we are facing. This situation, which permeates the Corinthian epistles, creates a challenge to the serious Bible student. That which is local and temporary in the situation has to be set aside, and that which is universal and permanent has to be applied to our lives. What makes this difficult is that Paul intended for everything he said to apply to the Corinthians. He did not label for us that which was related only to local culture and circumstance.

Unlike the book of Ephesians, which was intended to be distributed to all the churches, this letter was addressed to one church. This wonderful particularity is its great strength, but it is also what challenges the interpreter. A careless and lazy student can create confusion and disorder in the church by trying to apply to all times and all places a truth that may have been much more limited in its application. In my childhood I heard well-meaning preachers try to use passages from this letter to prove it was a sin for a woman to cut her hair. This may be laughable today, but as I prepare the material for this commentary I discover that many people are still trying to define relationships within the family with ideas that are much more a part of first-century culture than they are a revelation of God's perfect will.

For more than two decades I have gone again and again to a study of 1 Corinthians. It has become one of the most probing and practical books in the Bible for me as a pastor and as a Christian trying to serve God in an increasingly secular world.

SOME HELPFUL BACKGROUND TO 1 CORINTHIANS

The Recipients of the Letter

1 Corinthians was written to the church in Corinth which the apostle Paul had founded. The story of the beginnings of this church is recorded in Acts 18:1–7. Paul had come alone to Corinth after difficult experiences in Thessalonica and Berea (Acts 17:1–15) and a less than satisfactory reception in Athens (Acts 17:16–34). He supported himself by his profession of making tents, along with a Jewish couple, Aquilla and Priscilla, who had fled Rome because of Emperor Claudius' edict requiring all Jews to leave. Paul's prestige as a rabbi made it easy for him to be a participant in the activities of the synagogue, and each Sabbath he used this contact to persuade both Jews and Greeks that Jesus was the Messiah.

As people began to be converted, opposition arose within the Jewish community. So Paul turned to the Gentiles with the gospel. He stayed in Corinth almost two years, and a strong church was founded of both Jews and Gentiles who were converted. 1 Corinthians is full of references to this relationship—Paul's manner of presenting the gospel (2:1–3), Paul's role in the beginning (3:1–10), and Paul's reminder of the gospel which he had preached to them (15:1–3).

The church was a relatively young church with none who had been a Christian for more than six years. While some of the members did have the moral and ethical teachings of a Jewish background, most of the members had come out of paganism and were "starting from scratch." People whose churches work with internationals are beginning to discover what this is like. During this year I've seen people receive Christ whose only previous religious contact was with a non-Christian religion. In addition to having no vocabulary for communication, they often have no moral or ethical basis for thinking about the Christian life. Most of the members of this church in Corinth came from the lower classes in the town, and Paul reflects on this fact in his letter (1:26).

The church was located in a city where being a Christian was not an easy matter and where just knowing what a Christian ought to be like was difficult. Nothing in Paul's letter would indicate that there was any persecution of the church in Corinth. But while there were no efforts to restrict their freedom of worship, the very nature of the culture was a constant threat to the individual Christians and to the church's life.

Corinth was located forty miles west of Athens on the narrow neck of land between the Corinthian Gulf and Saronic Gulf. This assured its commercial success. Its two seaports made it wealthy since it controlled all the east-west commerce, and its land-bridge assured its control of all the north-south travel and business. It was the least Greek of the Greek cities and the least Roman city in the Roman Empire because of the great racial diversity of its population. There were people from all the known world. It had been destroyed and rebuilt, so it was a newer city with less restraining traditions.

The city had developed an unapologetic love of things and a love of pleasure. It was full of people who wanted to make money and have fun. Though the city in which I most recently pastored has many churches and synagogues, it is still very much like Corinth in its values and its lifestyle. While lip service is given to the "faith of our fathers," most people worship at the twin shrines of materialism and hedonism—the love of things and love of pleasure. On the hill overlooking Corinth was the temple to the goddess Aphrodite. Its male and female prostitutes made sexual intercourse a part of the religion, and they participated in the night life of the city when they were not at the temple. If the "church planning committee" of any church or denomination had been given an accurate description of Corinth, they would probably have listed it as the most unlikely place to start a church. But it was to people wanting to serve Christ in such a town that Paul wrote 1 Corinthians.

Paul continued to keep in touch with the believers at Corinth. He wrote to them after he left (5:9), and they sent him a letter asking specific questions concerning conduct and morality (7:1). Paul also received additional information from the three who had probably delivered the letter (16:17). In addition to this, he received other news of the church from members of the household of Chloe (1:11). He most likely had a report from Apollos, who worked with the church at Corinth, since at the time of the writing of 1 Corinthians he was in Ephesus with Paul (16:12). Unlike the letter to the church at Rome, which was made up mostly of strangers, Paul's relationship to those in Corinth was intimate, loving, and full of mutual reward.

The Occasion of the Letter

While the letter was precipitated by two specific occurrences, it was Paul's great love for the church at Corinth and his concern for the witness of the church that caused him to write. The need for the letter was created by a report he had heard and a letter he had received. Paul identified the source of his report as those of Chloe's household (1:11). This news was that some of the members of the church were quite reluctant to break with their background, causing some disturbing irregularities in the conduct of the believers. The problems included factions within the church, a case of incest, members suing each other, problems with sexual impurity, and the spread of a quarrelsome spirit. Paul felt that there needed to be reformation of conduct and this was one purpose of the letter.

But 1 Corinthians was also written to answer specific questions that the church wanted answered about the Christian life and church life. These included questions about marriage and divorce (ch. 7), the eating of food that had been offered to idols (ch. 8), the value of different spiritual gifts (ch. 12–14) and belief in the resurrection of the body (ch. 15).

Paul's quick response to the report and letter probably resulted from his awareness of what these pressures of a pagan society could do to persons and to churches.

The Date of the Letter

1 Corinthians was written between A.D. 54 and 56 by Paul from Ephesus (16:8). We know that it was written from Ephesus because Paul himself tells us in the letter that he was staying there. From what he said in the final chapter, it was more than just a passing visit because he spoke of the opportunities that were his (16:9).

Paul's arrival in Corinth has been set with some exactness at about A.D. 50. The edict of expulsion that Claudius had passed against the Jews was in A.D. 49. When the Jewish leaders took Paul to court it was before Gallio, who, separate documents show, was proconsul in Corinth beginning in the summer of A.D. 51. When he left Corinth, Paul went first to Antioch and then eventually to Ephesus, where he stayed for about three years. If he wrote the letter close to the end of his stay in Ephesus it would have been written between A.D. 54 and 56.

The question of the date and composition of 2 Corinthians is much more complicated. That, plus the whole question of the "lost letters" to Corinth, will be dealt with in the introduction to 2 Corinthians.

An Outline of 1 Corinthians

CHAPTER ONE

Getting Along with Others

1 Corinthians 1:1–31

The organizing theme of 1 Corinthians is how to live as a Christian in an increasingly secular world. But the letter is not an essay on the subject written for all Christians with a copy just happening to go to the church at Corinth. It was written especially for them, and the particular circumstances of their lives provided the agenda for the correspondence. It was not one of those "one size fits all" messages, but one which had been "tailor-made" just for them.

We, too, live in an increasingly secular world, a world in which persons try to define life totally apart from God. While the church has opportunities it has never had before, there are also pressures and problems and questions it has not experienced in its past. For example, the fact that advanced technology is converting many industries into factories full of robots raises questions about work, leisure, and meaning for life. The proliferation of nuclear weapons creates a morbid fear of the destruction of the human race which undermines the moral and ethical foundations of our society. And relationships are being redefined in such a way that the idea of marriage and the commitment it requires is being questioned.

All of this points to the truth of our need for a word from God that will give us a model for living the Christian life in a pagan world. And while the agenda for 1 Corinthians was created by the problems which the church of Corinth was having and the questions it was raising, there are enough similarities between their circumstances and ours to make this study of value to us. Then, too, Paul's two-step approach to dealing with either problems or with questions will help us in that before he addresses a specific question or suggests a practical solution to a problem, he states the theological basis for his answer. The "therefore" in Romans 12:1 is the word bridge

between the previous chapters which lay the foundations for understanding God's relationship with persons and the following chapters
which outline how Christians are to live. The principles on which
the actions are based can often be translated to today's problems
without doing damage to the original meaning of the Scripture because
they have their roots in a truth about God which does not change.
Often these principles can be applied with wisdom to our more contemporary problems.

Finally, the same Holy Spirit which worked in the mind and spirit
of the Apostle as he prayed about what to say to his friends in
Corinth is available to us as we seek to apply the teachings of this
particular book of the Bible to our lives.

RELATIONSHIPS ARE IMPORTANT

1 Paul, called to be an apostle of Jesus Christ
through the will of God, and Sosthenes our brother,

2 To the church of God which is at Corinth, to
those who are sanctified in Christ Jesus, called to be
saints, with all who in every place call on the name
of Jesus Christ our Lord, both theirs and ours:

3 Grace to you and peace from God our Father
and the Lord Jesus Christ.

1 Cor. 1:1–3

Paul begins this letter, which will eventually have in it some very
stern criticism, with a reminder of the relationships which he and
its recipients share. This is how he begins nine of the letters usually
attributed to him in the New Testament. Actually, he was following
the custom of first-century letter writing, which was to give the name
of the writer, the name of those receiving the letter, and a greeting.

Here, though, Paul gives a distinct Christian character to his introduction. The ordinary salutation of the day was "grace and peace."
But Paul gave a whole different dimension to it by adding "from
God through our Lord Jesus Christ." His expansion of a phrase that
ordinarily meant little more than "hello" became a reminder to them

of God's unmerited favor (grace) and of the wholeness and unity (peace) God brings into our lives through his Son.

Paul felt that it was important for his readers to remember the common relationship that they shared in God's call. He used the word *"called"* in relationship to himself and to them. He was called *"to be an Apostle of Jesus Christ"* and they were called *"to be saints."* The mention of his apostleship was an affirmation of the authority which God had given him, and it was particularly significant in view of the fact that there were those in Corinth who questioned his authority. It is equally interesting to note that when he wrote to churches where his authority was not questioned, he identified himself merely as "Paul" (Phil. 1:1; 2 Thess. 1:1; Philem. 1:1). On the other hand, whenever his authority had been questioned he referred to himself as an apostle (Rom. 1:1, Gal. 1:1, Col. 1:1). Paul was a wise communicator, and he always kept in mind those to whom he was writing when he introduced himself.

It is important, though, to understand that Paul did not use the term "apostle" lightly, for it defined his whole ministry. Paul understood clearly the call that was his because he knew that an apostle was a person sent by God for a specific purpose. The whole idea of apostleship is found in the statement of Jesus, "As the Father has sent Me, so send I you" (John 20:21). And the "specific purpose" for which God called Paul was first revealed through Ananias. Paul's mission was to take the gospel of salvation to "Gentiles, kings, and the children of Israel" (Acts 9:15–16). His task was not to set up programs or build structures but to carry a message of love and healing. Those of us in the church today who are called to be apostles to a hurting world would do well to model ourselves after Paul, for he knew that the need of the world was not as much for programs as for persons.

In verse 2 Paul tells his readers that the same God who called him to be an apostle had called them to be a different kind of people. This is really what the phrase *"sanctified in Christ Jesus"* means. The Greek verb form for "sanctified" means to set apart for God; as a noun, the word describes a thing or a person that has been devoted to the possession or service of God.

The root idea is that of separation. The Christian is to be different— separated—because he or she belongs to God. Paul goes on to stress the fact that his readers, the Corinthian church members, were *"called to be saints"* (v. 2), even as he was *"called to be an apostle"* (v. 1). He means that we are invited into the Christian life by God's invitation and not by some human initiative.

For Paul, "called" was a dynamic word. He recalls when God called him to preach the Gospel (Acts 1:1–19). And he remembers when God called many of the people to whom he was writing to salvation, not just as individual Christians but as the "church of God." For even as Israel was the congregation of God in the Old Testament days, so the church was God's congregation in the New Testament time. Paul wanted the members of this small congregation in Corinth to be reminded that they were a part of that larger purpose of God for mankind. Thus in an ordinary greeting Paul has reminded them of the relationship they have to each other and to God in such a way that it will be easier for them to hear his message to them.

It is important for us to remember that in all matters of communications relationships are very important. When I was a professor in a theological seminary, one of my graduating students had just been called to his first church, and he invited me to have lunch with him to celebrate the occasion.

While we ate, I kept him talking by asking him to tell me everything he knew about the church, the community, the leadership, the opportunities, and about the specifics of his move from the campus to his new church location. We also talked in general terms about preaching and pastoral care because his experience in both of these areas was limited. Then when we got onto the subject of the leadership role he would play with the congregation, he surprised me with a suggestion that had been given to him by one of his classmates. "I've been told," he said, "that if I want to make changes at the church, I'd better do it when I first get there because after I've been there awhile people will be less likely to follow my leadership."

At first I was shocked by the idea, but then I realized that in a nation where the average pastor serves his church less than three years, this would be an expected philosophy. However, I don't agree with this idea at all. It seems to imply that the more a pastor and the congregation get to know each other the less they can accomplish. Actually, the opposite is true, for it is the sharing of the common experiences of life and in working together through both good and bad times that relationships are built and a larger potential for leadership is created. After more than a decade of working with my congregation in Houston, I had a much better feel for where they were in their understanding and interest, what their real needs were, and how best to communicate with them effectively. The new broom may sweep cleaner but the old broom has the potential for sweeping more wisely.

BE THANKFUL FOR WHAT GOD GIVES

4 I thank my God always concerning you for the grace of God which was given to you by Christ Jesus,
5 that you were enriched in everything by Him in all utterance and all knowledge,
6 even as the testimony of Christ was confirmed in you,
7 so that you come short in no gift, eagerly waiting for the revelation of our Lord Jesus Christ,
8 who will also confirm you to the end, that you may be blameless in the day of our Lord Jesus Christ.
9 God is faithful, by whom you were called into the fellowship of His Son, Jesus Christ our Lord.

1 Cor. 1:4–9

It was Paul's habit to encourage and praise those with whom he worked and he did not make an exception in this letter. Even though he might write primarily a letter of reproof he always began it with a section of praise. Some people have even questioned Paul's sincerity in this section, knowing the kinds of problems he would be dealing with in the body of the letter. But when we read the verses more carefully we see Paul's focus is on what God has done in their lives. These brief words about what God had called them to become would be a great source of encouragement as they dealt with the very heavy burden of their shortcomings.

During the past ten years, I have led more than fifty seminars for people who have experienced failure in their marriages. From my personal experience with more than five thousand people who are divorced I've learned that few human experiences are more devastating to a person than the failure of a marriage. It's like experiencing the death of a loved one without having any of the usual support systems.

Others who have training and skills in the counseling field have helped in the seminars and provided insight into some of the psychological aspects of the grief that comes from the death of a relationship. My role as the pastor has been that of encourager. So in the midst of their pain and failure and anger I have tried to assure them that they are not outside God's love and concern, that they have worth because God loves them and that He will be with them. Thinking about God's love and concern can always give us a better context from which to deal with our failures.

Paul made several statements of thanksgiving for what God had done. First, you're the object of God's love and grace. *"The grace of God which was given to you"* (v. 4) means God's unmerited favor. So often in our sinful pride we try to earn God's favor, but this is impossible to do. And eventually we must face the truth that "there is none righteous, no, not one" (Rom. 3:10). Behind our effort to try to impress God is the feeling that God will not love us the way we are. And we fall prey to that feeling because we live in a world of people who make us try to earn their love by conforming to their expectations for us. Since we tend to go through life auditioning for the love of others, it seems only natural that we would have to do the same thing with God. But the greatest discovery in life is that nothing in our minds or hearts or actions is hidden from God, and He still loves us.

Second, Christ has brought you spiritual riches. When Paul wrote that *"you were enriched in everything in Him"* (v. 5), he was following a Biblical tradition of speaking of the God-man relationship in terms of wealth or riches.

Jesus spoke critically of the farmer who amassed material fortunes and was not "rich toward God" (Luke 12:21). The themes of spiritual bankruptcy and spiritual wealth are very prominent in the Bible, and for good reason. Those to whom Paul wrote this letter lived in a society that produced great material wealth but that created spiritually bankrupt people. In a society that thinks of little else but making money and having fun there is a constant deterioration in the quality of life. The worth of self and of persons diminishes and the quality of relationships deteriorates. Soon the distinctions between right and wrong fade and values become distorted; social pressure toward evil emerges. This was precisely the mood and pattern of life in first-century Corinth, but it is also a fairly accurate description of most cities in the world today.

Paul's claim is that in a world of such spiritual poverty Christ has enriched the lives of those to whom he is writing. Paul is pointing to some past action in their lives and could have referred both to their conversions and to whatever growth they had subsequently experienced. My first inclination upon reading this was to think that it must have been a tongue-in-cheek statement since Paul will soon be writing to them about their lack of unity. But Paul was not making a comparison between what they were and what they ought to be. Rather, he was thinking of the kind of people they were and the kinds of lives they had lived before Christ had come into their lives. Measured against their pagan neighbors or even against their former selves it was perfectly clear that Christ had enriched their lives. They had confirmed the gospel in their own experience. The life that grasps the truth of God is rich.

When Dr. Ray Collins died, his son Perryman called to tell me, and I went to his home to visit with Mrs. Collins and to plan the memorial service. Dr. Collins had lived a full life, having practiced medicine in Houston for sixty years. He had reared his children in the church and had watched his grandchildren grow to adulthood and give him great-grandchildren. So when at age ninety-four, after two very difficult years, he passed on, there was not in the gathering of his family as much a sense of grief at his death as there was a sense of gratitude for his life, and that the suffering was over. On the eve of his funeral I visited with his children and his grandchildren. As I left the funeral home I found myself elated as I thought about the quality of life that his family possessed. The following day after the funeral at the church I drove in the procession to the cemetery for the interment. The Collins's plot was in the same cemetery where the late Howard Hughes is buried, and as the procession passed the Hughes grave I thought of the difference between his life and Dr. Collins's. Howard Hughes was perceived as the richest man in the world but he died alone without support of family or friends and is remembered chiefly by the courtroom struggles for his money. Dr. Collins was a man whose life God had enriched, and it was a kind of wealth which lasts forever.

Third, God has given you great potential. Later in the letter Paul would devote three whole chapters to the understanding of gifts and their use in the church, but here in this early thanksgiving section he thanks God that they *"come short in no gift"* (v. 7). He is trying to encourage them with the realization that God has held back no gift that would help them to *do* His work and *be* His church in Corinth. Paul isn't suggesting that they are even aware of their gifts or have begun to develop them, but he wants them to see that by virtue of having accepted Christ, they have received special gifts. One of the great insights of the Scripture that we need to be aware of and to claim is that God has already given us the gifts which we need to do His will.

On one occasion I was a guest preacher in one of the large churches in Richmond, Virginia. While the church had a great history, the community in which it was located had changed and things were not going as well as in earlier days. There were deep feelings of concern, and one night I was asked to meet the men and women who represented the lay leadership of the church.

After expressing appreciation for the good the church was now doing, I asked, "Has God given any of you a special dream for the future of your church? Is there something you would like to see the church do in the name of Christ that it has never done before?"

More than a dozen persons out of the group responded with a resounding yes. They wanted their church to minister creatively to the needs of people in their neighborhood—to reach out in love to them as persons for whom Christ died. Our discussion that night went on and on with first one and then another making suggestions as to how they could fulfill their mission. As I listened, I was profoundly impressed with the thought that these very people already possessed the gifts and abilities they needed in order to fulfill their dreams. All they needed was the assurance that they could and that God would lead and guide them all the way.

Great untapped resources, whether in Corinth or in the churches of the twentieth century, are in the gifts God has given to His people.

Fourth, God has given you a basis of hope. Even in his greeting Paul reminds his friends of the ultimate hope they have in Jesus Christ. It seems strange to find a reference to the second coming of Christ right here in his opening words in the greeting. But what Paul is trying to do is to set the problems which they now face in the context of eternity. He wants them to be *"blameless in the day of our Lord Jesus Christ"* (v. 8) and gives as the basis of hope, not their good works but the fact that *"God is faithful"* (v. 9). It's easy to get so bogged down in today's failures that we lose sight of the ultimate victory we have in Christ.

My grandmother lived in our home for a couple of years while I was a high school student. She was a mountain woman who had been born in Chattanooga, Tennessee, but had spent most of her adult life in the hills of Arkansas and northeast Oklahoma. Grandmother and I spent many hours together. She loved to read, and often I would find some author she enjoyed and check a book out of the school library for her. But every time I brought her a book she would open it to the last chapter and read that first. This both amazed and upset me because it seemed to me that would take all the fun out of reading the book. One day I just couldn't stand it any longer, and I asked her why she always read the last chapter first. Without a moment of hesitation she said, "If I don't like the way a book ends, I don't see any sense wasting my time reading it."

As I have reflected on that since, I've come to believe that many Christians today need to take a page out of Grandmother's book. But the difference is that we already know how things are going to turn out; we know what's in our last chapter, and this means that we can live in the present with confidence. I believe Paul was wanting to assure his Corinthian friends right in the beginning that their future was as secure as the promises of God.

There is a kind of spiritual hand-wringing that suggests that those who engage in it think they are involved in a lost cause. They act as though some of the reversals that are experienced by the good are permanent. The hope of the Christian is based on the activity of God and allows us to believe that whatever may be the circumstances there will come a day when life will overcome death, when love will overcome hate, when good will overcome evil, and the Kingdom of God will triumph over the kingdoms of this world. It is the assurance of this future that allows us to live more triumphantly in the present.

The Things That Divide a Church

10 Now I plead with you, brethren, by the name of our Lord Jesus Christ, that you all speak the same thing, and that there be no divisions among you, but that you be perfectly joined together in the same mind and in the same judgment.

11 For it has been declared to me concerning you, my brethren, by those of Chloe's household, that there are contentions among you.

12 Now I say this, that each of you says, "I am of Paul," or "I am of Apollos," or "I am of Cephas," or "I am of Christ."

13 Is Christ divided? Was Paul crucified for you? Or were you baptized in the name of Paul?

14 I thank God that I baptized none of you except Crispus and Gaius,

15 lest anyone should say that I had baptized in my own name.

16 Yes, I also baptized the household of Stephanas. Besides, I do not know whether I baptized any other.

17 For Christ did not send me to baptize, but to preach the gospel, not with wisdom of words, lest the cross of Christ be made of no effect.

1 Cor. 1:10–17

Immediately following his opening words of encouragement, Paul begins with the problem of division within the fellowship of the church. The fact that he puts this problem first and continues the discussion for four chapters indicates that he feels it is of great importance.

There is nothing subtle or indirect in the way he approaches the problem. First, he states the problem as a fact that exists and not as a rumor. Paul is too careful in his dealing with the truth to bother with some unsubstantiated bit of gossip. Second, he gives the original source of the information. Some feel that *"those of Chloe's household"* (v. 11) is a reference to a slave who belonged to a lady named Chloe. Undoubtedly he had substantiated what they had shared with him by conversations with others, possibly those who had brought him the letter from the church at Corinth. Third, to show how intimate his knowledge was of the different factions in the church he repeats their divisive slogans, *"I am of Paul,"* or *"I am of Cephas,"* or *"I am of Christ"* (v. 12). This is a classic picture of a person dealing responsibly with a problem. In less than sixty words Paul states the problem, identifies his source, and repeats precisely and forthrightly what has been told him about the problem. But it is Paul's attitude and approach that is so remarkable. His words and his actions reveal that he is speaking as a Christian brother in behalf of Christ. What a perfect model for Christian confrontation!

From my thirty-five years in the ministry I have observed that the church of the twentieth century admires the spiritual courage of leaders such as Paul but it falls far short of copying their style of dealing with serious problems. We have such an anemic picture of Christian love that we avoid writing or saying anything that might upset someone or hurt his or her feelings. So concerned are we to avoid any issue which creates tension that we bury our heads in the sand and don't even bother to learn what the issues are. And our pathological fear of taking a firm and loving stand for Christ and His church has given us such finely tuned instincts for arbitration that we are deluded into thinking that we can reconcile any people or any ideas.

I can just picture the chairman of one of our "peace at any price" committees trying to counsel the Apostle Paul along these lines: "Paul, this is risky for you. You already have some people in that church who are critical of you, and this will just add fuel to the fire. You've been gone three years and don't realize how much the church has changed. Sure, there are some problems, but this isn't the way to deal with them. Your spelling out the issues will surface all sorts of destructive feelings and will end up adding to the problem rather than solving it. Besides, what the church really needs to unite it is a big project, like a major building campaign." Sound familiar?

It will be helpful for us as we seek to fulfill our own church mission today to examine the likely thinking of the several groups that were dividing the Corinthian church, but it is highly significant that Paul was able to write one letter to the whole church and all the various factions were able to listen. Had conditions deteriorated so they could no longer have fellowship with each other or worship together, it would have been much more difficult for the problem of division to be handled. There has been among Biblical scholars a continuing discussion as to the significance of the various groups that were splintering the church. The more traditional interpreters give the following characteristics.

The "Paul group" consisted of the church's "charter members." They were most likely Gentile converts, so one of the tenets of their faith would center on the freedom they had in Jesus Christ. They took great pride in the fact that they were in the church from the beginning.

It is easy for me to identify with the feelings of the Corinthian "old-timers," for the church where I have most recently been the pastor is eighty years old. And even though none of its charter members is still living today, there are people who were there when the fifth pastor was called in 1918. Quite naturally, they feel very special about their tenure in the church. In a similar way, this "Paul group" felt very special because they had been converted under the preaching of the Apostle himself, and those whom he had baptized wore the fact as a badge of distinction.

As we reflect on the characteristics of our churches today, almost 2,000 years later, it is interesting to note that this charter or "old-timers" group is usually very much in evidence. They are good people who are easy to love and are sometimes referred to as "the salt of the earth."

The "Apollos group" probably consisted of those church members who were especially drawn to the powerful preaching of Apollos. In Acts 18:21–28 he is described as being from Alexandria, eloquent and mighty in the Scriptures, fervent in spirit, and bold. Because he "knew only the baptism of John" Aquila and Priscilla became responsible for updating his knowledge and understanding. When Apollos wanted to go to Achaia, the province of which Corinth was the capital, he was given a letter urging the Christian brethren there to receive him.

Conjecture as to the nature of this group is drawn heavily from Apollos' place of birth. Alexandria was a city of vigorous intellectual activity and whose biblical scholars delighted in interpreting Scriptures by use of allegorizing. They could infer amazing meanings in what appeared to be the simplest verses. The combination of a fervent spirit and homiletical flair had strong appeal to this particular group.

The "Cephas group" was most likely made up of the Jewish Christians who had deep roots in the faith of their fathers. There is no indication that Peter ever visited Corinth, but he was undoubtedly looked up to by these Jewish Christians because of his identity with the church in Jerusalem. Members of this group were probably not too comfortable with the church members who had been converted out of paganism and who paid no attention to Jewish customs.

People with deep religious roots, like the Cephas group, always make a great contribution to the stability of the church at any time and in any place.

There is no general agreement as to the identity of the "Jesus group." Some feel that this may not have been a group at all but believe that by speaking of those who said "I am of Christ" Paul may have been making his own comment about the whole wretched situation. Paul could have been separating himself from all of the groups by stating with a bit of irony in his wording that he would rather identify with the Lord than with any of the Lord's servants. Though we have no indication as to what may have been its distinction, most likely the "Jesus group" was a fourth faction within the fellowship of the church.

In studying this passage of Scripture it is important that we not consider it as merely a lesson in church history. Instead, these verses should be examined in terms of our churches today, for in the Corinthian church we see a prototype of late-twentieth-century churches, all of which carry the potential for division. Sometimes the differences are ignored, not taken seriously, or glossed over, but they are real and they are there and we need to face them forthrightly and with courage.

Several years ago I taught 1 Corinthians to a group in our church on successive Wednesday nights. As we studied these particular verses, I was forced to think about all the differences within the church which had the potential of being divisive. While I labeled these groups differently, there was a great similarity between this inner-city church of the twentieth century and the one in first-century Corinth. For example, there is always the potential of tension between the senior adults and their needs and the young marrieds and their demands. There is quite a disparity between the interests of the old-timers and the newcomers, between those who work with internationals and those who feel the congregation ought to be homogenous. There is usually the potential for misunderstanding between those who want an authoritarian pastor and others who demand freedom and openness for lay persons. And then, of course, there is a group who wants to minister and another whose major emphasis is on evangelism.

Our first clue to Paul's understanding of the Corinthian church problem comes in the word he used for *"division"* in verse 10 and for *"contentions"* in verse 11. The verb form used in verse 10 indicates that the divisions were already present. *Schisma* is the Greek word for "cleft" or "division." It is used in the Gospels to depict a tear in a garment (Mark 2:21, Matt. 9:16), and it is used by John to describe the different opinions about Christ (John 7:43). A more picturesque word is *erides* in verse 11, translated "contention." The ancient Greeks used the word in their literature to mean battle strife, rivalry, and both political and domestic strife. The fact that Paul used the word in Galatians 5:20 to describe a work of the flesh which was opposed to all God was seeking to do would indicate how serious he viewed the problem to be.

The refutation of the divisions in the church that Paul introduces in verses 12–17 is picked up and developed in great detail in the first four chapters of the letter. It should be noted from the beginning that Paul did not direct his argument against any one faction but against all of the groups. He even refuted those to whom he was the hero by asking, *"Was Paul crucified for you? Or were you baptized in the name of Paul?"* (1:13). However, Paul does not get involved in either the beliefs or the practices of any of the groups but attacks the spirit of partisanship which he feels could ultimately divide the church. His larger concern was the quarrelsome spirit to which their differences had given birth. He uses his strongest argument first when he asks, *"Is Christ divided?"* (v. 13). The assumed answer is "no" with the inference that "your spirit is about to divide that which cannot be divided."

Paul introduced this passage with the clear goal for the fellowship of the church: *"that you be perfectly joined together in the same name and the same judgment"* (v. 10). He was not calling for uniformity of thought and action but for oneness of spirit. Later in the letter Paul will lead the church to celebrate the diversity of gifts, but here he was still calling for that spirit which binds the body of Christ together and allows it to perform its function. Those who have for a long time observed with a loving eye the actions of different churches have seen congregations deal with grave matters on which there were vigorous and differing opinions and come through it as stronger churches with a more loving fellowship. On the other hand, such observers have also seen the fellowship of other congregations torn and permanent scars inflicted over matters so trivial that in years to come the participants would have a hard time even remembering which side they were on in the argument. The difference between the two is that the first were able to preserve a oneness of spirit in the midst of differences. The church should prize the spirit which Christ has given her and take seriously any threat to its essential unity.

GOD'S WISDOM REPUDIATES DIVISION

18 For the message of the cross is foolishness to those who are perishing, but to us who are being saved it is the power of God.
19 For it is written:
"I will destroy the wisdom of the wise,
And bring to nothing the understanding of the
    prudent."
20 Where is the wise? Where is the scribe? Where is the disputer of this age? Has not God made foolish the wisdom of this world?
21 For since, in the wisdom of God, the world through wisdom did not know God, it pleased God through the foolishness of the message preached to save those who believe.
22 For Jews request a sign, and Greeks seek after wisdom;
23 but we preach Christ crucified, to the Jews a stumbling block and to the Greeks foolishness,
24 but to those who are called, both Jews and Greeks, Christ the power of God and the wisdom of God.
25 Because the foolishness of God is wiser than men, and the weakness of God is stronger than men.
1 Cor. 1:18–25

There are times when Paul seems to interrupt himself to explore a different subject before coming back to his original line of thought. A casual reading of verses 18–25 might lead us to think that Paul had picked up on his own mentioning of the gospel and is now turning aside from his discussion of divisions to pursue that subject. Rather, he is launching his criticisms by insisting that the party spirit in the church is caused by false wisdom, human pride, and by loyalty to human leaders. It is not the gospel he has preached that has brought division. The word of the cross that he had preached was the source of true wisdom and unity. Consequently, the divisions within the church must have come from that worldly wisdom which cannot accept the preaching of the cross. In this particular passage Paul uses the word "wisdom" in different ways. In verse 21 it quite likely means man-centered wisdom, while the same word in verse 24 refers to God's plan of salvation.

In this brief passage, the Apostle reminds the church for all times that while its gospel does not measure up to worldly standards, it is the only word of salvation to those who believe. The church in every century has had to resist, sometimes not too successfully, the temptation to try to "augment the gospel." For the first-century Jew, dying on a cross signified that one was under God's curse. The Old Testament idea was that God showed His happiness with an individual by pouring out material blessings and His unhappiness by sending judgment in the form of illness, loss, or trouble. The ultimate form of loss was death, and only criminals of the worst sort were crucified. Then Paul came along and proclaimed that the cross was not a curse but God's special revelation of His love and grace. Quite naturally the Jews stumbled over this.

On the other hand, people with a Greek background reacted differently to the cross. They were reared in a world of thought and reason, without any hint of the faith in God at work in their history that the Jews had in theirs. The Greeks were thinkers who loved to speculate on ideas and who needed rational evidence for anything they believed. It is this philosophy that gave birth to so much of the thought and scientific methodology that characterizes the Western world. While our religious heritage is with the Jews, our method of thinking about the universe comes from the Greeks, and as a result, we often ask the same questions of those who bring the gospel to us.

When I was preparing to fly to South Carolina to preach for a week in a church in a university town, one of the graduates of that university came by my office to talk. He knew of my upcoming trip and wanted to give me an orientation both to the school and the church. He summed up our whole visit in his first sentence: "The whole church is made up of professors and their families, students, and school-related people. They are suspicious of feelings and need everything to have a logical or rational approach." Our conversation reminded me how relevant Paul's discussion with the Corinthians is for our times.

Paul was very reluctant to adorn or dress up the basic facts of the gospel message he preached even though he knew it would be considered a scandal to some of his listeners and readers, while others would think of it as folly. We find it difficult to understand Paul's words "folly" and "scandal" because they create pictures in our minds that do not seem at all related to what Paul is saying. He means that to the unaided mind the gospel doesn't make sense but on the contrary seems to be "nonsense." How can a kingdom of righteousness be created as the result of an executed Christ?

One of the reassurances that Paul received was that to those who were being saved the message of the cross was the *"power of God"* (1:18). There is an important lesson for us here that is easy to overlook—as we preach and witness to the gospel of Christ, it is imperative that we have the same confidence in it that Paul did. And it is equally essential that we neither add to it or attempt to reduce it in any way. The message of the early church was simple and forthright: "God was in Christ reconciling the world unto Himself." Now I believe that while the gospel focused on the death and resurrection of Jesus, the idea of the cross reached back and included everything Christ was, and all He said and did. It was much more than a Palm Sunday sermon; the cross is also symbolic of the kind of life God calls us to in His Son (Luke 14:25–33).

The only gospel that can change our world today two thousand years after Jesus' earthly life, Good Friday, and Resurrection morning is the "word of the cross." But while I was a student in a state university, without realizing what was happening to me, I began to feel the need to prop up the gospel. Though there were some outstanding Christian teachers on the staff, some of my best professors from the standpoint of academics were persons who not only made no Christian profession but were articulate in their unbelief.

This was a new experience for me. And while I had heard two country preachers argue as to whether Paul was converted on the road to Damascus or when Ananias came to him, I'd never heard anyone suggest that what Paul mistook for a conversion and a call was probably either sunstroke or an epileptic fit. At the same time a brilliant astronomy professor insisted that he saw no indication of a personal force or being behind the universe as he understood it. Fortunately, a high school science teacher had grounded my thinking in the truth that our world is the handiwork of God. None of my Godless professors influenced me to abandon my faith in God or in the gospel I felt called to preach, but I did begin to feel the need for the respect of those to whom my beliefs and message sounded like foolishness.

OUR COMMON CALLING DRAWS US TOGETHER

26 For you see your calling, brethren, that not many wise according to the flesh, not many mighty, not many noble, are called.

27 But God has chosen the foolish things of the world to put to shame the wise, and God has chosen the weak things of the world to put to shame the things which are mighty;

28 and the base things of the world and the things which are despised God has chosen, and the things which are not, to bring to nothing the things that are,

29 that no flesh should glory in His presence.

30 But of Him you are in Christ Jesus, who became for us wisdom from God—and righteousness and sanctification and redemption—

31 that, as it is written, *"He who glories, let him glory in the LORD."*

1 Cor. 1:26–31

By referring to the makeup of the Corinthian church, Paul now illustrates the principle that God takes what is foolish to our world and makes it wise. While he did not completely eliminate the possibility that there were a few culturally and socially prominent members among them, he knew that there were not many. The congregation could claim as members a former ruler of the synagogue, a city treasurer, and perhaps one or two successful businessmen, but the majority were without educational, social, cultural, or religious credentials. They had little or no clout in society. It is not surprising that they had been drawn to Christ's preaching originally. Now, Paul is not suggesting that these are the only people God loves or that they are the only ones to whom the gospel was attractive. Rather, he is illustrating out of the makeup of the congregation the fact that God is able to take ordinary people and do extraordinary things in the world through them. The perspective of the centuries allows us to see what must have been very difficult for many to believe—that the most powerful force in first-century Corinth was neither the political power of Rome nor the cultural heritage of Greece, but the gospel of Jesus Christ which had gathered the church.

There are many places in the world today where the Christians all come from the edges of society—intellectually, socially, politically, and culturally. They would read Paul's words and feel that they were as descriptive of their present situation as they were originally to the Corinthians. But this is not true in those countries where Christianity has an "establishment" relationship with the world. I was in London, England, when the memorial service was held for the victims of the 1983 bombing at Harrod's department store. The service was conducted by the church of which the Queen of England is the head; the Prime Minister read the Scripture; and the entire procedure was covered by the nationalized media. In the United States of America the "prayer breakfast" has become a regularly scheduled event at every level of society and is attended by mayors, governors, senators, congressmen, and even presidents. There are many congregations who do not fit the description of the church at Corinth. And in these situations there is always the temptation to glory not in the gospel or in Christ but in our acceptance in the world. The church that I pastored during the last decade has many members who have prominent roles in society, but they draw the meaning for their lives from their common relationship with Christ. Even as the church uses the social status of its members to penetrate the upper levels of society with the gospel, it must be careful not to abandon the "people of the land," those faceless ones who are powerless but whom God calls to usefulness in His Son.

CHAPTER TWO

God's Wisdom in Christ

1 Corinthians 2:1–16

There are times in my life when I despair of the possibility of Christian unity. When I see denominations going their separate ways with hardly a conversation with the others and when I see different groups within the same denomination who seem to have no common ground for communication, I wonder what the future is for us. I guess my doubts are born of the false assumption that spiritual unity would have to come as man's accomplishment. Then I remember that God has a very large investment in His children's not being divided. The idea of wholeness and oneness is a part of the very character of God, is built into His revelation in Christ, and is central to the gospel which the church preaches. This means that everything which God is and does is on the side of Christians functioning as brothers and sisters.

In this second chapter of 1 Corinthians, after having chided the church for the divisions in its fellowship, Paul turns to those forces at work seeking to create a united congregation. He begins with the gospel which he had preached (2:1–5) and concludes with the wisdom of God (2:6–16).

THE PREACHING OF THE CROSS DRAWS US TOGETHER

1 And I, brethren, when I came to you, did not come with excellence of speech or of wisdom declaring to you the testimony of God.

2 For I determined not to know anything among you except Jesus Christ and Him crucified.

3 I was with you in weakness, in fear, and in much
trembling.
4 And my speech and my preaching were not with
persuasive words of human wisdom, but in
demonstration of the Spirit and of power,
5 that your faith should not be in the wisdom of
men but in the power of God.

1 Cor. 2:1–5

Paul now uses himself as an illustration of how God is able to
use the weak to confound the strong. If any of the readers had been
offended by his statement that "not many wise" had been chosen,
they could be comforted by the fact that Paul included himself in
the statement. The spirit of humility he asked of his readers he had
exhibited himself both in his message and in the manner of his life.
The remarkable correspondence between the minister and his gospel
is what gave it power, because the messenger must match the message.
It would have been ridiculous for Paul to have come to them with
a gospel which was "the foolishness of God" and to have attempted
to preach it with "words of wisdom."

One of the most difficult problems of those who seek to communicate the gospel to others is matching their lives with their message.
Often I am asked by someone to come to a meeting and give a talk
on some subject on which I have done a lot of speaking and writing.
When I decline because of my schedule sometimes they will say,
"You won't have to spend any time preparing." They always seem
a bit surprised when I tell them that my problem isn't getting my
talk ready but getting me ready emotionally and spiritually. Paul
reminds them that his manner of life matched his message.

We need to remember that Paul is laying a foundation for dealing
with the divisions in the church. In this section he wants to re-remind
them that neither the gospel he preached nor the manner in which
he preached it had in any way contributed to the schism in the congregation. He had come to them as a proclaimer—not to argue, discuss,
or persuade. Since the gospel is not a system of philosophy or logic
but a statement of God's revelation in Christ, the proper stance for
its messenger is that of a proclaimer. This is the stance of the evangelist
and the missionary who introduce the gospel to any person or people.

There are many who feel that Paul's deliberate decision to reject an approach to preaching which emphasized worldly wisdom is a reference to his own experience in Athens (which Luke records in Acts 17:16–34). They contend that he had made an effort there at a philosophical presentation of the gospel and had failed miserably. They feel that this is the background of his decision, once he arrived in Corinth, to know nothing among them *"except Jesus Christ and Him crucified"* (v. 2). While this is an old and oft-repeated interpretation, I don't think a good case can be made, for several reasons. First, all we have in Acts 17 is the introduction of the sermon, and while he does quote one of the pagan poets, Paul moves on to man's account-ability to God and the death and resurrection of Christ. Second, there were converts in Athens. But the best reason to reject this interpreta-tion is that there is no reason to suspect that there was ever a time in his ministry when Paul had the slightest question either about his message or the manner in which it was to be delivered.

A better understanding of his statement seems to be that he deliber-ately decided not to tailor his method of presentation to satisfy the expectations of his hearers in Corinth. Paul knew that the Corinthians loved big words, clever oratory, and complex logic. He also knew that there were those who gave them what they wanted. But Paul had decided that this would undermine the message that he brought. To match a simple gospel with a complex preacher would seem ridicu-lous, and to shape either the message or the presentation of that message to please the audience would be wrong. This is a hard and necessary choice, and it is not as easily made as many would think.

The desire to succeed and the need for the approval of the crowd present Christians with constant temptation to compromise. When I was the director of evangelism for my denomination, an aspiring young evangelist came to visit with me at a conference where I was speaking. He was just beginning his ministry, and we spent some time together talking about the direction he was heading in the work. He was young, bright, and attractive and showed great promise. But he was also extremely ambitious, and his desire for a certain kind of success revealed itself in one of the questions he put to me in all seriousness. "What do the people like today?" He elaborated on his inquiry by stating that he felt that people no longer "went for the hellfire and brimstone" approach and that the "psychological thing" seemed to be fading. I found a deep sadness coming over me as I realized the implication of his question. He wanted me to predict the next listeners' fad, and he intended to adapt himself to it. Paul knew exactly what they wanted in Corinth and decided not to do it. He wanted converts, not compliments. His calling was to be a witness, not a performer. Whether teaching a class, training our children, pastoring a church, or talking with a friend, it is important for our manner of life to match our message.

While Paul was not philosophical, there was a shrewdness to his preaching and writing that is well illustrated by his choice of the words *"the testimony of God"* (2:1). The better Greek texts seem to indicate that "mystery" would be a better translation than "testimony." It means the mystery that God reveals through Christ. Paul took a word that was commonly used by the mystery religions that were popular in Greece. They used "mystery" to mean religious secrets which were known only to an elite group of followers. Paul used the same word and changed the meaning to that which had formerly been unknown but had now been revealed to all believers.

Through the years I have heard teachers and preachers say that Paul had decided to stick with the "simple gospel," with the emphasis upon "simple." This is a mistake because the gospel is complex. It flows from the heart and mind and action of God. As Paul says later in this chapter, it goes beyond anything we have seen or heard or imagined (2:9). What Paul is reminding them is that by a deliberate decision his message had centered in Jesus Christ. And he had not presented Him as a great ethical teacher, or a moral example, or even as a great leader, but as the one "crucified Christ"—a contradiction in terms to the Jews and mere folly to the Greeks. Paul had come to them with the scandal of the cross and announced to them a salvation which required them to admit their own unworthiness and helplessness before God.

Paul's reference to his sense of insufficiency in verse 3 puzzles many. While his talk of *"weakness"* and *"fear"* and *"trembling"* is written to show the contrast between his powerlessness and the gospel's power, it does reflect what was going on in his life at the time he was preaching to the Corinthians. It could refer to his poor personal appearance and his unimpressive method of speaking (2 Cor. 10:10); he could have still been suffering the effects of the hostility of the Jews in Thessalonica (Acts 17:5, 13); or he could have been awed by the great wickedness of the city of Corinth. There seems to have been some thought of his physical safety since this was the point to Paul's special vision of the Lord in Acts 18:9–10. Paul's point was not so much to focus the attention on his inadequacies but to remind the readers that the power of the gospel was not drawn from its messenger.

The real proof of the power of the gospel is in changed lives. This "demonstration of the Spirit" was the thing that authenticated Paul's ministry. The gospel's most powerful argument is not in great sermons preached but in the changes it causes in lives. When I was a seminary student, I enrolled in a class in philosophy of religion in which we studied all the great rational arguments for immortality. We studied how all of the great minds of the different cultures through the centuries had dealt with the questions of death and afterlife. My thought was that when I became a pastor that all this knowledge would help me as I dealt with those who were facing death. When for the first time I sat in the hospital room with a woman who had been told by her doctors that she was dying and there was nothing they could do to prevent it, I realized how useless all of man's theories about death and dying are. When I watched this Christian woman draw upon the resources of the Risen Lord to face death without fear, I realized that the greatest argument for immortality in the world is one Christian who has found meaning in life and hope in death by the power of the gospel.

GOD'S WISDOM UNITES US

6 However, we speak wisdom among those who are mature, yet not the wisdom of this age, nor of the rulers of this age, who are coming to nothing.

7 But we speak the wisdom of God in a mystery, the hidden wisdom which God ordained before the ages for our glory,

8 which none of the rulers of this age knew; for had they known, they would not have crucified the Lord of glory.

9 But as it is written:

"Eye has not seen, nor ear heard,
Nor have entered into the heart of man
The things which God has prepared for those
    who love Him."

10 But God has revealed them to us through His Spirit.

For the Spirit searches all things, yes, the deep things of God.

11 For what man knows the things of a man except the spirit of the man which is in him? Even so no one knows the things of God except the Spirit of God.

12 Now we have received, not the spirit of the world, but the Spirit who is from God, that we might know the things that have been freely given to us by God.

13 These things we also speak, not in words which man's wisdom teaches but which the Holy Spirit teaches, comparing spiritual things with spiritual.

14 But the natural man does not receive the things of the Spirit of God, for they are foolishness to him; nor can he know them, because they are spiritually discerned.

15 But he who is spiritual judges all things, yet he himself is rightly judged by no one.

16 For *"Who has known the mind of the Lord that he may instruct Him?"* But we have the mind of Christ.

1 Cor. 2:6–16

Paul made a strong case in verses 1–5 that the gospel owes nothing to human wisdom and that both the messenger and the message are despised by the rulers of this age. But now he seems to be aware that people might take what he has written to mean that any kind of wisdom is bad. So in these eleven verses he makes an emphasis on the kind of wisdom that is good—divine wisdom. He teaches that there is such a thing as Christian wisdom. It is not to be confused with the world's wisdom. It centers in God's plan of redemption as revealed in Jesus Christ through the Holy Spirit. This wisdom is not understood or appreciated by the natural man.

This section was written because Paul did not want to create a kind of intellectual anarchy among Christians. This balance has continued to be needed in the church through all ages. Even today there are parts of the church that have a deep-seated anti-intellectualism. It is also true that in parts of the church, learning is respected and "loving God with all your mind" is taken seriously. But too often, in discussions that affect us all, the church has played the role of the frightened, insecure institution and not that of the people who gather weekly to worship the God of all true wisdom.

Paul did not believe that it was an act of intellectual suicide to become a follower of Jesus Christ. Instead he focused every aspect of his being on understanding what he called the "wisdom of God" (2:7). Because his preaching had purposely focused on the cross, his enemies had accused him of being too elemental and of dealing only with the ABC's of Christianity. Paul begins his answer to that accusation in this section and he also continues laying the foundation for dealing with the divisions in the church by discussing the natural man. He has previously denied that the divisions have been caused either by his message or his manner, and he now hints strongly that the root of the problem is in a worldly wisdom that is incapable of understanding divine wisdom.

This passage has several phrases that need some defining if we are to understand the gist of Paul's thought: *"those who are mature"* (v. 6); *"the wisdom of God"* (v. 7); *"hidden wisdom"* (v. 7); *"the spirit of the world"* (v. 12); *"the natural man"* (v. 14); and *"he who is spiritual"* (v. 15). One thing that makes studying the Bible interesting and challenging is that not only was it written in another language, but also in a different culture. Therefore, one writer will often use the same word to mean different things in different contexts.

The word "mature" comes from a Greek word which translated literally means "perfect." But it does not so much mean those who are without flaw as it does those whose parts are being fully developed. He is contrasting the mature with the "babes in Christ" in the next chapter (1 Cor. 3:1). The suggestion is that the real problem is not that the Apostle lacks wisdom, but that the church members are not at the place in their spiritual development that would allow them to understand. This condition creates a real crisis for serious preachers and teachers who would like to bring a greater depth to the understanding of those whom they lead. Our society has created a mentality that says, "Entertain me, but don't make me think and don't force me to grow." This creates a situation in which people never get out of spiritual kindergarten.

The *"wisdom of God"* is a reference to the gospel in all its implications. It is not just a sermon on the cross but involves all that is included in understanding God's redemptive purpose, the nature of God, and man's destiny. By *"hidden wisdom"* Paul means that which was hidden in the past but which has now been made known by a revelation of God. This wisdom is such that man was incapable of anticipating it, a plan which no one but God could have made, and which people cannot understand unless the Spirit assists them. It's important to understand that Paul did not have a "simple gospel" for babes and a different "wisdom gospel" for the mature. He was not suggesting that there is a deep knowledge which God has reserved for the spiritually elite. It is God's plan for all Christians to move toward maturity.

The phrase *"spirit of the world"* refers to the spirit of this age. In all of Paul's writings he contends that history is divided into "this present age" and "the age to come." By "this age" he means this world which is marked by rebellion against the creator—a man-centered world. By the "age to come" he means that Kingdom which God has already begun to create through Christ. While Paul was quite realistic about the powers of the world, his writing is infected with a great confidence concerning God's ultimate triumph in all things.

While Paul will begin to develop the idea of immature and carnal Christians in the next chapter, he introduces here the contrast between the natural and the spiritual person in this discussion of divine wisdom. To him *"natural man"* was all the persons who, because they had not received the Spirit of God in their lives, still had their understanding and their horizons very much limited to this world. It is not the suggestion that man at his worst cannot understand, but that man at his very best cannot understand spiritual matters unless the Spirit of God helps him. This truth has great implications both for Christian apologetics and for evangelism.

Many people in the church simply do not believe that what Paul has written is true. Consequently, they approach evangelism as though all they have to do is to tell the story of what God has done in Christ to save mankind. They assume without question that people are able to understand the message and receive it. In this passage Paul says that the message will not make sense to them nor will they be able to receive it unless they are assisted by the Spirit of God. Just as Christ came as a revelation of God's love, the Spirit must come to open our minds and hearts to the gospel. This is how he differentiates between a spiritual and a natural person. The spiritual man is the person in whom the Spirit is at work. This also underlines the essential part that the Spirit of God plays not only in conversion but in spiritual development.

CHAPTER THREE

Spiritual Maturity Creates Unity

1 Corinthians 3:1–23

Over lunch, several friends were discussing a church we all knew about which was so wracked with internal strife that it had become common knowledge in the community. Some members, who had no stomach for a fight, were drifting into neighboring churches. Those who remained were being pushed by the opposing groups to take sides, and the affair was becoming very unpleasant. The issue that had precipitated such a furor was the changing of the job description of the organist, who had been there for years and had built a small empire in her area of work. She had developed great skill in using a loyal following as a power base for budget, program, and calendar advantages. So when a special lay committee brought a report to the congregation suggesting a slight change in her duties, she took it as a personal rebuke and declared war. Since none of us were having to deal with the situation, most of us agreed with the one who said, "That doesn't sound like a big enough problem to split a church." Then one of the group reminded us of a truth that is too easily forgotten: "Any problem that has to be dealt with by people who are spiritually immature can divide a church, no matter how small it may appear."

Later, as I reflected upon the conversation, I realized how true that statement was. During the years I've been a Christian and a church member I've seen divisions created by who was going to play the piano, who would chair a certain committee, or over something as trivial as moving a Sunday school class from one room to another. I have also seen churches face with great spiritual maturity radical change in the community, new and different leadership, and every kind of hardship and seem to become stronger and more united. In this chapter the Apostle Paul ties the partisan spirit that is dividing the church to the failure of the members to grow up spiritually.

SPIRITUAL IMMATURITY DIVIDES

1 And I, brethren, could not speak to you as to spiritual people but as to carnal, as to babes in Christ.

2 I fed you with milk and not with solid food; for until now you were not able to receive it, and even now you are still not able;

3 for you are still carnal. For where there are envy, strife, and divisions among you, are you not carnal and behaving like mere men?

4 For when one says, "I am of Paul," and another, "I am of Apollos," are you not carnal?

1 Cor. 3:1–4

In the third chapter of his first letter to the Corinthians, while Paul is about to say some pretty devastating things to them about their spiritual condition, he shows that he does view them as fellow Christians by calling them "brethren." In chapter two, Paul had indicated that one reason he had not come to them with a philosophical approach was that true wisdom was divine in origin and not human. In this chapter he suggests that the reason he has not shared more of the divine wisdom with them is that they have not been spiritually mature enough to receive it.

Many of us think that the controlling factor in what we learn is the knowledge and ability of our preacher or teacher. Paul is suggesting that the spiritual immaturity of the Corinthian Christians had limited what he was able to teach them. I once heard a speaker say, "A great audience makes a great speaker." At the time I really didn't understand what he meant, but I've come to realize the truth in the statement. Whether one is preaching to a church, teaching a class, or talking to just one person, what is communicated is controlled by the interest, experience, understanding, and spiritual maturity of the listener.

The two terms that Paul used to describe them were *"carnal"* and *"babes in Christ"* (3:1). As Paul used the words, they mean the same thing.

To be carnal means not to be spiritual. They had received the Spirit, but their lives were still being controlled by their old nature. To be *"babes in Christ"* meant that they had truly experienced new birth, but that instead of having begun to grow up and mature they had remained in a state of spiritual infancy. In this condition they were neither able to cope with the adult problems that confronted them nor receive mature teaching from Paul about God.

In a renewal conference the leader gave each participant several pipe cleaners and instructed them to spend several minutes thinking about where they were spiritually in their lives and then to shape the pipe cleaners into something which symbolized their condition. When the time for the activity was over, each person was given a chance to tell a small group what he or she had made and how it symbolized his or her own spiritual condition. I was especially moved by a middle-aged man who had made a cradle. He explained it with a tone of shame and regret: "I'm a Christian who has never grown, so I thought this cradle best told the story." This was the condition of most of the Corinthian Christians, and it created a tremendous obstacle to Paul's leadership with them.

There is nothing wrong with being an infant or a child. Each week in my last church I had the joy of doing a sermon for the children in kindergarten and the first three grades. I had an old yellow rocking chair at the front of the church sanctuary, and at a certain time in the morning worship the children came and sat on the floor in front of me for "their sermon." It lasted less than two minutes and had only one very simple idea. As a means of catching and holding their interest, I usually had a picture or some object in my hand. But there were many subjects and ideas that were "off limits" to them because of their limited capacity. I did not resent this because it is natural for children to have the understanding of children. But if when they are grown physically and intellectually and have been Christians for many years, they still have only the child's capacity for understanding, I know they will not be able to function as God wants them to. This was Paul's problem in Corinth and, to some degree, it is the problem of many churches today.

The analogy in which Paul contrasts the different types of spiritual food was very popular with other Biblical writers. In 1 Peter, new Christians are urged, "like newborn babes, [to] long for the pure milk of the word, that by it you may grow in respect to salvation"

(1 Pet. 2:2). These words assume the naturalness of spiritual milk for spiritual babies as a way to stimulate growth. But the author of Hebrews is dealing with a Corinthianlike situation when he writes: "For though by this time you ought to be teachers, you have need again for someone to teach you the elemental principles of the oracles of God, and you have come to need milk and not solid food" (Heb. 5:12). Like Paul, he concludes that "solid food is for the mature" (Heb. 5:14). Throughout the New Testament "milk" is used to mean that first preaching of the good news of Jesus Christ. It is the message of the evangelist and the missionary that calls for a response of repentance and faith. It is the first and very important word.

In the same way "meat" is understood to symbolize that teaching which moves beyond our conversion and expands the implications of the gospel to every area of life. In a conversation we had, Billy Graham said, "I envy the work of the pastor. I'm called to preach the gospel and to ask for that first decision for Christ. But the pastor has the privilege of relating all the teachings of the Scripture to that convert as he grows." Dr. Graham was making the same distinction the Biblical writers made.

Through the years of my ministry I have been haunted by the number of people who take the first step of faith and fail to move on to spiritual maturity. If Paul were giving leadership to the church today, there would probably be many who felt that his ABC's were too deep for them. But while each Christian must accept some responsibility for how he or she responds to growth opportunities, I feel there are certain factors that contribute to the inordinate number of immature Christians. A flawed theology of evangelism will fill the church with "babes in Christ" who are unaware of the need to develop beyond where they are. An anemic understanding of the Biblical idea of discipleship will present Christian growth and development as an option and not as a requirement. And a total preoccupation with the numerical growth of the church has been known to have resulted in a neglect of the spiritual growth of the church members.

Now, for Paul at Corinth it was easy to tell who was spiritual and who was carnal: Where there was a spirit of love and unity they were spiritual and where there was strife and jealousy they were carnal. This is a much better system for judging maturity than many people use today. We have a tendency to equate being spiritual with how people talk or with the activities in which they participate. But Paul tied spiritual maturity not to activities but to character and attitude where the Spirit of God was creating in Christians the fruits of the spirit ("love, joy, peace, patience, kindness, goodness, faithfulness, gentleness, self control," Gal. 5:22–23). The person with these qualities could then be called spiritual. Conversely, when jealousy and strife were a part of a person's life, which was the situation in Corinth, then the "deeds of the flesh are evident" (Gal. 5:19). In these definitions of spiritual and carnal, Paul cuts through all the superficial human definitions and applies true wisdom.

When we don't grow, several things happen, all of which are bad. First, we lose sight of the real goal that Christ has for us, and that is to become spiritual persons. Then, we look a lot like people who are not Christians. Lostness and spiritual infancy look a lot alike. Finally, both the individual and the church suffer. Prolonged immaturity creates self-doubt, a prolonged dependence on leaders, and a bridge for sin in the life of the individual. It is only as we do grow that we are able to face adult problems, minister to others, and overcome temptations.

LEADERS WHO ARE A TEAM UNIFY

5 Who then is Paul, and who is Apollos, but ministers by whom you believed, as the Lord gave to each one?

6 I have planted, Apollos watered, but God gave the increase.

7 So then neither he who plants is anything, nor he who waters, but God who gives the increase.

8 Now he who plants and he who waters are one, and each one will receive his own reward according to his own labor.

9 For we are God's fellow workers; you are God's field, you are God's building.

10 According to the grace of God which was given to me, as a wise master builder I have laid the foundation, and another builds on it. But let each one take heed how he builds on it.

11 For no other foundation can anyone lay than that which is laid, which is Jesus Christ.

54

12 Now if anyone builds on this foundation with gold, silver, precious stones, wood, hay, straw,

13 each one's work will become manifest; for the Day will declare it, because it will be revealed by fire; and the fire will test each one's work, of what sort it is.

14 If anyone's work which he has built on it endures, he will receive a reward.

15 If anyone's work is burned, he will suffer loss; but he himself will be saved, yet so as through fire.

16 Do you not know that you are the temple of God and that the Spirit of God dwells in you?

17 If anyone defiles the temple of God, God will destroy him. For the temple of God is holy, which temple you are.

18 Let no one deceive himself. If anyone among you seems to be wise in this age, let him become a fool that he may become wise.

19 For the wisdom of this world is foolishness with God. For it is written, *"He catches the wise in their own craftiness"*;

20 and again, *"The LORD knows the thoughts of the wise, that they are futile."*

21 Therefore let no one glory in men. For all things are yours:

22 whether Paul or Apollos or Cephas, or the world or life or death, or things present or things to come— all are yours.

23 And you are Christ's, and Christ is God's.

1 Cor. 3:5–23

When the pastor of a church I know resigned to take another post the lay leaders decided that this would be a good time to poll the membership in order to get a feel for what it wanted in a new pastor. One of the professors of Church and Community at the seminary designed and administered the survey. While the results indicated a basic unity concerning the church's mission in the community, it was interesting how many of the expectations concerning the new leader contradicted each other. One member said, "The new pastor needs to be available to every church member all the time." Another said, "The pastor is too available. He needs to have more time alone to study." Some wanted a pastor who "was respected in the larger

Christian world and invited to speak," while in the same church there were those who expressed resentment at the pastor's ever being away "except for vacations." Some wanted a minister who was a good counselor and others wanted to be sure not to get someone "who was always counseling." Often problems are created in the church because of the different ways in which the members perceive the leaders.

In this entire section of his letter, Paul illustrates how the dissensions in the church had grown out of the fact that the members did not understand the true role of the apostles and teachers. He begins with a discussion of the way he and Apollos related to the church (vv. 5–9). The church was God's field, and Paul and Apollos were merely human instruments. They were servants who played different roles in introducing the Corinthians to God.

Paul uses an agricultural analogy in which he likened the role he played in preaching the gospel to planting the seed and Apollos' continuing role as watering the plants. They were not in competition with each other but were partners in a common venture, team members in a common task. And while their work was very important, it was subordinate to the role of God, who provided the increase. The inference is that divisions had been caused by giving more devotion to the servants than to the Lord.

This particular Corinthian problem continues to plague the church today. In every community there are Christians who are divided because of those who have a greater loyalty to one of God's servants than to that servant's Lord. The personality cult has been a part of our secular life in politics, business, education, and medicine. In each of these fields there are strong personalities who gather around themselves disciples to their way of thinking and acting. This fact of life has affected the church and has had a divisive effect. It results in ministers and churches and denominations competing with each other. The divided church is created by our forgetting that we are all servants and ministers of the one Lord and that both the field and the harvest are His.

When Paul's word is applied to us, it means that we are not only partners with everyone else who is at work in the church today but also with those who have gone before and those who will come. Just as there ought not to be any sense of competition between fellow pastors, the same spirit ought to prevail with predecessors and successors. Churches are often hurt by leaders who are so anxious to make a name for themselves that they cannot appreciate and applaud the work that was done by those who preceded them. I was the seventh pastor of the church where I was serving as I began the writing of this commentary. My immediate predecessor was there for thirty-three years before retirement. His predecessor was the pastor for almost twenty years. God used those two men to buy land, build buildings, win people and develop them in service, and to create in the church a sense of mission.

This same sense of partnership needs to be among the lay leaders of the church as well, producing the feeling that each has a unique role to play and that God will join them all together to accomplish his purpose. If you were to look on the surface at the five men who chaired the diaconate while I pastored South Main, you would wonder if they had changed the criteria with each new nominating committee, because they were different in age, experience, education, vocation, and personality. As each of them took office I was at a different place in my ministry, and the church was at a different place in its needs. It was amazing to see how the character and personality and interests of each new chairman matched exactly what the church needed at the time. They were supportive of each other and thought of themselves not as competitors, but as "laborers together."

Paul describes quite accurately the relationship when he says that different servants at different times do their particular task, but that the God who is their Lord continues to give the increase. The source of real unity among Christian workers is that we are all servants of the same Master, and the source of unity in the whole church is that we are all products of God's grace. Since it is God who convicts of sin, convinces us of the truth of the gospel, and calls us to faith, then our greatest loyalty ought to be to Him and not to one of His servants, no matter how important a role that person may have played in the work of the church and in our lives.

In verses 10–15, Paul shifts his analogy from agriculture to building and the emphasis from God's part in the work to the need for those who work in the church to be responsible. It is interesting to watch Paul walk a tight line between man's part and God's. He states plainly that *"neither he who plants is anything, nor he who waters"* (3:7). But so no one will feel that his or her work is not important, he turns to a discussion of the need for those who lead the church to function responsibly. He felt it was wrong to say, "It's all up to God," and equally wrong to say, "It's all up to me." We are *"God's fellow workers"* (3:9) in the work of the Kingdom.

Paul considered himself the wise master builder of the Corinthian church by virtue of his having begun the work there and having nurtured it during its first year and a half. He was there in advance of the first convert and had laid the very foundation of the church. But even as he began to write about the great care which needed to be exercised in building upon that foundation, he felt the need to remind the church what the foundation was—Jesus Christ. The gospel that Paul had received and had preached to them was of Christ's death, burial, and resurrection (1 Cor. 15:1–5). And while the church might have a variety of builders and different materials, it had only one foundation and that was Jesus Christ. This was the church's real basis of unity then, and it remains so today.

In verse 12 Paul concedes the possibility of a different quality of work being laid upon the original foundation. One has only to read the words *"gold, silver, precious stones, wood, hay, straw"* (3:12) to stimulate pictures of things valuable and things worthless, things that are costly and things that are cheap, things permanent and things temporary. When Karen was appointed a missionary to Mexico, because we were her home church, we had a special service in which we as a congregation set her aside for the work God had called her to, much as the church at Antioch of Syria had set Paul and Barnabas aside. At the close of what had been a very moving hour of worship, at least a dozen of the older members of the church came and one by one, shared with me what had been their part in Karen's life. One took care of her in the preschool area, another worked with her during her teen years, one led a choir she was in, another first introduced her to the idea of missions in a mid-week mission study group. There was in the expression of satisfaction of each the feeling that all the work, the time, the energy, the study, and the commitment had been worth it. Karen was their "gold, silver, and precious stones."

Paul's writing suggests that it is not always possible at the time to tell the difference between the various kinds of work that are done. While the untrained eye could easily tell the difference between gold and straw, it isn't that easy to evaluate what is being developed and accomplished in the church. That which seems deep may actually be quite shallow, and something that creates great excitement may just as soon be forgotten. Jesus illustrates this idea in the parable of the soils when He discusses the seed sown in shallow ground (Matt. 13:20–21). At the same time something that seems quite ordinary may turn out to be extremely important, and that which creates conflict may prove to be most redemptive. Paul does not elaborate or illustrate his point but he does promise that eventually everyone will know the difference because the work will be tested. The analogy he used for the test was fire, which would not destroy the gold, silver, or precious stones but would consume the wood, hay, and stubble (3:13).

The "day" that Paul says will declare the true value of what has been built refers to the time when Christ shall come again and the world will be judged. The "day of the Lord" in the Old Testament was a term that meant God's coming in both judgment and deliverance. All of us who work in the church need to do so with the awareness that there will come a time when what has been done will be tested and its true worth revealed. It can be a day of reward or a day of loss.

Along with the fact that all we do will be judged, Paul now discusses the possibility of either reward or loss. Those of us who are nervous about any discussion of future rewards have missed a very obvious teaching that permeates both the Old Testament and the New Testament.

When the disciples asked Jesus what they would get out of following Him, Christ answered without hesitation that in the present world they would be a hundred times better off and that in the world to come they would experience eternal life (Mark 10:28–31). While Jesus rejected the common notion that our rewards would be materialistic, He affirmed the fact that there is a relationship between what we become and do and the reward we receive. This was not a contradiction of His teachings about salvation by grace through faith. Rather, His discussion here is not about salvation but about the works of saved persons building up the church.

CHAPTER FOUR

Those Who Share the Gospel

1 Corinthians 4:1–21

Nothing is more beautiful to watch than the dynamic that develops between those who give spiritual leadership and those who are led. Janette is a talented laywoman who for years has taught the Scriptures in a home Bible study. Most of those who have been in her classes are rich in this world's goods but at a spiritual level are seeking something. Through the years literally hundreds of them have become believers as a result of her teaching and her personal interest in helping them find faith. It has been interesting for me to watch the kind of bonding that takes place between Janette and those in her classes. At times they are almost worshipful of her and she has to remind them of her own humanness, and at other times they take her so for granted that she wants to skip a month just to remind them of the commitment of time and energy she has made to them. To a degree this is what Paul is doing in 1 Corinthians 4. He's reminding the Corinthian church of his role as an apostle and of their relationship to him in that role.

FAITHFUL STEWARDS

1 Let a man so consider us, as servants of Christ and stewards of the mysteries of God.

2 Moreover it is required in stewards that one be found faithful.

3 But with me it is a very small thing that I should be judged by you or by a human court. In fact, I do not even judge myself.

4 For I know nothing against myself, yet I am not justified by this; but He who judges me is the Lord.

5 Therefore judge nothing before the time, until the Lord comes, who will both bring to light the hidden things of darkness and reveal the counsels of the hearts; and then each one's praise will come from God.

1 Cor. 4:1–5

Paul brings this first section of his letter to a close by telling the readers how they are to think of the apostles. Paul used two different words to describe the apostles in 4:1, and they show the contrast of the relationship the apostles had with God and also the relationship they had with the church. The word translated "servants" came from the description of a particular Roman slave. On the great galley ships there were slaves whose work was to row the ship. Those slaves who were on the lower bank of oarsmen were called "under-rowers." They labored only as the master directed. Paul felt that he and the other apostles did only as God directed them as His servants. In a sense, every Christian needs to see himself or herself in this relationship with God, whatever our position in the work.

The second word Paul used was translated "steward." In contrast to the "under-rower," the steward was a slave with great authority and large responsibility in the household, having to direct activities and to make decisions. Paul also felt that he and the other apostles had been given authority by God to preach the gospel and to give leadership in the churches. In this role they were accountable to God for how they handled their responsibility.

This is a difficult concept for Christians today to accept and implement. During the years I worked at one of my denominational offices and preached in many different churches, I observed various attitudes toward pastors and staff members that fell short of Paul's ideal. Frequently I encountered people who thought of their minister primarily as an employee. There was the "since we pay his salary we have a right to tell him what to do" attitude. Once I even heard two Christian businessmen, who were not happy with their pastor, use terms that I had only heard in connection with losing football coaches. They said, "I think we should buy up his contract and ship him out." It is true that those of us who lead the church as clergymen are hirelings, but we are God's hirelings.

But Paul gave a marvelous criterion for evaluating God's servants and stewards. It was to be *"found faithful"* (v. 2). Some have translated it to be found "trustworthy." Graham was a quiet man, never pushing himself, seldom making speeches in the business meetings. Yet over and over he ended up either as a member or a chairman of significant committees and task forces. Once, a person who did not know him well noticed the number of ministries and programs he had been involved in and asked why the church turned to him so often when there were so many who seemed to have less to do. Several people made the same reply: "Because he's trustworthy. If he accepts a task, then he does it. It's as simple as that." The master needed to be able to trust his steward with his most valuable possession, and God needs to be able to trust His ministers with His most valuable possession, the gospel of Jesus Christ. He trusts us not to dilute the gospel or change it. He is depending upon us to share it with everyone.

In the second part of this message Paul made it clear that the Corinthians were not to judge the ministers. It is clear that Paul rejected the Corinthians' evaluation of his ministry. Now, of course, everyone who does God's work must face the judgments of others. Paul was not so thick-skinned that he could totally ignore the criticisms of others, but he had learned to put it into a larger perspective. While we often learn helpful things from those who are critical of us, we must never let them become the sole judge of our ministry. This is easier if we remember who commissioned us and the One to whom we are responsible.

We also read here that Paul rejected his own judgment of himself and his ministry! While Paul was a very strong person with tenaciously held views, he never pretended to be perfect. In his letter to the church at Philippi he confessed, "I count not myself to have apprehended" (Phil. 3:13). At the same time there is the possibility in verse 4 that Paul is creating a hypothetical situation, a situation in which he evaluates himself and finds he has a clear conscience. He seems to be saying, "Suppose I judge my work and find it completely satisfactory, is that enough?" The answer that he assumes is "no." Neither having others feel good about us nor feeling good about our own ministry is enough.

Paul claimed that the only one who was really capable of judging was God. They, the Corinthians—and we late twentieth-century church members—are His servants. Only God knows all the circumstances and the innermost thoughts of our hearts and minds. Somehow, I believe that if we could view our leaders this way, we would be better church members and more effective Christians. And if those who are church leaders would take the same position Paul did we would be more secure and more effective. The criticisms of others need to be forgotten in the context of the praise that *"will come from God"* (v. 5).

HUMBLE SERVANTS

6 Now these things, brethren, I have figuratively transferred to myself and Apollos for your sakes, that you may learn in us not to think beyond what is written, that none of you may be puffed up on behalf of one against the other.

7 For who makes you differ from another? And what do you have that you did not receive? Now if you did indeed receive it, why do you glory as if you had not received it?

8 You are already full! You are already rich! You have reigned as kings without us—and indeed I could wish you did reign, that we also might reign with you!

9 For I think that God has displayed us, the apostles, last, as men condemned to death; for we have been made a spectacle to the world, both to angels and to men.

10 We are fools for Christ's sake, but you are wise in Christ! We are weak, but you are strong! You are distinguished, but we are dishonored!

11 Even to the present hour we both hunger and thirst, and we are poorly clothed, and beaten, and homeless.

12 And we labor, working with our own hands. Being reviled, we bless; being persecuted, we endure it;

13 being defamed, we entreat. We have been made as the filth of the world, the offscouring of all things until now.

1 Cor. 4:6–13

In this short passage of Scripture there is an amazing mixture of ideas and emphases. In verse 7 there is one of the great statements on the doctrine of grace. *"What do you have that you did not receive?"*

is a question that will create genuine humility in each of us, for everything that is lasting and worthwhile we have received at the hands of God. Paul knew that pride could be so divisive in the life of the church and that humility had a way of drawing people together. I have observed this in the life of the church. Those persons who were filled with a sense of self-importance could create a crisis in the fellowship over the most insignificant of things. But individuals who lived with a sense of gratitude for God's grace in their lives could deal in a harmonious way with the most volatile of issues.

These verses also contain one of the most sarcastic statements in all of Paul's writings. In his letter to the Colossians, Paul used the analogy of the victorious Roman army to illustrate Christ's victory over all the forces of evil in the universe (Col. 2:15). In our passage in Corinthians he draws upon the same picture of the victorious Roman army, but with a totally different application. He pictures the Corinthian Christians as having the arrogance of the victorious Roman generals while he likens the apostles to the captives who are dragged along at the end of the parade. He is trying to contrast the Corinthians' pride and arrogance and feeling of superiority with the way that he himself has functioned in his relationship with them. And he chides the Corinthians for forgetting all the sacrifices the apostles had made in their behalf.

Completely apart from what this passage tells us about the spiritual immaturity of the Corinthians, verses 9–13 give us one of the finest pictures of the difficulties that the apostles faced. Paul lists in words that tear at the brain what the price tag had been for him to be a faithful steward of the gospel. It is a story of danger, of *"men condemned to death"* (v. 9). It is a story of ridicule, *"a spectacle to the world"* (v. 9). It is a story of contempt, *"fools for Christ's sake"* (v. 10). It is the experience of privation: *"we both hunger and thirst, and we are poorly clothed, and beaten, and homeless"* (v. 11). And while going through all of this in order to preach the gospel, Paul was supporting himself by the work of his *"own hands"* (v. 12).

As I read Paul's description of his sufferings, I wondered how many people would be faithful to Christ today if there were the possibility of that cost. Then I remembered that in many parts of the world today there are Christians who can identify with what Paul experienced. When these twentieth-century "fools for Christ's sake" visit the United States, they are sometimes offended by both the materialism and the spiritual pride they observe. They want to say to us, "What do you have that you did not receive?" (4:7).

At a dinner in the home of a friend, I met a group of Christian leaders from Moscow. It was the first group of Russian Christians I had ever been around. Their amazement at our privileges made me realize that I had taken too much for granted. When told that the Governor of Texas was a committed Christian, they were shocked that Christians could hold office. When told of one church's program of evangelism, they expressed amazement that we were allowed to invite others to become believers. All of us Americans ended the evening with a new sense of gratitude to God for all His gifts and a new commitment to use them for His glory.

SPIRITUAL PARENTS

14 I do not write these things to shame you, but as my beloved children I warn you.

15 For though you might have ten thousand instructors in Christ, yet you do not have many fathers; for in Christ Jesus I have begotten you through the gospel.

16 Therefore I urge you, imitate me.

17 For this reason I have sent Timothy to you, who is my beloved and faithful son in the Lord, who will remind you of my ways in Christ, as I teach everywhere in every church.

18 Now some are puffed up, as though I were not coming to you.

19 But I will come to you shortly, if the Lord wills, and I will know, not the word of those who are puffed up, but the power.

20 For the kingdom of God is not in word but in power.

21 What do you want? Shall I come to you with a rod, or in love and a spirit of gentleness?

1 Cor. 4:14–21

As Paul brings the entire discussion of disunity in the church to a close, he makes a strong appeal for unity on the basis of his unique relationship with the Corinthian church (vv. 14–17) and closes this part of the letter with a warning (vv. 18–21). There is in the first passage a warm fatherly admonition for the majority and in the second a stern rebuke for the few causing trouble. In reading the letter I get the feeling that Paul was trying to compensate for the harsh tones of the sarcasm and irony in the previous paragraph. He wanted to close his dealing with divisions on a different note.

The analogy that Paul used to distinguish himself from all the others who had played a part in their spiritual pilgrimage was the difference between an instructor and a parent. In his use of *"my beloved children"* (v. 14) we see his feelings of love and tenderness for them. In Ephesians he counsels fathers not to be so harsh with their children that they would provoke them to wrath (Eph. 6:4). Here Paul, functioning as a spiritual father, follows his own advice as he calls upon his paternal relationship with them as a basis for unity.

The word *"instructor"* is translated different ways in various Scripture versions, sometimes "tutor" and at other times "guide." It was usually used of a slave who was responsible for guiding the conduct of a child from age six to manhood. He was usually an older and most trusted slave who not only delivered the child to the school each day, but guided the child in the development of his character and his lifestyle. A child might have any number of "instructors" of this sort in the process of growing up.

When Paul wrote *"You might have ten thousand instructors in Christ"* (v. 15), he was exaggerating for emphasis, but the point was well made. Just as a child might have many instructors but only one father, so the Corinthians might have many people who would help them as they matured in the Christian faith. But they would have only one spiritual father and that was Paul.

There is a special bond that God created between spiritual parents and their children, and it is a wonderful basis for unity. I attended the Silver Anniversary of a church in Anchorage, Alaska. The church has had only one pastor. He had come to Alaska as a carpenter-preacher and the church had been formed out of the converts to his witness. As I listened to him speak of the church's history, I sensed a different sort of relationship than that which most pastors have with a congregation. He was different because he was the spiritual father for most of the members.

CHAPTER FIVE

Don't Condone Immorality

1 Corinthians 5:1–13

This chapter introduces a section on the need for the church to be more sensitive about its witness in the world. The Apostle Paul knew that one of his best arguments for the power of the gospel was a life that was changed. But he also knew that the secular world would be scrutinizing the Christian community with the hope of finding some blatant inconsistency with which to discredit the church. Paul felt that great care had to be exercised to draw a clearer line between the Christian and pagan lifestyles, and he wrote to the Corinthian Christians about their attitude toward a case of incest (5:1–13), about dragging church matters into secular courts (6:1–11), and about controlling their sexual appetites (6:12–20). While the cases he cites are obviously tied to the Corinthian situation, the basic problem with which Paul is dealing is still the church's problem today—the need to be more sensitive as to how our lives affect our witness in the world.

     1 It is actually reported that there is sexual immorality among you, and such sexual immorality as is not even named among the Gentiles—that a man has his father's wife!
     2 And you are puffed up, and have not rather mourned, that he who has done this deed might be taken away from among you.
     3 For I indeed, as absent in body but present in spirit, have already judged, as though I were present, concerning him who has so done this deed.
     4 In the name of our Lord Jesus Christ, when you

are gathered together, along with my spirit, with the power of our Lord Jesus Christ,

5 deliver such a one to Satan for the destruction of the flesh, that his spirit may be saved in the day of the Lord Jesus.

6 Your glorying is not good. Do you not know that a little leaven leavens the whole lump?

7 Therefore purge out the old leaven, that you may be a new lump, since you are truly unleavened. For indeed Christ, our Passover, was sacrificed for us.

8 Therefore let us keep the feast, not with the old leaven, nor with the leaven of malice and wickedness, but with the unleavened bread of sincerity and truth.

9 I wrote to you in my epistle not to keep company with sexually immoral people.

10 Yet I certainly did not mean with the sexually immoral people of this world, or with the covetous, or extortioners, or idolaters, since then you would need to go out of the world.

11 But now I have written to you not to keep company with anyone named a brother who is a fornicator, or covetous, or an idolater, or a reviler, or a drunkard, or an extortioner—not even to eat with such a person.

12 For what have I to do with judging those also who are outside? Do you not judge those who are inside?

13 But those who are outside God judges. Therefore *"put away from yourselves that wicked person."*

1 Cor. 5:1–13

As Paul moves from the problem of factions in the church to several moral issues, the first one he confronts the Corinthians with is a case of flagrant immorality within the life of the church. This had apparently been going on for some time and was common knowledge in the church.

Almost everyone agrees that the phrase *"a man has his father's wife"* (v. 1) would mean that he had a sexual relationship with his step-mother. Whether his father was divorced from the woman or was no longer living is not indicated, but the fact that Paul gives no instruction to the church as to how to deal with the woman would indicate that she was not a Christian and hence not under the authority of the church. This type of relationship was forbidden in Jewish law (Lev. 18:7–8) and, as Paul indicated, even the sexually promiscuous pagan society forbade it.

Evidently, at this point the young Corinthian church took a rather casual attitude toward sexual morality, but this particular case seemed to be worse than usual. But, unfortunately, the church was crippled in its ability even to recognize the problem, to say nothing of its paralysis in dealing with it, because that dividing line between the pagan world and the church had almost been obliterated. There are some who feel that a Gnostic distortion of the gospel might have been at the root of the problem because the Gnostics believed that what was done with the body was unimportant and irrelevant to one's religion. While it is true that Gnostic doctrines plagued the church during its early days (reflected especially in Colossians), I do not think this was the background of this particular problem in Corinth.

Rather, the problem within the Corinthian church was how to resist the pressure of conforming to an immoral society. After all, they had only recently been a part of that world, and they brought into the church deeply ingrained habits of thought and action which stood in stark contrast with the ideals that God had for them in their new relationship with Him. In addition they were being asked to live the Christian life, not in some remote and isolated colony of Christians, but in a world and culture that took a very casual attitude toward sexual morality.

How to live a moral life in an immoral world is a constantly recurring problem for Christians. This is no antique issue but one with which every church and each Christian needs help in today's world. While Biblical faith views sex as the gift of God which can bring happiness and fulfillment within the marriage relationship, there are many in our secular society that treat sex as no more than a physical appetite to be satisfied. This attitude, wherever it is found, expresses itself in relationships that are casual, temporary, physical, and self-fulfilling, in contrast to the Biblical mode. This casual attitude toward sex has infiltrated television, movies, magazines—even our conversations during coffee break. It is the very atmosphere in which we live our lives, and we are more affected by it than we realize.

This rather terrifying truth is headlined for me so often in comments that are made to me or in the questions I am asked. A bright, attractive teenager in a church in Washington, D.C., asked, "You don't really think there's anything wrong with 'making out,' do you, as long as you're careful?" And then there was the middle-aged deacon who asked why we didn't just drop the "until death do us part" from the wedding ceremony. In a divorce seminar one of the women stated emphatically, "I have no intention of ever marrying again, but I don't plan on doing without sex." Then I recall so well the casual way in which the young woman seated by me on the plane said that she had been reared in the same denomination as mine and that she was a topless dancer. Our problem and the problem of the Corinthian Christians is the same: how to live moral lives in an immoral world.

Both Paul's attitude and his action may be offensive to some twentieth-century Christians, but a close examination of his thoughts and suggestions may give us fresh insights.

First, Paul was shocked by the sin itself. When we live day after day in a world where immorality is accepted, there is danger that we become so infected and influenced by that culture that almost nothing shocks us. For example, twenty years ago a motion picture was released that created a public furor because of its casual treatment of virginity. Letters were written to newspaper editors, certain theaters banned the picture, and sermons were preached against it. There was a surge of shock at the casual way the film treated sexual relationships. But today people watch suggestive or even pornographic movies in their homes on cable television, and the networks are releasing programs in prime time that compromise Christian marriage and family values. We are losing the capacity to be shocked. By contrast, Paul was shocked at what was happening at Corinth, and he felt something must be done about it.

Second, Paul was shocked at the attitude of the church. What was happening, plus the church's attitude toward it, created a deathlike experience for Paul, and he was in mourning. But the church was not even aware that there was a problem. Whether being *"puffed up"* (v. 2) meant that their spiritual pride had kept them from being aware of the problem, or that they were actually proud of a situation they ought to be mourning, is not clear. It was probably a combination of both.

Spiritual pride has a way of blinding us to reality, and we often take pride in things we ought to repent of. I can almost imagine someone rationalizing the situation in a way that would sound familiar to modern Christians. "Ours is a broad-minded church. As long as he stays active in the church and does his part I don't think it's anyone's business what he does in private. Besides, while he's a lot younger than she is they seem to have a meaningful relationship. What they really need from us is affirmation and not judgment." Sound familiar?

The action Paul suggested to remedy this critical situation was severe and must have created great consternation and pain in the hearts of those who heard it. He obviously felt the need to be very specific in his writing since he couldn't be there with them in person. The Apostle Paul well understood the techniques of written communication, and while he had already made up his mind as to what should be done (v. 3), he wasn't about to let the church off the hook when it came to their responsibility. He urged them to gather as the church (v. 4) and to excommunicate the offending brother (v. 5). He gave two reasons for the wisdom of this action (vv. 5–6).

Paul's suggestions, which were really instructions, must have put them into shock. Even this far removed from the actual situation, because of my knowledge of the dynamic of relationships in a church, I sort of catch my breath at the sweeping implication of Paul's solution to their problem. But if we look a little closer at the way it was to be done and the purpose for which it was to be done, we will see the wisdom in it and find some principles for church discipline in our own day.

Verse 4 gives instructions for the atmosphere of the meeting which is to be held. While Paul wanted them to think of his being present in spirit, he suggested also that they gather *"in the name of our Lord Jesus Christ"* (v. 4). They were not to come together in a quarrelsome and fractious manner or as a lynch mob or a vigilante group. They were to assemble as those who had confessed "Jesus is Lord," and in the *"power of our Lord Jesus Christ"* (v. 4). Paul wanted them to see they wouldn't be able in their own wisdom and strength to do what was necessary, but in Christ's power they could.

There was a time in recent history when a congregation came together to "church" a person. In one tradition it was called "excommunication" and in another "withdrawing fellowship," but it meant the same thing—putting the person out of the church. The fact that this is so seldom done today might mean that we are more loving and forgiving, or it could mean that we are less concerned with the integrity of the Christian life within the body of the church. I am convinced that a part of the reaction to church discipline as it was practiced earlier in this century, is a reaction to the punitive spirit in which it was done.

When my cousin, who is the age of my mother, told me of those deacons, who like secret agents, peeked through the windows at school dances to record the names of the church youth who were present and how on Sunday these names were called from the pulpit and the church was asked to "discipline" the guilty, I knew why her enthusiasm for that church had grown cold. From reading Paul's instruction to the church at Corinth I think he would have been offended at any approach to discipline that disregarded the spirit and power of Christ.

Paul's exact phrase in verse 5 was *"deliver such a one to Satan."* This should not be thought of as removing him from God and giving him to the devil, or moving him from the ranks of the Christians to the ranks of the non-Christian. At the time Paul was writing, the world was considered Satan's realm. Those who read this statement probably understood it to mean, "Put him out of the church." J. B. Phillips picks up on this idea when he translates the verse: "The man who has done such a thing should certainly be expelled from your fellowship!" Paul did not tell them exactly how to do this so it can be assumed that they knew the procedure.

Paul did not view the action as punishment but as having a redemptive purpose both for the man and for the church. As painful as the experience would be, Paul felt that it might bring the man to his senses and cause him to see what he was doing and repent. As long as our friends within the Christian community help us rationalize our sins, we are not likely to do anything to change. But when in love we are confronted with what we are doing and are forced to look at ourselves through different eyes, we more likely begin to examine our lives. This is what happened to King David. Until he had to look at his lust and adultery and murder and deceit through the prophet Nathan's eyes, he never considered changing. But if a discipline such as Paul urges is to be effective, it must be redemptive.

To love the church and an individual enough to do what Paul suggested takes courage, deep confidence in God, and a mature love for people. Our own "don't rock the boat" mentality tries to parade itself as being more sophisticated, more loving and accepting, and less judgmental than these first-century Christians. But I wonder. Is it possible that we are less concerned than they for the witness of the church and the quality of life among its members?

Paul felt that this disciplinary action was for the church's good as well. Not only might the person be salvaged, but the action could also save the church. Without questioning Paul's love for the person involved, I'm inclined to think Paul felt the witness and even the existence of the church was at stake. To fail to take this stand would eventually lead to the spiritual contamination of the whole church.

The analogy of the leaven, used by Paul in verses 6–8, came from the process of preparation for the Passover. Here he compares the immorality that cannot be tolerated and must be rooted out from the church with the leaven that had to be discovered and gotten rid of before the time of the Jewish Passover. On the first day of Passover all leaven must be removed as a symbol of Israel's liberation from the sins of Egypt. No leaven could be present in the bread that was eaten in the Passover meal lest there be risk of contamination. Paul was saying, "If this is not handled promptly and incisively, it will eventually permeate the whole church." Paul had learned that a church will eventually adjust to what it tolerates, and he had a dream of a different kind of church.

This has been the history of the church. If we do not raise our voices against violence in every form, we will become violent people. If the church gives no commitment to efforts at peace, we become a warring people. If the church will not speak out against the idolatry of materialism, it will become materialistic. Whatever evil we allow to exist unchallenged in our midst will grow like a malignancy within the fellowship of the church. Consequently, the effort to leave things as they are in the interest of peace represents a cowardly and unwise posture, because evil is contagious.

The contemporary church needs to salvage from this very difficult experience within the Corinthian church some guidelines for a redemptive approach to church discipline. I believe there are three questions that should be raised.

First, does the action calling for discipline threaten the life and existence of the church itself? Depending on the particular church, I can see where the answer could be "yes" in one situation and "no" in another. For example, in a small and new congregation that is trying to witness for Christ in a hostile environment, if one of its members is involved in immoral activities, the congregation may decide that a failure to take quick, decisive, and public action might cause the fragile organization to collapse if the offending member is not expelled from the church. On the other hand and under the same circumstances, an old and well established church might choose first to have the minister or one of the lay officers of the church visit with the offending member and try to "redeem" him or her.

The second question: Is there danger that the sinful act will infect the whole church? This will always be a judgment call, but it is a good question and must be wrestled with. And it is a question a church must answer when it seeks to minister to persons who have experienced failure in some area of their lives. For example, when our church began to minister to people who had been in prison, I sensed there were those in the congregation who were fearful that it might look as if we condoned the actions of those who had broken the law. And when we started a special ministry to the formerly married, there were those who were concerned that we might be weakening our stand on marriage.

While such questions may have been born of fear, they are important as we also ask ourselves whether or not a particular activity would be harmful for the church as a whole. We decided that in these instances there was such a strong commitment to the Christian lifestyle in the congregation that our involvement in such ministries would not water down the church's witness. But we readily acknowledge that other churches might not be in a position to answer the way we did.

Third question: Will allowing a specific activity to go on lessen the distinction between the church and the world? This is a most difficult question because the very existence of the church in the world creates a climate for compromise. In the last verses of this chapter Paul deals with a misunderstanding in the church on this particular point. Evidently he had written a letter on this issue which preceded 1 Corinthians because he clearly states, *"I wrote to you in my epistle not to keep company with sexually immoral people"* (v. 9). What other epistle? There has been much speculation about this. Some interpreters believe it to be an earlier letter that has been lost while others feel he is referring to a part of 2 Corinthians. (Read the Introduction to 2 Corinthians for a discussion of the sequence of Paul's visits to Corinth and of various theories about the order of his correspondence with them.)

The one thing we do know is that those who received the letter misunderstood at least one thing Paul said. He seems to have said that they were not to have anything to do with a church member who was living in immorality, and they took him to mean they were not to have anything to do with anyone who is immoral. Paul clarifies his position by stating that he was referring only to those church members who were openly involved in the sins which he lists (5:11). The other church members were to cut them off from such social contact as eating with them.

Paul gave a different standard for relating to those outside the church. He made it clear that he knew it would not be possible to function in this world if we limited our social contact only to "good" Christians. He stated frankly that to do that we would have to *"go out of the world"* (v. 10). In spite of this, however, there are those who believe and practice the notion that a Christian's whole life should be lived within the fellowship of the church, and when it is necessary to buy such things as automobiles or furniture we should turn to the "born-again yellow pages" so we will not even have to trade with the lost. But doesn't this miss Christ's point, that we are to be salt and light in the world?

On the surface Paul's standard seems to suggest that we treat immoral lost people better than we treat immoral church members. But his point is entirely consistent with the idea that we are not to judge the world, but we are responsible for the life of the church. We are to move about in the world without a judgmental or censorious attitude as stewards of the gospel. But in the church we are to impose upon ourselves a stern discipline so that our lives will not contradict the gospel we share. An ever-present danger in our church life today is that we are lenient with ourselves and judgmental of the world. And it is this attitude that so often makes it hard to get a hearing for the gospel. Paul's approach is better. Now he moves on to two other moral problems.

CHAPTER SIX

Don't Compromise the Witness

1 Corinthians 6:1–20

In this chapter Paul continues to warn the church in Corinth about the way in which it deals with certain problems affecting the witness of the church. Paul was concerned that two church members would have a disagreement and instead of settling it in the Spirit of Christ, would take each other to court (6:1–11). He was also concerned that there were some who saw no relationship between their faith in Jesus Christ and what they did with their bodies (6:12–20). As I read about these issues with which he was dealing, I wish it were possible for us to get his insight into some of the more complex issues that the church faces today, issues in which the witness of the church is also at stake. The issues are increasingly difficult to sort out and to be consistent on as illustrated in the life of one family. Because the wife felt that there was a religious dimension to the whole question of abortion she circulated a petition both on her street and at church urging a ruling against abortion on demand. While she was doing her best to protect the life of the unborn child, her husband went to work at the government-operated plant which assembled nuclear devices and as he passed pickets at the gate who were calling for a world-wide ban on nuclear arms, in his mind he classified the pickets as Communists. Neither of these were issues for the church and for Christians at the time of Paul, but they are today, and how the church deals with them may affect not only her witness but the future of mankind.

SETTLE YOUR OWN DIFFERENCES

1 Dare any of you, having a matter against another,
go to law before the unrighteous, and not before the
saints?

2 Do you not know that the saints will judge the world? And if the world will be judged by you, are you unworthy to judge the smallest matters?

3 Do you not know that we shall judge angels? How much more, things that pertain to this life?

4 If then you have judgments concerning things pertaining to this life, do you appoint those who are least esteemed by the church to judge?

5 I say this to your shame. Is it so, that there is not a wise man among you, not even one, who will be able to judge between his brethren?

6 But brother goes to law against brother, and that before unbelievers!

7 Now therefore, it is already an utter failure for you to go to law against one another. Why do you not rather accept wrong? Why do you not rather let yourselves be defrauded?

8 No, you yourselves do wrong and defraud, and you do these things to your brethren!

9 Do you not know that the unrighteous will not inherit the kingdom of God? Do not be deceived. Neither fornicators, nor idolaters, nor adulterers, nor homosexuals, nor sodomites,

10 nor thieves, nor covetous, nor drunkards, nor revilers, nor extortioners will inherit the kingdom of God.

11 And such were some of you. But you were washed, but you were sanctified, but you were justified in the name of the Lord Jesus and by the Spirit of our God.

1 Cor. 6:1–11

Paul seemed to have a list of things he wanted to discuss with the Corinthian church. This list was apparently made up from reports he had received about what was going on in the church.

Paul was shocked to learn that church members were suing each other in the secular courts. Every time I read these verses I am reminded of church squabbles that have spilled over into the courts and into the papers and have wondered how what Paul wrote to the Corinthian church applied to them today. In recent years I've seen a church that had been growing and ministering in an effective way become the object of ridicule as a disgruntled group within the church went into the courts to force the pastor and lay leaders to make public certain financial records. And I watched one of the great churches of our time almost destroy itself in a long, expensive, and bitter court battle between factions within the church over the property. While there are vast differences in both the church and society of Paul's day and ours, can we find some guiding principle in his message to the Corinthians that will help us?

Paul felt that Christians ought to be able to settle their own problems without resorting to a public display in the secular courts. His conclusion was strengthened by his Jewish background and his concern for the church. In the history of their relationship with Rome, the Jews had secured permission to apply their own laws to themselves. For this reason a faithful Jew would not even consider having what was a "Jewish problem" decided on by a gentile court. There was even a procedure set up for dealing with differences within the Jewish community. This was Paul's background, and it was also the background of the Jewish members of the Corinthian church.

But the Greek members of this church had a very different heritage. There was among the Greeks a natural love of litigation. The fondness for the contest, for debate, and for oratory made going to court almost a form of entertainment. While there was in the Greek system a method of settling disputes before they got into court, evidently these particular church members were not availing themselves of this quieter way of solving their problems.

Not only was Paul's background different, but he approached problems from a different perspective. The church members were completely absorbed with their own private concerns, while Paul, from his position of maturity, was anxious for the church. First, he was concerned about their need to grow spiritually. That they were not able to settle their problems outside the court was evidence of a failure within the fellowship of Christian discipline. Later in the letter Paul would be writing about the importance of discovering and developing their spiritual gifts and learning to love each other. So he must have seen the factious spirit, the sexual immorality, and the disputes in the courts as obstacles to spiritual growth.

Second, Paul was concerned about the reputation of Christians in Corinth and the witness to persons who were outside the church. He knew the *"low esteem"* (v. 4) in which Christians and the church were held by a pagan society, and he felt that their suing each other would only confirm the worst suspicions of the unbelievers. This is a matter of continuing concern for Christians today, because there are always those on the outside who seem to delight at every opportunity to discredit a Christian or a church.

Christians today can get guidance from Paul's counsel, but we need to be very careful not to push his point too far or try to apply it in situations that are radically different. First, I don't think Paul was intending to suggest that justice was impossible in the secular courts or that Christians should never sue anyone. Paul himself received excellent treatment at the hands of Gallio, who was the deputy in Corinth. Gallio's fairness and wisdom and courage saved Paul from the consequence of a Jewish insurrection (Acts 18:12–17). Paul also wrote in the letter to the Romans that the secular powers were "ordained of God" and should be obeyed (Rom. 13:1–2).

It will be helpful for those who try to transpose Paul's instruction to the Corinthians in this instance over into contemporary society to remember two things. First, there are many Christians who are part of our judicial system who bring a larger dimension to justice and truth as a result of their faith in Christ. Second, Paul probably was not able to anticipate his advice being applied wholesale in a highly complex industrial society.

I have a Christian friend who owns a chemical company where an explosion and fire caused damage to the plant and serious injury or death to several persons. Involved in the deaths and injuries were several employees. When I first learned of the tragic accident I wondered just how David would handle what had happened. I knew that it would be a time of great personal pain and loss for him because he was a person who prized his employees, and to the degree that it was possible, took a real interest in their families and in their personal lives. I knew from a flow of articles and books on the general subject of the Christian ethic in the marketplace that he was not a man who kept business and religion separated in his life. Knowing this, I wondered how he would deal with that avalanche of lawsuits and claims that seemed to me to be inevitable. Shortly after the accident I learned that he was a part of a Christian organization who sought to get Christians to negotiate legitimate settlements out of court. They have two reasons: to spend the money on the real victims rather than on all the expenses of the trial and to show that it is not necessary to take a Christian to court in order to get him to do what is right. While it is a very idealistic approach for a society so complex, there is a great deal of interest in the idea and in many cases it is working. David's case is too fresh to know what the outcome will be, but if it should fail it will not have failed because he did not try.

What Paul was working with was a much simpler situation. He suggested that when two church members have a quarrel, it ought not to end up in a lawsuit, even if one of the brothers has to suffer wrong. When kept in the context in which it was written, that is still good advice.

Verses 9–11 serve both as a conclusion to the first part of the chapter and as an introduction to the verses that follow. They read like a roll call of the disinherited. Paul didn't mean to leave the impression, I am sure, that anyone who had committed any of those particular sins could not become a Christian. Rather, he preached a gospel of liberation in which those who repented of sin and turned to Christ were forgiven and made to be children of God. But here he was actually giving the background of some of the church members as indicated by his words, *"And such were some of you."*

After listing at least some of the pagan sins and declaring that those who continue to make them the practice of their lives will not inherit the Kingdom of God, Paul goes on to remind them of the experience which they had in Christ that had separated them from the pagan world. He did this to motivate them to take their calling seriously.

Paul used three words to describe what had happened to them: they were "washed," "sanctified," and "justified." It's interesting that the verb Paul used for "washed" is used only one other place in the New Testament—in connection with Paul's own conversion: "Arise and be baptized, and wash away your sins, calling on the name of the Lord" (Acts 22:16). The Corinthians had experienced that same cleansing.

The terms "sanctified" and "justified" were used almost as synonyms. The first means to be spiritually set aside by the act of God to be His people and serve His purpose. The second is one of Paul's favorite words for what God does to make persons His children.

Sometimes just remembering what God has done in our lives both motivates us and puts things in a larger perspective. I remember vividly a certain Monday night deacons' meeting in our church. The business and discussion had been long and drawn out. Everyone seemed tired and anxious for the meeting to end so they could go home. But when the business was finally concluded the chairman announced that he had asked three of the newly ordained deacons to share a word of witness. I could almost feel the current of resentment that seemed to flow through the room. But as those three new deacons shared their unique pilgrimage with God, everyone in the room became caught up. Their witness served as a catalyst for the rest of us to remember how God had dealt with us. When the meeting was finally dismissed there was a wonderful sense of joy and unity, and everyone stood around and visited.

DON'T LET YOUR BODY LEAD YOU ASTRAY

12 All things are lawful for me, but all things are not helpful. All things are lawful for me, but I will not be brought under the power of any.

13 Foods for the stomach and the stomach for foods, but God will destroy both it and them. Now the body is not for sexual immorality but for the Lord, and the Lord for the body.

14 And God both raised up the Lord and will also raise us up by His power.

15 Do you not know that your bodies are members of Christ? Shall I then take the members of Christ and make them members of a harlot? Certainly not!

16 Or do you not know that he who is joined to a harlot is one body with her? For *"The two,"* He says, *"shall become one flesh."*

17 But he who is joined to the Lord is one spirit with Him.

18 Flee sexual immorality. Every sin that a man does is outside the body, but he who commits sexual immorality sins against his own body.

19 Or do you not know that your body is the temple of the Holy Spirit who is in you, whom you have from God, and you are not your own?

20 For you were bought at a price; therefore glorify
God in your body and in your spirit, which are God's.

1 Cor. 6:12–20

Paul now goes back to the theme of sexual laxness which he had discussed earlier. There is one general principle here which speaks to us with great relevance: *"Glorify God in your body"* (v. 20). The practical application here is related to not having sexual intercourse with prostitutes, but the overall principle had as large a relevance then as it does now. While the Puritans may have lived as though there were no such thing as sex, our generation, like the Corinthians, acts as though there is nothing but sex. This is why Paul had so much to say about it and why this portion of his letter has a special word from God to us.

"All things are lawful for me" (v. 12) should have quotation marks in the text because it was a popular saying of the day. It may have had its source in Gnosticism or in a misunderstanding of something that Paul had said or written. Gnosticism was a Greek philosophy that espoused the idea of a "dualism" between the body and the soul. The soul was recognized as good and of God, but the body was considered bad and not of God. In fact, the body was viewed as the jail that imprisoned the spirit. This notion affected behavior in two diverse ways. Some people decided the body needed to be punished, so they denied it practically all of its appetites. This was called asceticism and was behind many of the monastic movements.

But the more popular reaction was not to neglect the body but to indulge its every appetite with the feeling that what one did with one's body had nothing to do with the soul or with one's religion.

In this age of bumper stickers, I saw one recently that was very "Corinthian." It said, "If it feels good, do it." Today there are people who never heard of the Gnostics, who treat sex as an appetite to be satisfied as casually as the need for food is met by having a snack.

When Nancy, my oldest daughter, was in high school, her teacher invited me to speak to a class that had been studying moral values in American literature. Rather than use the occasion to talk about the distinctives of my own religious heritage, I decided to talk about what all the various denominations have in common in their view of wholeness: that God created our body with its appetites, our mind with its reason and questions, our emotions with their responses, and our will with its capacity for decision and that Christ came to create wholeness in our lives.

When I had completed my talk, a young man near the rear of the room asked a question that was more a statement than anything else. "If God made the body with its appetites, then why are you preachers always hassling me about sex?" My presentation had been so general in nature that I hadn't even mentioned "sex" or made any derogatory remark about anyone's lifestyle, and I reminded the student of that fact. But evidently someone had been hassling him, and he was not to be denied a chance for rebuttal. He went on, "My sexual needs are just like all my other needs. If I get hungry I drop by McDonald's for a quarterpounder with cheese, and if I feel the need for sex I get a date with a girl who is willing. Now what's wrong with that?" It was a classic statement of a very old philosophy. And it deserves our attention because in many ways the inability to make the moral distinctions between "fast food" and "fast sex," which characterizes so much of our thinking, has crept into our churches even as it had in Corinth. Possibly Paul's response can be helpful to us.

The statement "All things are lawful for me" (v. 12), could have come from a misunderstanding or a misapplication of Paul's teaching about the freedom which we have in Christ. In contrast to the law which bound persons, Paul saw the gospel as a liberating word and the church as a liberating community.

This note of freedom in Christ flows through all of Paul's writing. His statements concerning Christian freedom were usually made as a polemic against the narrow legalism of Judaistic religion. But there were those in the Corinthian church who used their freedom to create new slaveries. The same persons who had celebrated the freedom from guilt which God's forgiveness brought, used that freedom to indulge their appetites and became slaves again—this time to their own desires.

Like so many Christians of my age, I was reared in a church that defined the Christian life negatively. A good Christian didn't drink, dance, smoke, play cards, or go to Thompson's movie theater. Too often the sermon's main function was to produce a guilt trip, and those of us who answered the call to give up "worldliness" discovered that the observable sins we quit were replaced by one that was less visible and more deadly—spiritual pride. We also discovered that a life emptied of worldliness is still empty and needs something to fill it. Even as a boy I had felt that there was some irreconcilable conflict between this narrow judgmental approach to religion and the love and patience and forgiveness I had experienced in my relationship with Christ.

When during college I began to be exposed to preachers and teachers and others who interpreted the Christian life in positive terms, it was a very freeing experience. When exposed to the idea that it's the One to whom you commit your life that makes you a Christian and not something you've quit doing, all I'd experienced or observed affirmed it as true. When it finally came to me that the focus of the gospel was more on the love of God than the sinfulness of man, I was ready to celebrate. It's a very heavy and intoxicating experience as a sinner to realize that we can stand before a holy God and be made free from the penalty and power of sin over our lives.

Next I began to realize that freedom had responsibilities and also that freedom could be abused. The Corinthians did it, and so do we. Now I'm sensing the need to discover that the love which forgives makes tough demands and that our character is determined by how we use our freedom. We do not need to return to those days when we tried to earn God's love by things we did or didn't do, but we need to learn to let His unconditional love create in us a holy life lived in response to His love. The move from legalism to love, to responsible discipleship, tells the story of my life, and it's the last of the three I'm working on now.

In his rationale for sexual purity in these verses Paul gives the best insight into what's wrong with casual sex. He is addressing the tendency of members of the church in Corinth to visit prostitutes. But what he had to say to them is relevant to anyone today who enters into a sexual relationship outside the context of a marriage commitment, whether it is a teenager experimenting with sex, a single adult engaging in a one-night stand, or a married person having sex with someone besides his or her marriage partner.

Paul makes a clear distinction between how the appetite for food and the need for sex are to be met. He quotes the popular saying that *"food is for the stomach, and the stomach for food"* (v. 13), reminding his readers that ultimately both the stomach and the food will cease to be. But he contends that sexual intercourse, unlike eating food, involves the whole person, a person who has continuity in the resurrection. He didn't mention that it was a violation of the seventh commandment. Rather he took the position that to deal so casually with sex is a violation of the whole Christian view of persons.

It is the Christian view of persons that makes so many attitudes and actions relating to sex in our society so wrong. Everything about the pornography business—whether it's hard porn or soft porn and whether it's a vulgar pamphlet sold in an adult bookstore or a successful girlie magazine—has as its basic problem that it uses sex in a prostituting way. And this same demeaning view of sex has infiltrated the world of advertising when it uses sex to sell a product.

Paul's next argument used the Christian view of union with Christ as an argument against casually joining one's body with a harlot. The passage he quotes is from Genesis 2:24, and it describes the relationship of Adam and Eve to each other. This is the same passage Jesus quoted when he reminded his questioners of what God intended for marriage to be (Matt. 19:1–10). He reminded his readers that in their relationship with God, they established a union with Christ, and in their relationship with the harlot, they formed a physical union. It was wrong to join the body in which Christ dwelt with a harlot. I doubt that Paul is suggesting that when a church member joined himself to a prostitute that he was actually married to her. Rather, he was merely reminding them of the intimacy of the sexual relationship and how it stood in contradiction with one's relationship with Jesus Christ.

While Paul applied the general principle to only one area, if it is to be more relevant to us today we need to relate it even more broadly. If the principle is "Glorify God in your body," then there are many more areas of application besides the one Paul mentioned. Stated positively, a commitment to health and the eating and exercise habits involved would take on religious dimensions. Stated negatively, it would also mean that the abuse of our bodies with alcohol or other drugs or by overeating represents a failure to take seriously the truth that our bodies are the temple of Christ. At a more subtle level it would mean that a Christian cannot justify a pace of life that creates a stress that strains the heart and causes early heart trouble.

Paul's advice to *"flee"* (v. 18) is still good advice. It meant not just to avoid these temptations but to run away from them. Each of us, no matter how circumspect our lives, will face many temptations. But we ought not to underestimate their power to attract nor overestimate our ability to resist. The question which comes to me is where to "flee"? Because our society is so permeated with a lesser view of persons and a self-centered view of the body, I've decided that it isn't a place away from where I am. I can't move to a different town or take a different job. What I can do is relate all of my life to God and find in that relationship a perspective from which to deal with everything, whether it's the temptation to immorality or too fast a pace in my life.

CHAPTER SEVEN

Sex, Marriage, and Divorce

1 Corinthians 7:1–40

With chapter 7 the agenda changes and it is likely that the interest of the readers picks up. Through the first six chapters Paul dealt with disturbing situations he had heard about from various sources within the church. Now he begins to answer questions which persons in the church had asked. When I teach a class or lead a seminar I always try to "split the time" with the participants. Instead of using the entire time for my lecture, I try to leave half of the time either for response or for questions from the group. I usually try to create a situation in which people who wish to remain anonymous can turn in written questions to be added to those which are asked openly. Almost without exception the discussion period is more interesting both to the group *and* to me than is the lecture. Not only are people more interested in answers to questions they ask, but I do a better job of responding to the specific interests and attitudes of real people.

By reading the rest of 1 Corinthians it's almost possible to reproduce the questions the church members had asked. Paul seems to have a list before him as he writes, and he appears to quote from his list from time to time. The seventh chapter's questions were about marriage and singleness. The next three chapters (8–10) deal with questions about eating meat offered to idols. Chapter 11 answers questions raised about worship and conduct in church. The following three chapters (12–14) deal with a number of questions relating to spiritual gifts and their manifestation in the church. Chapter 15 is the classic chapter dealing with questions about the resurrection from the dead. The closing chapter deals with what would be called today "housekeeping matters," such as the plans for the offering, personal plans, and final exhortations and greetings.

GUIDELINES FOR SEXUAL INTIMACY

1 Now concerning the things of which you wrote to me: It is good for a man not to touch a woman.

2 Nevertheless, because of sexual immorality, let each man have his own wife, and let each woman have her own husband.

3 Let the husband render to his wife the affection due her, and likewise also the wife to her husband.

4 The wife does not have authority over her own body, but the husband does. And likewise the husband does not have authority over his own body, but the wife does.

5 Do not deprive one another except with consent for a time, that you may give yourselves to fasting and to prayer; and come together again so that Satan does not tempt you because of your lack of self-control.

6 But I say this as a concession, not as a commandment.

7 For I wish that all men were even as I myself. But each one has his own gift from God, one in this manner and another in that.

8 But I say to the unmarried and to the widows: It is good for them if they remain even as I am;

9 but if they cannot exercise self-control, let them marry. For it is better to marry than to burn with passion.

1 Cor. 7:1–9

It is impossible to read these verses without coming to the conclusion that the Apostle Paul felt that while marriage was allowable, celibacy was superior. In the previous chapter he clearly condemned a sexual relationship with a prostitute, and here he broadens the admonition with a statement that could rule out marriage: *"It is good for a man not to touch a woman"* (v. 1).

While Paul holds to the preference of being single throughout the chapter, he concedes that marriage may be necessary as an expedient alternative to sexual immorality (v. 2). He also recognizes that everyone does not have his *"own gift from God"* (v. 7), which allows him to resist sexual temptations and to concentrate completely upon God's work. But Paul's answers to his readers' questions create a whole new set of questions in the minds of today's readers of this passage.

One question is whether Paul's position was in conflict with his own Jewish background, especially his teaching about celibacy. When one reads the entire chapter, one finds at least three traditional Jewish teachings about marriage that Paul affirms. First, marriage was to be monogamous. One husband and one wife for life was the ideal. Second, premarital or extramarital sex violated God's ideal for the marriage. Third, the sexual demands in the marriage were the same for both husband and wife. This represented a radical statement for the first century—and for today's society as well. These statements build a wall around marriage and magnify its importance. But in Paul's background marriage was considered the norm and not an expedient relationship. It was a sacred *obligation* rather than something that was *permitted*.

A second question is: Doesn't advising that it *"is better to marry than to burn with passion"* (v. 9) give us a sub-Christian view of marriage? My New Testament professor during seminary days had a wonderful marriage of many years and delightful children whom he dearly loved. In the process of leading us to an understanding of a certain passage he often used illustrations either out of the wonderful Christian home in which he had been reared or from the experiences within his own family. When he came to this chapter in 1 Corinthians, he upset some of the students by saying rather critically of Paul, "There are a lot better things which can be said about marriage than that it's not a sin." All that we know from the Scriptures, beginning in Genesis and going through the Bible, tells us that the professor was right. Then how do we deal with what Paul wrote in this chapter?

We need to remember some things that are very elemental in all interpretation of the Scripture passages. First, Paul was not writing a general treatise on marriage. He was answering very specific questions which had been asked of him. Second, we must understand his answers in terms of some of the very twisted views that some of his readers had about marriage. Third, we have to isolate from the whole situation those aspects which were obviously local and temporary. Fourth, all that he said to them must be interpreted in the light of the feelings that he had about the imminent return of Christ to the earth and the inevitability of persecution in the days ahead. Finally, we need to realize that it was not possible for Paul to respond to their questions except in the light of his own personal experience with marriage. All of the above needs to be kept in mind, or we will find ourselves using this passage as "proof-text" for something that does not seem in tune with the rest of Scripture.

THE RELIGIOUSLY MIXED MARRIAGE

10 Now to the married I command, yet not I but the Lord: A wife is not to depart from her husband.

11 But even if she does depart, let her remain unmarried or be reconciled to her husband. And a husband is not to divorce his wife.

12 But to the rest I, not the Lord, say: If any brother has a wife who does not believe, and she is willing to live with him, let him not divorce her.

13 And the woman who has a husband who does not believe, if he is willing to live with her, let her not divorce him.

14 For the unbelieving husband is sanctified by the wife, and the unbelieving wife is sanctified by the husband; otherwise your children would be unclean, but now they are holy.

15 But if the unbeliever departs, let him depart; a brother or a sister is not under bondage in such cases. But God has called us to peace.

16 For how do you know, O wife, whether you will save your husband? Or how do you know, O husband, whether you will save your wife?

1 Cor. 7:10–16

From the moment Paul became a follower of Jesus Christ he began trying to relate this relationship to all of life. While the church has tended to think of Paul as her theologian, Paul's doctrine was always given not for idle speculation, but as a basis for living. The overriding emphasis of his writing is that *all* areas of our lives are to come under the influence of our relationship with Christ. This was not an idea that came naturally to me, because my early introduction to Christianity was focused more on eternity than on the present time. I heard more debates on who would be in heaven than how we should live on earth. So I worked out a neat little compartment in my life called "religion" and walled it off from the rest of my life.

In my "religion" section were the ideas that Paul had written to the Romans: we are all sinners (Rom. 3:10; 3:23); God still loves us (Rom. 5:8); and if we believe in Christ and confess Him as our Lord He saves us (Rom. 10:9–10). Somehow it had not yet dawned upon me that God intended these truths to become the foundation for how I live my whole life. I was still to discover Paul's "therefore" in Romans 12:1 which formed the bond between our relationship with God in Christ and the lives we live in this world. One of the liberating discoveries of my life has been that God is interested in helping us bring order and meaning to every situation, circumstance, and relationship in life.

Paul's first principle was: one's faith in Christ ought to strengthen one's marriage and not create unhealthy tensions for it. One of the first questions Paul had to deal with was from Christians who were married but who wondered if maybe they would be able to better serve Christ with their whole being if they were to withdraw from the marriage. For different reasons—all of them wrong—they had begun to wonder if their marriages stood in the way of their serving Christ. Though Paul, in this very chapter, makes a strong case for the celibate life, he urges them not to withdraw from their marriages. He also counseled them that if, for any reason, they did separate, not to consider divorce but to work on reconciliation.

There are many ways in which one's relationship to Christ can be of great help in giving solidity to a marriage. One's faith can furnish the ideals for the marriage and be to the relationship what the compass or the sextant is to the navigator. Our faith describes what our marriage is intended to do and be, and this gives us something with which to measure our progress. The Biblical teaching that one's marriage was to be the primary human relationship of one's life called for a commitment, and the teaching that the ideal marriage was for all of life urged a long-term investment of self. For the Christian partner to have experienced God's love and forgiveness becomes a resource for dealing with problems with the unbelieving spouse. To hold before us God's plan for marriage also gives us a basis for analyzing and rejecting the many inadequate models for relationships being promoted in our society today.

I can understand how easy it is for Christians, in the name of obedience to Christ, to neglect their marriages. Most of us realize that those who do not nourish their relationship weaken it, but we somehow feel that if we neglect it for the sake of the church the effect will be different.

Several years ago I was devastated by some divorces among close Christian friends. Just knowing and loving both parties in the divorce creates extra pain, because there is always the pressure to take sides and to try to fix blame. But more than anything else, I found myself, for the first time in my marriage, feeling exposed to the possibility of failure and being vulnerable. Though I had never verbalized it to others, I admitted to myself that somewhere in the back of my mind I felt that involvement in the life of the church immunized our marriage from problems. I remember the very day when I decided that neglecting my marriage for the church had the same effect upon it as it would if I were an executive with one of the local companies and neglected my marriage for the business. That awareness made me decide to give my marriage a higher priority and begin to draw upon the resources of my relationship with Christ to give strength to my marriage.

Barbara and I agreed that we needed to give our marriage more thought and time and a higher priority. We decided to set a day each week aside to be with each other, a time that belonged neither to the church nor the children but to us. Thursday seemed like the best day for both of us, so we began to use that as our day. We had access to a farm just over an hour from our house, and we made that our place for retreat. We developed rituals connected with both the coming and the going. If we drove up late Wednesday night after I had finished everything at the church, we would stop in Sealy at Mason's Corner Truck Stop for a late snack. If we went on Thursday morning, we'd stop at the Ricebelt Restaurant in Katy for an early breakfast. But whether early or late, we were together, and we caught each other up on all the things that were going on in our separate worlds. Rather than having a set plan for how we spent the day, we let that depend upon the season of the year and our interests. The more we did together, the more we enjoyed doing things together. Just being together was fun, even when we were doing nothing but doing it together. Of course, we didn't make it every Thursday because there were illnesses, special children's schedules, and crises at the church which had to be dealt with, but for more than five years we have worked to make time to nourish our marriage and it has paid great dividends.

Paul's second principle was: even if your spouse isn't a Christian, do what you can to stay in the marriage. Many of the persons to whom Paul was writing had not come to Christ out of Judaism, with its high ethical standards for the family. They had been converted from paganism and felt that at conversion they needed to break all social ties with that pagan world, including marriage to a pagan. This one situation spawned such questions as: Are the children holy in God's sight? Should we leave our lost spouse? Is it all right to stay?

Paul laid out several guidelines. First, becoming a Christian is never grounds for divorce. If at all possible, the Christian should stay in the marriage. Second, any separation should be initiated by the unbeliever and not by the new Christian (v. 15). While Paul felt that the believer should acquiesce to the unbeliever's leaving, this does not mean that Paul took a casual view of marriage. Third, Paul assured the believers that their children were all right in God's sight. Fourth, he reminded the Corinthian Christians of their responsibility to model the Christian life before their unbelieving mates and of the possibility that the example of their love and life would lead to the spouse's conversion. While Paul said it was not only all right, but desirable, to stay in the marriage, he recognized the possibility that some pagan spouses would leave their Christian mates. But this separation did not put the believer outside the church. In this case Paul recommended continued singleness or reconciliation as the ideals. At no time did he discuss the possibility of a second marriage.

Today Christians who are married to unbelievers have some of the same questions. It is not easy for a Christian to love the church and its mission and to find meaning within the fellowship of Christian friends when he or she is married to a person with a different value system and a different agenda. Even when there is genuine love, much respect, and a shared life, this is true. To take Paul's advice seriously will often mean that the Christian will have to make sacrifices in his or her involvement in the church rather than jeopardize the marriage. This is not an easy decision to make, and there are no real assurances that one's mate will ever become a Christian. But it is what Paul suggested, and I have seen good results come from it many times.

What do you think Paul would have answered had he been asked: "Should a Christian consider marrying a pagan?" While this particular question was not asked, I feel sure that his answer would have been, "Absolutely not."

The mixed marriage he wrote about was created when one partner in a marriage between unbelievers was converted to Christianity. He felt that it was not good for individual Christians or for the witness of the church for marriages to be broken on religious grounds. I doubt that he could have conceived of a serious Christian entering into such an important relationship with a person who was not a Christian.

BEING CONTENT WITH PRESENT STATUS

17 But as God has distributed to each one, as the Lord has called each one, so let him walk. And so I ordain in all the churches.

18 Was anyone called while circumcised? Let him not become uncircumcised. Was anyone called while uncircumcised? Let him not be circumcised.

19 Circumcision is nothing and uncircumcision is nothing, but keeping the commandments of God is what matters.

20 Let each one remain in the same calling in which he was called.

21 Were you called while a slave? Do not be concerned about it; but if you can be made free, rather use it.

22 For he who is called in the Lord while a slave is the Lord's freedman. Likewise he who is called while free is Christ's slave.

23 You were bought at a price; do not become slaves of men.

24 Brethren, let each one remain with God in that calling in which he was called.

1 Cor. 7:17-24

The basic idea of these verses is that it's best for people when they are converted not to seek to make changes in their social or marital status. With Paul's feeling about the shortness of time before Christ's return and the possibility of imminent persecution, he urged these new converts to find their real contentment in their calling in Christ and not in a changed status in society.

On the Indianapolis Speedway, when there is some problem on the track that endangers the race drivers, a yellow light is flashed. This is not a signal for them to stop, but a signal for them to hold their places as they go around the track. They are neither to lose ground nor gain ground but stay in place. Paul felt that the circumstances under which new converts would be living justified his "flashing the yellow light." What he wrote was never intended to be used to make Christianity a preserver of the *status quo*, but it was wise advice for the circumstances that prevailed in the Corinthian church at that time.

But behind his counsel for a special situation is a very profound truth: the calling we have in Christ transcends the importance of our status in society. In the passage Paul said one should stay either Jew, Gentile, free or bond; the inference included also single, married, widowed, or divorced. In one church there were people of different social, economic, and educational status but they were "one in Christ." This was the relationship that was to be the clue to their attitudes and activities. But the experience creating a basis for contentment in each of these was that each had been bought with a price (v. 23) and had been called to be faithful to the commandments of Christ.

I can still remember the sense of excitement I felt as a teenaged boy to whom life had brought some harsh realities when there was born in my mind and heart the intoxicating idea that God had a purpose for my life. From a human standpoint I really didn't have much status. In a community where most people owned property, we rented. At a time when divorces were not common, I lived with my divorced mother. At a school where most of the people lived in town, I lived in the country and rode the school bus. At a time when the social life was organized either around playing on the team or marching in the band, I barely could get to classes with the aid of crutches. But I was probably one of the happiest and most excited persons in the senior class for the very reason Paul discusses here. I had found the meaning for my life in Christ's calling, and it had made as nothing those things that would have seemed to make a real difference. On the surface many changes have taken place in my life during the past years—socially, educationally, and economically. But the common thread that ties my life together and has given stability in every circumstance has grown out of my call to serve Christ.

CREATING STABILITY IN UNCERTAIN TIMES

25 Now concerning virgins: I have no commandment from the Lord; yet I give judgment as one whom the Lord in his mercy has made trustworthy.

26 I suppose therefore that this is good because of the present distress—that it is good for a man to remain as he is:

27 Are you bound to a wife? Do not seek to be loosed. Are you loosed from a wife? Do not seek a wife.

28 But even if you do marry, you have not sinned; and if a virgin marries, she has not sinned. Nevertheless such will have trouble in the flesh, but I would spare you.

29 But this I say, brethren, the time is short, so that from now on even those who have wives should be as though they had none,

30 those who weep as though they did not weep, those who rejoice as though they did not rejoice, those who buy as though they did not possess,

31 and those who use this world as not misusing it. For the form of this world is passing away.

32 But I want you to be without care. He who is unmarried cares for the things that belong to the Lord—how he may please the Lord.

33 But he who is married cares about the things of the world—how he may please his wife.

34 There is a difference between a wife and a virgin. The unmarried woman cares about the things of the Lord, that she may be holy both in body and in spirit.

But she who is married cares about the things of the world—how she may please her husband.

35 And this I say for your own profit, not that I may put a leash on you, but for what is proper, and that you may serve the Lord without distraction.

36 But if any man thinks he is behaving improperly toward his virgin, if she is past the flower of her youth, and thus it must be, let him do what he wishes; he does not sin; let them marry.

37 Nevertheless he who stands steadfast in his heart, having no necessity, but has power over his own will, and has so determined in his heart that he will keep his virgin, does well.

38 So then he who gives her in marriage does well, but he who does not give her in marriage does better.

39 A wife is bound by law as long as her husband lives; but if her husband dies, she is at liberty to be married to whom she wishes, only in the Lord.

40 But she is happier if she remains as she is, according to my judgment—and I think I also have the Spirit of God.

1 Cor. 7:25–40

Verses 25–28 in this passage were written in response to a specific question "concerning virgins." While several possible interpretations have been given as to what virgin Paul refers to, it probably refers either to a father or guardian of an unmarried daughter, or to a man who was betrothed to a virgin but whose marriage had not yet been consummated. Whichever it was, Paul's answer is consistent with his advice in the rest of the chapter. He argues that in the light of the *"present distress"* (v. 26) that the best thing to do is to stay as one is, although to prevent immorality it is not a sin to marry.

The question that keeps coming to me is this: since the crisis situation to which Paul alluded does not exist in our day, what relevance does this passage possibly have to us? I think there is more relevance than meets the eye at first reading. Our crisis is not the same, but we do live in a time of great crisis for Christians. Ours is a time of moral uncertainty, and that fact is undermining the efforts of many to build Christian marriages. The rapidly changing roles of men and women in society are creating tension and conflict in relationships. The failure of so many marriages is causing many young couples to have doubts about ever getting married. The fear of a nuclear holocaust has caused some young marrieds to say to me, "Should we even consider bringing children into a world so close to destruction?" The combined pressure of urban life and the two-paycheck family is creating stress that will change the shape of the family as we know it. With Paul's goal of achieving and maintaining stability in uncertain times, how should the church address itself to these more contemporary questions about the family?

With our situation I can imagine Paul writing to the church in Fort Worth (or Seattle or Kansas City, or any city) and saying, "Because of the present distress, I have several bits of advice. First, don't marry so young but take time to grow up. Second, make sure you marry the right person, someone with common interests, common goals, common values, and a common faith in God. Third, before you marry be sure you know what marriage is, and instead of using the pagan concept of 'romantic love,' discover all the richness of God's ideals for marriage. Fourth, work to make a good marriage. This present pagan world will keep on trying to undermine your relationship. Finally, draw from all the resources within Christ and within the church for strengthening your marriage." Would this be the kind of advice Paul would give today?

It is in this passage that Paul spells out his reason for feeling that being single is preferable to being married (vv. 32–35). Simply stated, his position was: unmarried persons *"care about the things of the Lord"* (vv. 32, 34) and married persons *"care about the things of the world"* (vv. 33, 34). While it is true that the ordinary cares of the family would be heightened and intensified during a time of persecution, and that a person who is married might have his or her interests divided, the statement still seems to idealize singleness and to caricature being married.

I've spent approximately half of my life as a married person, having married at age twenty-seven and having been married for thirty years. My experience is that being married, rather than distracting me from God's work, has enriched my understanding, strengthened my commitment, and broadened my interests. Marriage has given me a support system within the relationship for my faith in Christ and for my service in the church. I have no experiential way of knowing what my experience would be with marriage during a time of severe persecution, but for times like these I believe a good case can be made for serving Christ in an acceptable way within the context of a Christian marriage.

CHAPTER EIGHT

Let Love Control Knowledge

1 Corinthians 8:1–13

I was introduced to the basic teaching of this chapter in between my freshman and sophomore years in college while I was attending a summer conference for students in North Carolina. The morning format for the week had a lecture by a Bible teacher, followed by a large number of seminars on various subjects of interest to the students, and we were asked to take our choice. My first choice was the subject of "Dealing with the Gray Areas of Life" since the brief explanation said that some of the areas of right and wrong on which Christians did not always agree would be discussed. Evidently others were interested too, because when I got to the room it was so packed that I couldn't get in and had to wait and catch the second session. The wait was worth it. It was so long ago I've completely forgotten who the leader was but I still remember his outline. First he wrote on the top of the chalkboard "Things which are always wrong for everybody" and led us in making a list. Then he erased the board and wrote at the top "Things which are always right for all people to do." Neither of the discussions on these topics were as easy as I would have anticipated, mainly because the lists of things always wrong or always right that each of us had were not the same. So the leader took all those disputed activities and put them under the heading of "Things which seem wrong to some Christians but not to all" and led us in a discussion of both how to handle the gray areas and how to relate to fellow Christians who don't feel the way you do about everything. He drew the principle from his understanding of 1 Corinthians 8. This principle still has relevance for today.

> 1 Now concerning things offered to idols: We know that we all have knowledge. Knowledge puffs up, but love edifies.

2 And if anyone thinks that he knows anything, he knows nothing yet as he ought to know.

3 But if anyone loves God, this one is known by Him.

4 Therefore concerning the eating of things offered to idols, we know that an idol is nothing in the world, and that there is no other God but one.

5 For even if there are so-called gods, whether in heaven or on earth (as there are many gods and many lords)

6 yet for us there is only one God, the Father, of whom are all things, and we for Him; and one Lord Jesus Christ, through whom are all things, and through whom we live.

7 However, there is not in everyone that knowledge; for some, with consciousness of the idol, until now eat it as a thing offered to an idol; and their conscience, being weak, is defiled.

8 But food does not commend us to God; for neither if we eat are we the better, nor if we do not eat are we the worse.

9 But beware lest somehow this liberty of yours become a stumbling block to those who are weak.

10 For if anyone sees you who have knowledge eating in an idol's temple, will not the conscience of him who is weak be emboldened to eat those things offered to idols?

11 And because of your knowledge shall the weak brother perish, for whom Christ died?

12 But when you thus sin against the brethren, and wound their weak conscience, you sin against Christ.

13 Therefore, if food makes my brother stumble, I will never again eat meat, lest I make my brother stumble.

1 Cor. 8:1–13

When as a young Christian I was reading through the New Testament for the very first time, I didn't have the slightest idea what Paul was talking about in 1 Corinthians 8. Nothing in my experience equipped me to understand either the problem of the Corinthians or Paul's answer to them. Even when a teacher explained to me what the situation was in Corinth, I still did not grasp the broader implications of their struggle and the great wisdom of Paul's answer and its relevance to us today. In recent years I've realized that they were dealing with every Christian's problem—how to be a follower of Christ in a pagan world. How can a Christian stay in this world and not be compromised by its values and its lifestyles?

The questions came to Paul out of a difference of opinion in the church about whether or not it was permissible for a Christian to eat food that had been sacrificed to some god. Most people today, unless they have spent time in the remote areas of one of the world's undeveloped countries, have not been exposed to any form of worship that includes the sacrifice of animals, although it was an everyday experience for first-century Christians. There were several situations in which a Christian might be asked to eat this meat that had been offered to one of the gods. He might be invited by a friend to a special meal at the temple, an event that might have no great religious significance. There were many in those days who no longer believed in the existence of the gods, but who continued to participate in some of the festivals at the temple for social reasons. Or a Christian might be invited to have dinner in the home of a neighbor or friend who was not a Christian, in which case he could almost be assured that the meat served was from an animal that had been dedicated to one of the gods. Or even in his own home, when a Christian sat down to a meal prepared in his own kitchen he could never be sure that the meat his wife had purchased at the corner market had not been sacrificed to some idol.

Before looking at the two sides in the church that represented different positions on eating meat offered to idols, we ought at least to mention the one thing on which they were all agreed: that it is a sin to worship idols. The insistence that God's children should have no other gods before them was the theme of the Old Testament prophets, and that same insistence was assumed in the preaching of the first century. Those who became Christians had no question about the necessity to break away from the religious implications of idolatry. But the whole of society was permeated with the social implications of the worship of pagan gods, and it was at this point that the questions began to arise.

It was this situation that precipitated the question to Paul about whether or not it was a sin for a Christian to eat meat offered to an idol. For one group in the church the practice raised no question.

Though they may have had a pagan background, they were so strong in their belief that there was but one God and that He had revealed Himself in Jesus Christ that they did not view the gods to which people sacrificed animals as having any reality. The idols were now just so many pieces of wood or stone or metal. While they might not accept an invitation to dine at the temple, they saw absolutely nothing wrong with eating meat that had been offered to one of the idols in the home of a friend or in their own homes. Not only was their conscience clear, but they had almost a spirit of condescension toward the church members who did not agree with them.

A second group had a more difficult time handling the whole situation. They were also converts to Christianity who had come to faith in Jesus Christ out of a background of paganism. But they had been seriously involved in the worship of idols and in the various ceremonies surrounding that practice, including the meals in the temple. When they became Christians they accepted as true the fact that there is but one God and that the idols that had been a part of their previous life were nothing. But while they could accept this in their minds, at an emotional level they had problems. Even though they knew that the gods to whom the meat had been offered were not real, every time they ate the meat they felt guilty. They began to wonder if feeling guilty didn't mean that what they were doing was a sin, and they articulated their fears within the church.

While I have not been exposed to this form of idolatry, I have often seen people with problems of conscience over something that to me seemed relatively innocent but that did not to them because of their past associations.

I met Tom when I was in Las Vegas conducting a School of Evangelism during a Billy Graham Crusade. Tom was a recent convert to Christianity, having come into the church out of a lifetime of involvement in the gambling industry. He had been a very successful dealer at the blackjack table at one of the casinos. As a new Christian anxious to grow in the faith, he had enrolled as a layman in the school, and this is how we met.

At one of the intermission times, Tom cornered me and asked for help in what he considered to be a very big problem. The weekend before he and his wife had attended a marriage enrichment retreat sponsored by his church. During the recreation periods different couples took advantage of all the various free-time activities—swimming, skiing, hiking, and just sitting around visiting. What had really upset Tom was that when he went back into the lodge to pick up his sweater, he noticed two of the couples sitting at a table playing cards. As he recounted the experience to me he said, "So much of my life has been involved in playing cards as a part of the gambling industry that I not only couldn't bring myself to play, I really wonder if it's wise for any serious Christian to play cards." His situation was very similar to the one in which Paul was confronted by the Corinthians. It was an activity that one group of Christians could participate in without any problem and yet another group from the same church could not because it violated their consciences.

Paul's answer is given in this chapter and in 1 Corinthians 10:14–33, and the two sections are separated by Paul's example of how he has put into practice in his own life the principle he is going to ask them to follow in dealing with the problem. In verses 1–3 Paul indicates, even before he gets into details of his discussion, that Christians always need to let love, not knowledge, be the last word. Knowledge doesn't always make us considerate of others but has a tendency to make us proud. Even our knowledge about God can do this to us. I can still remember the vain look on the face of a young graduate student who said to me, "I have a difficult time having any respect for someone who does not have a well-thought-through doctrine of God." He had allowed all the theology he had learned to become a barrier between himself and those who were without his knowledge. Learning how to submit our knowledge to love is the theme Paul is going to bring into the discussion.

In verses 4–6 Paul takes the side of those who see nothing wrong with eating meat offered to idols. He agrees with them that there is "only one God" (v. 6) and that an "idol is nothing" (v. 4). He goes so far as to suggest that there is absolutely no religious significance to what is eaten or not eaten: *"Food does not commend us to God: for neither if we eat are we the better, nor if we do not eat are we the worse"* (v. 8). In the tenth chapter of 1 Corinthians Paul does introduce the idea that there may be some demonic connection with idol worship, but in this statement he agrees with the basic understanding of idols held by the group that has no conscience against eating meat offered to an idol. But he did not agree with their spirit and with the attitude their knowledge had created toward what he called their "weaker brothers."

Probably all of us have misused the knowledge we've had in this way. Years ago I was speaking in a small rural church out from Danville, Virginia, and was going with the young pastor and his wife to eat lunch with one of the fine women of the church, a wealthy widow. As we were walking up on the porch, the pastor whispered to me, "Kenneth, whatever you do while we are here, please don't say anything about bowling." Before I could ask why, the door opened and we were ushered into her lovely home for an excellent meal and a wonderful time of fellowship. My only distraction in an otherwise pleasant time was wondering why the pastor had warned me not to mention bowling. As we drove away later that evening, I asked that he tell me. He related how the lady had been reared in a small mountain community where the pool hall and the bowling alley were in the same building, and it was the place where the less savory element of the community hung out. She had come to associate bowling with disreputable people. One day, in all seriousness, she had said to her pastor, "I hope I don't live long enough to see my pastor coming out of a bowling alley." While I did not agree with her that a moral issue was at stake in bowling or not bowling, I could not let my knowledge create in me a condescending attitude. My love for her needed to take precedence over whatever superior knowledge I might have.

Paul's "however" in verse 7 introduces a second reality. Not everyone in the church knew there was only one true God. Paul reminds his readers that what is safe for one Christian may not be safe for another because of his different background, different temperament, or different level of maturity. This was a fact in the Corinthian church just as it is a fact in every congregation of believers today. There were church members whose consciences would not let them eat meat offered to idols, and there was nothing they could do about it. They would do great violence to themselves if they went against their consciences.

Paul made those who had the greater knowledge the object of his counsel. He suggested that they start by substituting love for their fellow Christians for their knowledge of what was right or wrong. Paul, more than any other writer in the New Testament, taught Christians to celebrate the freedom that they had found in Christ. But in this passage he suggested that no Christian has a right in the exercise of his or her freedom to undermine the faith of another

Christian. He warned not to let this *"liberty of yours become a stumbling block to those who are weak"* (v. 9). His plain advice is that those who know there is nothing wrong with a certain behavior are still to refrain from it in order not to create problems for the weaker brother. Paul goes so far as to say that if eating meat creates a problem for a brother that he *"will eat no meat while the world stands"* (v. 13).

In the midst of Paul's discussion there is a valuable lesson that he clearly assumes: that each Christian needs to be concerned about the effect of his or her conduct upon the spiritual life of fellow Christians. And in this concern love is a higher motive than knowledge.

When I was first introduced to this principle for ordering my life, I reacted to it much in the same way I'm sure some of the Corinthians did. I thought, "Why should I have to act differently just because their conscience is weak? Why don't they get a strong conscience? It's not fair!" But these questions, while very natural, are questions raised not out of love for our fellow Christians but out of love for our own personal liberty.

While Paul did place the larger burden for action upon the stronger members, his letter was also designed to strengthen the conscience of the "weaker brother." He didn't want them to use their weak conscience as a way to manipulate the actions of others and to have their way. Since everyone in the church heard the whole letter when it was read to the congregation, those who felt it was wrong to eat meat offered to idols must have been offended by some of the things Paul wrote. Paul's statement that God was not really concerned with what we ate or didn't eat must have made some feel uncomfortable. Those of us who have a conscience against something need to be sure that it is based on a truth of God and is not just some unfounded fear or feeling.

Once when I told a speaker that he was "over my head" he told me, without apology, that I needed to "lift my head." The same principle is true with our consciences. While we need to obey them we need constantly to be strengthening and informing them, as well. The root of the problem for the weaker brothers was not their lack of sincerity but their limited elementary knowledge of the Christian faith. This trapped them with all sorts of fears. One of the best ways for the weaker Christian to lay aside fears is to grow in his or her understanding of the nature of the Christian faith. This will be a liberating experience and will help his or her conscience to become strong and informed.

The principle that Paul gives for handling this problem can be of help to any church of any era because it can apply to many diverse circumstances. Christians agree that there are certain activities and actions that are always right. It is always right to tell the truth, to love your neighbor, to minister to others, to worship God.

At the same time, there are certain activities on which there is agreement that they are never right for a Christian: taking what belongs to another, lying to someone, or taking another's life. But there are many questions raised where there is no clear Biblical injunction, such as social drinking, use of birth control, or serving in the military.

Often the gray areas are a reflection of the area or of the times and have little to do with the Biblical faith. When I was a teenager I heard many ministers say that it was a sin to attend movies, but Dr. Hendricks, who pastored the county seat church, saw nothing wrong with attending movies. An association of churches in West Texas wouldn't allow boys and girls to swim in the pool at the church camp at the same time, while the churches along the coast didn't have a qualm about what their West Texas brethren thought was a sin. When a missionary couple came home from Peru and were visiting the churches to report on their work, one church wouldn't let the wife stand behind the pulpit to speak because they felt it violated the teaching of the Scripture, while another church in the same city not only let her stand behind the pulpit, but listed her in the bulletin as "preaching the sermon." Since serious Christians have different opinions on these and many more issues, Paul's admonition to make love the principle of our action is a good one. If we love one another and we prize the fellowship of the church, we will not let this kind of difference become the occasion for division.

On the surface, the principle of action which Paul has suggested seems too much. Maybe Paul sensed as he wrote, or dictated, the letter that those who would be hearing it would say, "That's not fair. We're the ones who are right, and we are the ones who are having to give in." So instead of completing his line of reasoning with practical application, he answers the response he anticipated from them by pointing out that his own life was lived by the very model he was recommending for them. His discussion of the nature of his own ministry is covered in chapter 9.

The Model for Leadership

1 Corinthians 9:1–27

Chapter 9 does not really introduce a new subject, as would seem the case from reading it, but is rather a continuation of the Apostle's argument set forth in chapter 8. In that chapter he had urged the more mature Christians in the church to exercise their freedom in Christ in a responsive way. Because there were those in the church who were critical of Paul's ministry, he could justifiably have anticipated that those people even questioned his apostolic authority. Consequently, this entire chapter is a defense and description of his ministry in which Paul illustrates in his own life models of what he has asked them to do. There was none of that "do-as-I-say-and-not-as-I-do" mentality in Paul. He knew that once he asked the mature Christians to lay aside some of their rights, they would begin to scrutinize his life.

LAYING ASIDE RIGHTS

1 Am I not an apostle? Am I not free? Have I not seen Jesus Christ our Lord? Are you not my work in the Lord?

2 If I am not an apostle to others, yet doubtless I am to you. For you are the seal of my apostleship in the Lord.

3 My defense to those who examine me is this:

4 Do we have no right to eat and drink?

5 Do we have no right to take along a believing wife, as do also the other apostles, the brothers of the Lord, and Cephas?

6 Or is it only Barnabas and I who have no right to refrain from working?

7 Who ever goes to war at his own expense? Who plants a vineyard and does not eat of its fruit? Or who tends a flock and does not drink of the milk of the flock?

8 Do I say these things as a mere man? Or does not the law say the same also?

9 For it is written in the law of Moses, *"You shall not muzzle an ox while it treads out the grain."* Is it oxen God is concerned about?

10 Or does He say it altogether for our sakes? For our sakes, no doubt, this is written, that he who plows should plow in hope, and he who threshes in hope should be partaker of his hope.

11 If we have sown spiritual things for you, is it a great thing if we reap your material things?

12 If others are partakers of this right over you, are we not even more? Nevertheless we have not used this right, but endure all things lest we hinder the gospel of Christ.

13 Do you not know that those who minister the holy things eat of the things of the temple, and those who serve at the altar partake of the offerings of the altar?

14 Even so the Lord has commanded that those who preach the gospel should live from the gospel.

15 But I have used none of these things, nor have I written these things that it should be done so to me; for it would be better for me to die than that anyone should make my boasting void.

16 For if I preach the gospel, I have nothing to boast of, for necessity is laid upon me; yes, woe is me if I do not preach the gospel!

17 For if I do this willingly, I have a reward; but if against my will, I have been entrusted with a stewardship.

18 What is my reward then? That when I preach the gospel, I may present the gospel of Christ without charge, that I may not abuse my authority in the gospel.

1 Cor. 9:1–18

Paul was using one of the most basic of all principles of leadership: he himself practiced in his own life what he preached to others.

The secret of the power and influence of the leaders of the first-century church wasn't just in the things they said but the fact that they were themselves an incarnation of their own message. I watched with great interest the impact of Mother Teresa of India when she visited our country—her ministry to the poor, the sick, and the dying. Her visit received wide coverage in the media and everywhere she went she was met by adoring masses. It was obvious that the great impact she was having on all who came into contact with her was not in the things that she said about the needs of the poor and dying, for all those things had been said countless times by others. The extraordinary power came from the integrity of her life, the fact that she had herself laid aside everything in order to give herself in a loving ministry to the poor and to the dying.

Paul's key argument was that both as a Christian and as an Apostle he had many rights he had not claimed. While he does state the proof of his apostleship in the first verse, this is not so much a defense of his apostleship as a preparation for a listing of the privileges that could have been his because of his position. He had seen the living Christ on the road to Damascus and he had done the work of an apostle in Corinth. As far as Paul was concerned, that settled it. Now he would recite for them the rights he could have claimed but didn't.

He mentions specifically three privileges, introducing them with three questions where it is assumed that the answer is "yes." *"Do we have no right to eat and drink?"* (v. 4) is most likely a reference to the fact that as a Christian he has the same freedoms that all mature Christians have. While there are some who think this could be a reference to his right to be supported by the church, it is more likely a reminder that Christ has freed him also from the strict dietary laws which had been part of his background.

His claiming the right *"to take along a believing wife"* (v. 5) is probably a reminder that he, like the other apostles, could be married and have his wife with him to assist in the ministry. However, the text is unclear enough that some have felt this was a reference to any married woman who might serve as an assistant in the work of the ministry. If you read a dozen different translations, you will find that the majority lean toward the "wife" interpretation. As far as the purpose of Paul's argument is concerned, the specific interpretation makes no difference because he was merely pointing out that he had the same rights that the other apostles had.

His third right, and the one he devoted the most time and space to, was the right to be supported financially by those to whom he ministered. He states his claim in a question: *"Is it only Barnabas and I who have no right to refrain from working?"* (v. 6). While Paul supported himself, he did not suggest that his approach should be the norm. Rather he made a very strong case for ministers being supported by the churches where they served. He argued the case from nature: the soldier, the husbandman, and the shepherd (v. 7). He argued the rightness of it from the law (vv. 8–10). He illustrated his position out of the practice in the temple (v. 13). He clinched his argument by appealing to the teachings of Christ that *"those who preach the gospel should live from the gospel"* (v. 14). Anyone who feels that there is something basically wrong with a church providing a salary for a staff member needs to read carefully Paul's magnificent argument in this chapter.

But Paul did not list these three rights to make people feel sorry for him or even to suggest he would now like to claim the rights. He was illustrating that not only was he asking them to lay aside certain liberties for a good reason but he himself was already doing what he was asking them to do. This is very clear in his statement in verse 15: *"I have used none of these things, nor have I written these things that it should be done for me."* There is one difference in Paul's action. Instead of laying aside privileges because of the conscience of the weaker brother, Paul lays privileges aside *"lest we hinder the gospel of Christ"* (v. 12). He lays aside his privileges for the sake of the gospel. To me that is a far superior reason to any other.

I have known scores of people who have followed the example of the Apostle and who have laid aside privileges to which they were entitled for the sake of the gospel.

Mary Ann is married to a very successful professional man. Unlike some women for whom it is necessary to work outside the home, she is free to do whatever she wishes with the time not used in caring for her family. Mary Ann has decided to use her freedom in order to perform a ministry in Christ's name to a very special group of people. The city in which she lives has a major medical facility which treats cancer patients from all over the world. Through her church she has become involved in a ministry to cancer patients who are from out-of-town. She's one of a number of Christians who are involved, and what I say about her is true also of others. But I've singled her out both because I've been able to observe firsthand what she does and because she illustrates so wonderfully this principle Paul articulated of laying aside privileges for the sake of the gospel. She cleans up an apartment for the family of a cancer patient. She picks a patient up at the airport. She takes a bottle of detergent by for a couple who haven't had time to purchase one. She visits the daughter of a pastor from New Mexico after he calls to express his great concern for her declining condition. As she does all this she is happy and fulfilled and thankful for the privilege of doing it and embarrassed if anyone brags on her. In the years I've known her I have never asked her to help anyone but that she did it and thanked me for letting her do it. She has forgotten her "rights" for the sake of the gospel.

While there are many lay persons like Mary Ann, I have also known a host of persons who worked for the church vocationally who had that same spirit. Uncle "Doc" was my mother's brother. His name was really James Oscar, but for some reason I was never aware of it because everyone called him "Doc." During his lifetime he was what today is called a bi-vocational preacher. That is a fancy name for a minister who is not paid enough to live on by those to whom he ministers, and who is required by the necessities of life to earn additional income in some other way while giving his main energies to the church. Uncle "Doc" was a carpenter and a farmer. He served the churches in which he preached with such unselfishness and love for the people, and yet he never really had anything of substance. The people whom he served were actually able to do better by him than they did, but for some reason or another no one gave leadership to the idea. It bothered me, and I mentioned it to Uncle "Doc" one day when he was taking me to the doctor. He said, "Kenneth, if my goal in life were to make money, I wouldn't be a preacher. I know that the church ought to take better care of me than it does, but if I spend a lot of time pushing them to do right by me it will hinder the effectiveness of my ministry." When God began to deal with me concerning a call to preach it was in the light of what I saw in my uncle's life that I came to surrender to God's call. Uncle "Doc" was a powerful example to me of how a preacher ought to think about his rights and privileges.

Not all preachers are like my Uncle "Doc." I was once asked to be the host for a famous preacher who was coming to our city for an occasion. Unlike my uncle, this preacher was full of demands that he felt his status as a religious celebrity entitled him to make. He wanted a certain kind of car to pick him up at the airport. He insisted on special hotel accommodations. There were detailed instructions as to how he was to be publicized and how he was to be introduced. I almost felt I was handling royalty and that what we really needed was a protocol officer. As I found myself resenting what I was being put through, I remembered what my Uncle "Doc" had said and realized how right he was. Insisting on our "rights" sends a message that suggests we are more interested in ourselves than in the work. It also dulls the spirit of sacrifice that lies at the very center of the Christian faith.

In the last three verses of this section, Paul opens his heart and discusses the sense of urgency he has about his sharing of the gospel. It was not something he chose but a thing he felt had been chosen for him. Every person who has come to feel that God is calling him to preach the gospel can understand Paul's *"Woe is me if I do not preach the gospel!"* (v. 16).

When, after having been out of high school for a year with rheumatoid arthritis, I returned for my senior year, I had this same sense of necessity. During that year of sickness I had come to believe that God wanted me to spend my life preaching the gospel. I will never forget how difficult a time the vocational counselor had in her efforts to guide me toward college. She kept wanting to give me tests to see what vocation would be best for me to choose. What I could not adequately explain to her was that I felt that what I should do with my life had already been chosen.

Paul felt that God rewarded him by allowing him to preach the gospel. He must have anticipated that someone among his readers in Corinth would hear what he had said and ask, "If Paul doesn't claim his rights as a Christian and as an apostle, then what's his reward? Will he have to wait until the end of time?" Verse 18 seems to be the answer to just such a question. *"What is my reward? . . . That when I preach the gospel, I may present the gospel of Christ without charge"* (v. 18). Paul seemed to indicate that the reward for what he was doing was built into the doing of it.

I grew up in a religious atmosphere where there was so much emphasis upon controlling behavior by either the desire of reward or the fear of punishment that I reacted against it and began to look for a better motive for the Christian life. One of the best discoveries that I made was that God has made life so that reward is not an arbitrary decision on God's part but is built into obedience. One of the big discoveries of the Christian life is the sense of fulfillment which comes in the process of doing what we feel God wants us to do.

When our son Troy was in his early years of high school, he brought home an excellent report card. When I told him how proud I was of him, he said that his friend's father gave him a hundred dollars for every *A* he brought home as a final grade. Now, I wasn't about to get involved in that kind of deal and told Troy so, but I asked, "Is there some reward built into doing the work and making an *A*?" He told me that he really did have a sense of accomplishment in having pulled it off. I believe that God has made life so that those who think less of their own rights and privileges and more about others and the Kingdom of God, feel fulfilled here and now.

EVERY PERSON'S SERVANT

19 For though I am free from all men, I have made myself a servant to all, that I might win the more;

20 and to the Jews I became as a Jew, that I might win Jews; to those who are under the law, as under the law, that I might win those who are under the law;

21 to those who are without law, as without law (not being without law to God, but under law to Christ), that I might win those who are without law;

22 to the weak I became as weak, that I might win the weak. I have become all things to all men, that I might by all means save some.

23 Now this I do for the gospel's sake, that I may be partaker of it with you.

1 Cor. 9:19–23

For years I've been interested in what it takes to be a good leader, and I'm convinced that these verses contain more helpful insight on what it takes to give real spiritual leadership than any other passage in the Bible. Paul begins by declaring the liberty that is his in Christ, *"I am free from all men"* (v. 19). He wasn't thinking of financial or political freedom but spiritual freedom, the freedom that had come to him through Jesus Christ. To Paul the gospel was a liberating word and the church was a liberating community, and he was the benefactor. Faith that does not free us is a false faith, and a church that binds people instead of loosing them is not a true church. Paul was free from the penalty and power of sin and free to have fellowship with God the Father.

In Paul's life, as is true for each of us, there is a sense in which he was already free and also a sense in which he was being made free. God had already done something for him at the time of his conversion, and God was continuing to work in every area of his life to bring the freeing influence of the gospel to bear upon him. Even though he was a Christian after the Damascus road experience, Paul, like others of the apostles, had to grow in his understanding of how the gospel related to all of life. We make a very bad mistake when we assume that once we are Christians all of our ideas are right. We bring into the family of God many values and attitudes and understandings that need to be exposed to the freeing spirit of Christ.

The freedom that Paul celebrated was real, and it permeated every area of his life. He was free from the smothering effects of the culture that had created him. When defending himself before the Jews, as he began to give his Jewish credentials, Paul sounded extremely orthodox. But Christ freed him from that sense of exclusiveness which characterized so many. One of the reasons God moved the center for world evangelization from the church in Jerusalem to the church in Antioch of Syria had to do with the fact that Simon Peter and many of the disciples in Jerusalem still understood Christ's commission to mean that they were to go only to "the Jews" who were in Jerusalem, Judea, Samaria, and the uttermost parts of the world (Acts 1:8). Paul had been freed from his narrow background and could preach to the whole world an "unhindered gospel."

It is easy for people to confess Christ and join the church, but not to continue to reflect the ideas and the attitudes of the family in which they were reared and the community where they grew up, is difficult. Sometimes I have looked out upon the congregations I have pastored and have been absolutely amazed at the diversity racially, educationally, politically, and socially. In my last pastorate, there were blacks, whites, Cambodians, Koreans, Hispanics, Japanese, and a host of other ethnic and national groups represented. Often I think about how different my attitude is from the community in which I was reared. That small rural community of the early 1930's had well-developed prejudices against Indians, Blacks, Jews, Democrats, and people who lived in town. While leaving home and going to school would have softened some of the attitudes, it has been coming to know Christ and growing in that knowledge that has done the most to free me from the culture that nurtured me.

Paul was free from the expectations of his peers, and he was free to risk. One of the things that made him so effective in the work was that he did not need the consensus of the other apostles in order to do something. There is no more subtle or deadly tyranny than the group, and the Christian who must have its approval is not truly free. Years ago I had the responsibility of designing the programs of evangelism for my denomination. My colleagues and I worked to find innovative ways to train the laity to share their faith. What we did was not really original, but it was different for our churches. We didn't want to design an approach without tying it very closely to the types of churches that had the reputation for being adventuresome and creative in trying pilot projects. This would allow us to evaluate and rewrite and redesign. I was amazed that the very churches that had complained about always being asked to do the "same old stuff" were reluctant to try the new program until after they could find out how it had gone in some other churches. They were afraid to try it because it was their habit always to check around with their peers before doing anything. Had Paul been this way the Gentiles still wouldn't have heard the gospel.

The freedom that Christ brought to Paul and to us needs to be as broad as our lives. We need to be free from personal ambition. Nothing bogs down the work of Christ more than introducing to the agenda a desire for something for yourself. I had a friend who once served on a nominating committee that was expected to have an easy job filling the position, but instead they continued to meet for what seemed like ages. One day when my friend was grumbling to me about never being on another committee, I asked him pointblank what was taking them so long. "We have two members of the committee of six who want the job," he said, "and they keep undermining everyone the rest of the committee gets interested in."

We need to be free from the fear of failure. The anxiety caused by the possibility of falling on our faces keeps us from the real risk-taking that is a part of the life of liberty. It is not an accident that in baseball those who set the records for the most home runs also strike out a lot. In life, those who "swing for the fences" always run the risk of failure. But never to try anything where there is a chance of failure is to lose all the sense of adventure in life.

We need to be free from the intimidation of our enemies. One marvelous characteristic of Paul was that though he often had a response for his detractors, he never let his enemies control the agenda of his life. There are many Christians, unfortunately, who can be controlled by anyone who lets them know that he or she is upset with them. We need to be free from compromising sin. Known sin, unconfessed and unforgiven, forms a jail for the spirit and impedes our life and God's work.

We need to be free to love everyone God loves. The world in which we live is quite selective in whom it loves, and when we show that same partiality we are not free. We need to be free to give our money, our time, and ourselves. People who get their kicks from getting and holding onto are not free.

We need to be free to make commitments. The people who affect an air of superiority because they have made no commitments to persons or causes or institutions are really slaves to their own self-centeredness and fear.

We need to be free to disagree. The effort in so much of the life of the church to get everyone to act as though they think alike is sick and enslaving.

I'm convinced that all these freedoms are my heritage in Christ and within the church.

In the same verse where Paul declared his freedoms, he announced that he had made himself a *"servant to all, that I might win the more"* (v. 19). What people do with their freedom is a clue to their character. Paul decided that he would use his freedom to voluntarily become a slave or a servant. His model for this position was his Lord who taught His disciples, "Whoever desires to be first among you, let him be your slave—just as the Son of Man did not come to be served, but to serve" (Matt. 20:27–28). Christ saw himself as the fulfillment of the Suffering Servant prophecies of Isaiah, such as Isaiah 53. On the night of the Passover Feast, that same night in which He instituted the Lord's Supper, the Scriptures tell how He played the role of the servant and washed the feet of His disciples (John 13:1–12). Actually, Paul felt that Christ's whole life from beginning to end was an act of servanthood, and this is nowhere better reflected than in the great hymn to Christ in Philippians 2:5–11. Even the most cursory study of Paul's life would attest to the fact that he truly was a servant and a good model for us.

It is easier to celebrate "the theology of servanthood" than it is to become a servant. A friend jokingly said to me once when we were discussing this, "The only thing wrong with being a servant is that everyone treats you like a servant." We laughed about it, but afterwards I reflected that this is the best reason it is so hard. Others get the limelight and the credit and the attention, and the servant does the work. The very idea of being a servant is a challenge to pride, to ego, to self-centeredness. While lip service is still given to the idea that we should be servants, I'm convinced that most people have rejected the idea with their actions. As I look around me in the churches it seems that we have taken more of our definitions of success and our models for leadership from the business community than from the Galilean or from Paul. The pastor goes to motivation seminars, reads books on management, and thinks of himself as an executive. While this may be the way to lead a business successfully, it does not reflect the Biblical example for spiritual leadership. The words of our Lord that greatness comes through being a servant of all have not been revoked.

It is in the context of being a free person who has made himself a servant that significant leadership can be given. Challenging goals can be set. Paul's goal was to win over as many as possible (v. 19). This posture also creates great flexibility and the ability to identify with people where they are. There is not a finer statement of what it means to really love people than Paul's declaration in verses 20–22 that he is able to identify with all kinds of people. He included in his illustration the Jews, the Gentiles, and the weak, but a study of his life as recorded in Acts would indicate that he was at ease with women, with people of all sorts of vocations, nationalities, and lifestyles, as was true of his Lord. Paul was not a chameleon who took on the moral and spiritual climate of his environment. Rather, he was a people-lover who did not let cultural or religious differences become barriers between him and persons for whom Christ died.

Because he was the servant of Christ he was able to identify with and love different kinds of people as his Lord had.

The church would be more effective in her evangelism if all those of us who are members could learn really to identify with all kinds of people. Most of us come equipped, even before we are converted, to like people who are like us. That's why most churches are made up of one kind of people. I used to be a student of the church in the transitional community, and I studied the histories of a number of congregations that moved. The members who had moved the church usually reported that they did so because there weren't any people living around the church. Actually the population density in most of the communities I studied was higher at the time the church moved than it had been when the church was founded. What they meant was that there were "fewer people like us around the church." The inability to identify with and love and minister in Jesus' name to all kinds of people has caused the death of many individual congregations. And the individual Christian who cannot reach across the barriers of age, sex, race, culture or reputation and love people needs to learn Paul's valuable lesson of freedom.

DEVELOPING SELF-DISCIPLINE

24 Do you not know that those who run in a race all run, but one receives the prize? Run in such a way that you may obtain it.

25 And everyone who competes for the prize is temperate in all things. Now they do it to obtain a perishable crown, but we an imperishable crown.

26 Therefore I run thus: not with uncertainty. Thus I fight: not as one who beats the air.

27 But I discipline my body and bring it into subjection, lest, when I have preached to others, I myself should become disqualified.

1 Cor. 9:24–27

In these verses Paul begins by putting the price tag on spiritual leadership, and he closes with a solemn warning. The cost for spiritual leadership is spiritual discipline. The analogy he uses first is that of the track meet. Corinth hosted one of the most famous of the Greek athletic events, second only to the Olympic Games. It was impossible for anyone in the city not to be aware of the strict disciplines and the strenuous training. But Paul felt that the Christian race was different in at least two ways. The crown the runners received was a wreath which soon wilted, while the reward of the faithful Christian would last forever. Also, in the races only one person could win, while in the Kingdom of God, every child of God has the potential for success. But there was one thing that Paul felt that each Christian had in common with the athletes—he or she needed discipline.

Several years ago as I watched the television coverage of the winter Olympics, I came to be fascinated with a special-interest feature telling how the speed skaters trained. I had watched the races and they went so fast that even the longest distances were completed in just minutes and the shorter races within seconds. Then as I watched the documentary on their training procedure I realized that the racers had trained every day for four years for those brief moments at the games. I began to think about all the ordinary pleasures of life they had cut out in order to keep in shape and to sharpen their skills and techniques. They did that for the chance of winning a medal that only three out of the hundreds could get. If a man or woman could pay that kind of price for a gold or silver or bronze medal, what price ought those of us who are stewards of the gospel of Christ pay?

There is something in us that makes us want the rewards of accomplishment without paying the price. Because writing does not come easily for me, I understand the statement I heard recently when a famous author said to a reporter, "Most people really don't want to write. They want to have written." The feeling was being addressed by the son of a close friend who, when asked what he wanted to be when he grew up, said, "I'd like to be a returned missionary." He liked the honor and adulation and thought it would be nice to skip language school and the rigors of the work and just enjoy the results.

We live in a day of "instant everything," but there is no such thing as spiritual leadership without spiritual discipline. Growth involves consciously cutting out of one's life everything that does not aid in reaching the goal. It involves patiently building into the life those skills and habits of thought and action that make the goal reachable.

In the last two verses of this chapter, Paul changes his analogy from the track meet to the boxing ring and introduces into his discussion of his ministry a very disturbing thought. The picture he paints with words is that he is not some shadow boxer who shows off his muscles by poking at the air but that he is in a real fight. Then as you read, you realize that the enemy he is describing is not some external foe who threatens his leadership but his own desires. His words *"I discipline my body and bring it under subjection"* (v. 27) obviously included all of the appetites of the body that had to be controlled, but they also included everything Paul meant in other places when he used the term "flesh." That more-inclusive term described anything, whether physical or spiritual, that might undermine his effectiveness as God's servant. He was saying that he stayed in a constant battle with himself in order to prevent doing anything that would disqualify him in the work.

The first time I read Paul's words *"lest, when I have preached to others, I myself should be disqualified"* (v. 27), it bothered me that he would even hint at the possibility. To me it was inconceivable that one who had suffered so for Christ, who had been so faithful in his stewardship and who had been used of God in such a marvelous way, could even consider doing anything that would eliminate him from the work. But the more I thought about it I realized that I had not really accepted Paul's humanness, while he had. This was Paul's way of reminding his readers, "Don't forget that we are all human. Never lose sight of the fact that we are just instruments of God." The advice is needed by each of us, because one of the great temptations of life is to handle the sacred things of God until we forget that we are clay. It's at that time that we are most vulnerable to temptation. So Paul begins the chapter on his ministry with the ringing declaration that he is free, but he closes it with the somber reminder that he is also human. Having used his own life as a model of what to do with one's freedom, he will go back to the original question about idolatry in chapter 10.

CHAPTER TEN

Learn from the Past

1 Corinthians 10:1–33

I grew up with that unfortunate stereotype of history as something dry and irrelevant, and as a result, I shied away from all the courses on history it was possible to avoid. Then as a graduate student, with the help of two exciting professors I discovered what history is all about. Over a three-year period I was exposed to the history of the church, of missions, of theology, of thought, and of interpretation. It was being introduced to history that created the context for my other studies and that helped me to see my place in God's plan more clearly.

People who forget history tend to keep making the same mistakes and keep having to start over rather than being able to build upon the wisdom and the accomplishments of the past. In Paul's continued appeal to the Corinthians for unity, he reminds them of the lessons that can be learned from history. A study of God in His relationship with Israel in times past will reveal what builds up and what is destructive, what works and what doesn't, what frees and what enslaves, and what pleases God and what brings His judgment.

Don't Feel Secure in Ceremony

1 Moreover, brethren, I do not want you to be unaware that all our fathers were under the cloud, all passed through the sea,

2 all were baptized into Moses in the cloud and in the sea,

3 all ate the same spiritual food,

4 and all drank the same spiritual drink. For they

drank of that spiritual Rock that followed them, and that Rock was Christ.

5 But with most of them God was not well pleased, for their bodies were scattered in the wilderness.

6 Now these things became our examples, to the intent that we should not lust after evil things as they also lusted.

7 And do not become idolaters as were some of them. As it is written, *"The people sat down to eat and drink, and rose up to play."*

8 Nor let us commit sexual immorality as some of them did, and in one day twenty-three thousand fell;

9 nor let us tempt Christ as some of them also tempted, and were destroyed by serpents;

10 nor murmur as some of them also murmured, and were destroyed by the destroyer.

11 Now all these things happened to them as examples, and they were written for our admonition, on whom the ends of the ages have come.

12 Therefore let him who thinks he stands take heed lest he fall.

13 No temptation has overtaken you except such as is common to man; but God is faithful, who will not allow you to be tempted beyond what you are able, but with the temptation will also make the way of escape, that you may be able to bear it.

1 Cor. 10:1–13

From the general tenor of Paul's words here, it seems there were individuals in the church in Corinth who felt that the fact that they had been baptized and had partaken of the Lord's Supper made them immune to the temptations of idol worship. Just as a person who has taken shots that immunize him or her against a contagious disease is not afraid of catching it, the Corinthians felt that once they had been baptized and had taken the Lord's Supper they were immune to any danger.

Never did this frame of mind seem more dramatically pictured than in the experience of one of the leaders of the city who reached out to me in a time of crisis for help. I sat in his office high above the street's noise. In addition to an oil drilling company, he owned extensive real estate and a fleet of barges that carried cargo along the intercoastal canals. He had translated his money into power and status in the community, and he had access to congressmen and judges who had been elected with the assistance of his money and influence. Though he was married and had an expensive portrait of his family displayed in a spot of honor behind his massive desk, he had kept one or more mistresses in conveniently located condominiums, without ever considering a divorce from his wife.

I was there in an effort to help his teenage son, whose bizarre behavior I interpreted as a signal for help and possibly an effort to get the attention of his father. The businessman couldn't understand how "something like this" could happen to him. Then he spelled out the formula that he felt should have protected him: "I was christened as a baby by devout parents; at twelve I went through confirmation class and took communion; I pledge generously every year to the parish budget; and I've done the same thing for my son that my parents did for me. What happened?" His question was an invitation for me to tell him what Paul told the Corinthians, "Don't find your security in the ceremonies of religion. Find it instead in the Living God Himself."

To illustrate the folly of trusting in the ceremonies of religion to protect a Christian from temptation, Paul reaches back to the early history of Israel for an illustration. While many of the church members in Corinth were Gentiles, Paul seems to assume that they had been so thoroughly integrated into the family of God that they now shared with the Jews a common ancestry. Their only Bible up to now was the Old Testament. Paul makes the crossing of the Red Sea a kind of eating of the manna, and the drinking of the water that God provided a Lord's Supper type of experience. His point was that the Israelites were baptized "into Christ." Yet, Paul reminds his readers, the majority of those who had this experience did not please God with their lives and as a result died in the desert.

We cannot trust in religious ceremony that does not usher us into a different kind of life. In spite of the nation's grand experiences with God, Israel had participated in the worship of idols and in gross sexual immorality; they had been unwilling to trust God for their provision, and as a result, they had died in the desert. Paul intended for this to be a warning to the Corinthians.

If Paul's warning was "Don't rely on the ceremonies of religion to protect you," his affirmation was "God is interested in how you live your life." In verses 6–11 he lists a number of lessons to be learned and acted upon if we are to make it in our world. While the wording of some of the verses may be tied to the particular situation in Corinth, they are very relevant to people trying to live the Christian life in a secular world. Paul states most of them negatively as prohibitions, but when they are reversed and stated positively, they give an excellent basis for an ethical lifestyle. "Don't lust after evil things" (v. 6) becomes: "Learn to desire what is really good for you." "Do not become idolaters" (v. 7) can best be translated for today: "Don't let anything replace God in your affection." "Let us not commit fornication" (v. 8) is a positive call to put our sexual drives and their expression into the context of love and commitment. "Let us not try the Lord" (v. 9) recalls a time when the Israelites grew impatient about God's provision and is for us a positive call to learn to trust Him for our needs. "Do not complain" (v. 10) is a reference to the frequent murmurings of the Israelites and is a call for us to keep a positive and wholesome spirit.

It is difficult at times to match up the lifestyle God wants us to live with the various ceremonies and rituals that are so much a part of our lives. I still recall a mother who came to me on the evening on which the last of her four children was baptized into the church. As she took her handkerchief and wiped some perspiration from her brow, she breathed a deep sigh of relief and said, "At last, they are all in the church and I can stop worrying." Knowing her four children and knowing the kinds of pressures and temptations that lay ahead of them, I wondered if she had not relaxed a little too soon. Still ahead for them was the pressure to make materialism their god, to treat sex as nothing more than an appetite to be satisfied in any way they wanted, the temptation to create their own dream world by the use of drugs or alcohol, and scores of other temptations. Although the mother in her happiness about her children's commitment to Christ did not really hear me, I told her that only the first step had been taken and that the real work was just beginning. What her children would need now would be a way of dealing with the trials and temptations they would face as they worked at building Christian lives.

Paul's concern for his friends is that they are setting themselves up for a great fall, so he gives them some very pointed and practical advice, which is still good today. First, we need to be realistic both about the trials we must face and our own strength to resist. *"Let [the man] who thinks he stands take heed lest he fall"* (v. 12) is a warning against unfounded pride and a call to be humble about our own spiritual strength. It is such an easy thing for Christians to make the enemies which we face seem like "straw men" who can be pushed aside easily with a verse of Scripture or a religious platitude, when actually they are powerful, persuasive, persistent opponents who often invade our minds and hearts and take us captive before we even know they are near. The evil we face in life is a master at disguise and frequently changes the labels on things to confuse us. I've heard what God calls fornication redefined and referred to as being "sexually liberated," and I've watched Christians be seduced by a materialism so subtle that they had a religious feeling about it. One of the best defenses we have is to become realistic about the temptations of the world in which we live and to be honest about our own limited spiritual resources to resist.

Second, Paul told his readers not to feel exempt from trials. He assured them that *"no temptation has overtaken you except such as is common to men"* (v. 12). These words have assurance for two different groups. Those who feel that because they are Christians they will not have to face certain temptations are reminded that there are trials that are common to everyone. Paul alludes to this truth later when writing to the church at Philippi and says that he had been "thoroughly initiated into the human lot with all its ups and downs, fullness and hunger, plenty and want" (Phil. 4:12). This statement comes as a shock to all those who have felt that they had in their relationship with Christ an exemption to problems. On the other hand, to people who are going through difficult times this passage is a source of assurance that they are not alone. Sometimes we are all a bit paranoid about the suffering we go through, and we look around and get the feeling that everyone else is having it easy while we, alone, are having a hard time. This word is a reminder of the common lot we all share as human beings.

Finally, Paul gave his readers two great words of assurance about their trials and temptations. First, God would set some limits on what He would allow to happen to them: God *"will not allow you to be tempted beyond what you are able"* (v. 13). There is in this statement the idea that is found in other places in the Bible that God knows us, our strengths and our weaknesses. This doesn't mean that we will never be overcome by evil but that our failure will not be the result of having more than we can handle. The great promise of this passage is that there is nothing any of us will face in life that will be so overwhelming but that if we turn to God He will help. Second, Paul assures us that *"with the temptation [He] will also make the way of escape, that you may be able to bear it"* (v. 13). This promise is one that I have tested over and over and have found to be true. There have been times when I tried in my own strength to deal with problems and they became worse, but on every occasion that I have asked God for help He has given it.

Don't Flirt with Idolatry

14 Therefore, my beloved, flee from idolatry.

15 I speak as to wise men; judge for yourself what I say.

16 The cup of blessing which we bless, is it not the communion of the blood of Christ? The bread which we break, is it not the communion of the body of Christ?

17 For we, being many, are one bread and one body; for we all partake of that one bread.

18 Observe Israel after the flesh: Are not those who eat of the sacrifices partakers of the altar?

19 What am I saying then? That an idol is anything, or what is offered to idols is anything?

20 But I say that the things which the Gentiles sacrifice they sacrifice to demons and not to God, and I do not want you to have fellowship with demons.

21 You cannot drink the cup of the Lord and the cup of demons; you cannot be partakers of the Lord's table and of the table of demons.

22 Or do we provoke the Lord to jealousy? Are we stronger than He?

1 Cor. 10:14–22

Paul now turns from the dangers of overestimating one's own strength to the incompatibility of being a Christian and worshiping an idol. If the history of Israel proved that being strengthened by the means of grace provided by God Himself did not permanently secure one against the temptation of idolatry, then the common sense thing to do would be to *"flee from idolatry"* (v. 14). Many of today's Christians who read the Bible find it difficult to believe that worshiping other gods would ever have been a problem either for Israel or for first-century Christians. That's because they have never stopped to analyze what the attraction was. For one thing, Israel wanted to be like the other nations, even in its religion. Being different is a burden that is still difficult for God's people to accept. Then, too, they wanted a god who was visible, who could be located, before whom they could stand. There was something a bit too ethereal about the God who insisted that He was a spirit. The instinct to have an experience with the Living God and to memorialize it by erecting a building is still with us. But one of the real attractions of most idol worship is that it often speaks to the more base elements in the nature of people. This is why we are always tempted to use our religion to justify pride, prejudice, lust, and materialism.

The earliest mention of the Lord's Supper comes here and in the next chapter, but Paul's purpose is neither to detail how it was instituted nor to show how it was used in the early church. Rather, he gives it as an argument for Christian unity and against Christians having anything to do with the worship of idols. The sharing of the cup and the bread refers to the way in which each Christian shares in the benefits of Christ's sacrifice, and the observance of the Lord's Supper in the context of worship binds the whole body of Christians together as one. The great reality celebrated in the Lord's Supper is our unity together with Christ. This unity of the Christian body ought to express itself in love for one's brother or sister, however irksome the demands made by a weaker conscience. In looking around for an analogy Paul reached back to the history of Israel and to their sacrificial meals. The participation of both priests and worshipers symbolized the fact that they all participated in the benefits and thus were "partners in the altar."

While Paul did not think other gods actually existed, he did think that the act of worship of an idol was demonic. To him this was not a meaningless act but a positive evil, because it gave to something man-made the devotion, affection, and glory that rightly belongs only to the Living God. Paul hinted that this act of worship brought the worshiper into a relationship with that lower order of beings which are opposed to God. Paul felt that there was such a contradiction between joining one's self to Christ and the believing community in the Lord's Supper and joining one's self to idols in worship that he could not conceive of any true believer doing it.

As I study this passage and seek meaning for my life today, I have no temptation to join in the worship of a man-made idol. If I were traveling and found myself in a country where there were persons who actually worshiped some physical object, I would be more inclined to take a picture of it than to bow down and worship. But does this mean that I am no longer susceptible to the temptation to worship idols? No, all it really means is that I'm not tempted to worship *that* kind of idol. Like the prophet Isaiah I have figured out the inconsistency of cutting down a tree and using part of it to make a fire and cook a meal and part of it to make a god to pray to and say, "Save me, for thou art my god" (Isa. 44:17–18).

If an idol is whatever takes the place God should have in my affection, then all of us continue to be tempted to worship idols. Just as in a primitive society a person might make an idol of any material, in our day we may make an idol of anything—our work, our family, our body, our house, our hobby, or even our religion. If anything besides God gets our best thoughts, our tears, our feelings, and our energy—are we not just more sophisticated idolaters?

The temptation to idolatry does not come to us with a clear label which warns "beware of idolatry." It comes so naturally blended into the life we live that we don't recognize it. I became painfully aware of this at the time I was struggling with the decision of whether I should resign a pastorate of more than a decade and return to the seminary classroom to teach. Even as the deepest part of me said I should do it, there was a part of me which began listing all the "practical" reasons for not doing it: our personal support system was in Texas; my seminary salary would be substantially lower; the thoughts of sorting out all the things which had accumulated; and finally, the warm security of a congregation that loved me. Eventually, I had to admit to myself that though I had been called to be a "pilgrim," I had in fact become a very comfortable "settler." It shook me a bit to realize that even as I sought God's wisdom concerning the decision, I was in danger of putting some very good things in my life first, ahead of God's will for my life. Is not this the constant temptation of our lives and the reason that none of us should consider ourselves above being tempted to idolatry?

PUT FREEDOM IN PROPER CONTEXT

23 All things are lawful for me, but all things are not helpful; all things are lawful for me, but all things do not edify.

24 Let no one seek his own, but each one the other's well-being.

25 Eat whatever is sold in the meat market, asking no questions for conscience' sake;

26 for *"The earth is the LORD's, and all its fullness."*

27 If any of those who do not believe invites you to dinner, and you desire to go, eat whatever is set before you, asking no question for conscience' sake.

28 But if anyone says to you, "This was offered to idols," do not eat it for the sake of the one who told you, and for conscience' sake; for *"The earth is the LORD's, and all its fullness."*

29 Conscience, I say, not your own, but that of the other. For why is my liberty judged by another man's conscience?

30 But if I partake with thanks, why am I evil spoken of for the food over which I give thanks?

31 Therefore, whether you eat or drink, or whatever you do, do all to the glory of God.

32 Give no offense, either to the Jews or to the Greeks or to the church of God,

33 just as I also please all men in all things, not seeking my own profit, but the profit of many, that they may be saved.

1 Cor. 10:23–33

Paul is now ready to bring the discussion of meat offered to idols to a close; it has covered much of chapters eight through ten. While he steadfastly refused to lay down a rule that would apply to all Christians and under all circumstances, he did give some valuable insights into the method by which we are to make decisions in those gray areas in which there is not general agreement. The approach he suggested can be summed up under three headings.

First, put God's glory above every other consideration. This is the positive statement that helps put things into context. Obviously God is not glorified when a person gives to an idol the honor that rightly belongs to God, nor is He glorified when one causes strife or ill will within the community of believers. Paul's statement to *"do all [things] to the glory of God"* (v. 31) is our best antidote to strife and to self-centered action. It is the perspective that will best guide us in dealing with issues that are volatile and that have such potential for harming the Kingdom. It's easier to agree with the wisdom of the principle than to apply it to life.

Years ago, when I was a young professor, I was asked to address a group that was having a meeting on our campus. The day on which I was to speak was one of those days in which anything that could go wrong did. So when I showed up for my assignment I was tired and frustrated from the start. My mood wasn't helped any by some rather irresponsible statements that were made by the speaker who preceded me on the program. I gave the speech that I had prepared, but evidently some of my feelings of anger and frustration came through in my talk. One of those in the audience was offended and went home and wrote a stinging letter to me with a copy going to the seminary president. The substance of what he reacted to was of such little consequence that I cannot even remember what it was. Had I used Paul's principles I would have written to the person and thanked him for writing, explained the circumstances under which I had spoken, apologized for letting my feelings become too involved in the presentation, and asked him to pray for me. That's not what I did. Instead, I did to him exactly what he had done to me. I reacted to the feelings in his letter, line by line, with a copy going to the president. And for not thinking first of the glory of God I created a lifetime enemy and did harm to the Kingdom.

While Paul was writing mainly about the subject of food offered to idols, the way in which he stated the principle, *"or whatever you do"* (v. 31), suggests that it has a much broader application. Can you imagine what would happen in all situations of strife within the church if we would agree from the very beginning to binding arbitration with the agreed-upon principle being "whatever will give God the most glory." Because of the neglect of this principle, so much good is left undone, and so much strife is begun.

Second, consider others ahead of yourself. This is the same position that Paul took earlier, with only a small change. In verse 23 he repeats word for word a quotation he had used in 1 Corinthians 6:12, but here he broadens the application. Earlier he developed the idea that if a person exercises every freedom he has without regard for others, he or she is likely to become enslaved again. In this passage Paul argues against exercising one's freedoms without restraint because it may not build up the body of Christ. There is in all authentic Christianity a healthy tension between individual freedom and corporate or community responsibility. Keeping a good balance between the two is not easy.

In his counsel not to seek our own way but to seek *"the other's well-being"* (v. 24), Paul used a very precise colloquial expression which does not mean "neighbor" or the person who is near me or like me. Rather, the word he used literally means the one who is *not like me*, the one with whom I am most likely to disagree. This is the person whom I'm to consider above myself. To give deference to a friend who is like me and who likes me would be natural, and it would not require a great deal of spirituality. But to place limits on my own actions in order to help a weaker brother who is different and is always differing with me is not within my power unless God helps me.

Paul's last word in his summary was that we are to keep always before us God's never-ending purpose, to save individuals. In the account of Paul's life in Acts and in the writing of Paul in the Scriptures, he comes across as a person of strong convictions who is able to function well without the approval of his peers. Yet he closes this chapter with the statement that he tried to *"please all men in all things"* (v. 33). On the surface this seems to be in conflict with his statement to the Galatians: "If I still sought men's favor, I should be no servant of Christ" (Gal. 1:10). But we need to remember in this statement and in others like it that Paul is saying that it is wrong to try to please others just to curry favor with them or to avoid conflict or persecution. His conviction on that never changes, and it represents an approach to ministry that has great integrity and is needed in the church today. On issues of substance where the gospel itself is at stake or the mission of the church is endangered, it would represent the worst sort of cowardice if a person tried to please everyone.

But in this case, Paul's motive was to try to please as many as possible in order to *"win the more"* (9:19) to Christ. While the gospel itself was a scandal to some, Paul felt that his life ought never be a stumbling block keeping others from faith in Christ. This is just another way of seeking the "glory of God," because as individuals become believers, God's larger purpose is accomplished and He is glorified. With chapter 10 Paul puts a period to the discussion of meat offered to idols and moves to a variety of questions relating to how men and women should conduct themselves in the church's worship services.

CHAPTER ELEVEN

Let Worship Unite You

1 Corinthians 11:1–34

At a recent meeting one of the speakers said, "This issue of the role of women in the church is one of the most divisive facing God's people today." He went on to claim that the whole question had been created as a spinoff of the feminist movement and that it had its roots in a totally secular view of life. While the majority of those present agreed with his analysis of the situation, they must have forgotten that in his first letter to the Corinthians, Paul discussed what was the proper role for women in the service of worship. It would seem from his writing that women had a larger role in the worship service of the early church than they do today, and he had no objection to their praying or prophesying, which was another word for preaching or proclaiming. But he does deal with a problem that was more related to a custom than to a deep theological issue— that of women wearing veils in the service (11:1–16). He also dealt with the importance of not bringing differences into the service (11:17–22) and the real meaning of the Lord's Supper (11:23–34).

The experience of worship ought to unite God's people. Often, as a leader of worship, I have looked out on the congregation and have been struck by all of the differences and all the potential for strife that exists within the church. Then we join in celebrating what God has done in Jesus Christ to save us and there is created in the process of singing, saying, and listening to Scriptures, prayers, and sermon a wonderful sense of oneness. Because this experience that was intended to unite had become the occasion of strife, Paul wrote this chapter.

BE SENSITIVE TO TRADITIONS AND CUSTOMS

1 Imitate me, just as I imitate Christ.
2 Now I praise you, brethren, that you remember

me in all things and keep the traditions as I delivered them to you.

3 But I want you to know that the head of every man is Christ, the head of woman is man, and the head of Christ is God.

4 Every man praying or prophesying, having his head covered, dishonors his head.

5 But every woman who prays or prophesies with her head uncovered dishonors her head, for that is one and the same as if her head were shaved.

6 For if a woman is not covered, let her also be shorn. But if it is shameful for a woman to be shorn or shaved, let her be covered.

7 For a man indeed ought not to cover his head, since he is the image and glory of God; but woman is the glory of man.

8 For man is not from woman, but woman from man.

9 Nor was man created for the woman, but woman for the man.

10 For this reason the woman ought to have a symbol of authority on her head, because of the angels.

11 Nevertheless, neither is man independent of woman, nor woman independent of man, in the Lord.

12 For as the woman was from the man, even so the man also is through the woman; but all things are from God.

13 Judge among yourselves. Is it proper for a woman to pray to God with her head uncovered?

14 Does not even nature itself teach you that if a man has long hair, it is a dishonor to him?

15 But if a woman has long hair, it is a glory to her; for her hair is given to her for a covering.

16 But if anyone seems to be contentious, we have no such custom, nor do the churches of God.

1 Cor. 11:1–16

Now Paul is addressing three questions that are related to worship: whether it was proper for women to participate in worship bareheaded (11:2–16); how members should behave during the Lord's Supper (11:17–34); how the various spiritual gifts were related (12:1–31). There is indication earlier in the letter of an inquiry having been made by the Corinthian Christians, and these issues may have been raised in that letter or Paul may have learned about the situations from those who had reported to him about the divisions in the church.

There was a time when those who studied this passage might have been able to say that Paul was addressing an issue that was peculiar only to that church and that day without the conclusion being questioned, but that is no longer true. First, the role that Christian women should have in the worship service is being discussed with renewed interest today. The questions being asked today are not about keeping the head covered but whether it is all right for women to receive the offering in worship, or serve the Lord's Supper, or teach or preach in the worship service. Second, there are many who feel that the arguments that Paul used to convince the women of Corinth that they should keep their heads covered have been used in our day to try to prove the inferiority of women in society, in the family, and in the church.

Paul's answer was clear concerning the need for women to wear veils in the worship service. It had been the custom in the synagogue and in some pagan temples for women in attendance to cover their heads. In the Jewish tradition, the covering represented a distinction in dress to acknowledge the difference between men and women. The women were also seated separately from the men and were not allowed to recite the lesson aloud with the men. Some of the members in Corinth were from this Jewish background and had unconsciously brought with them much of their tradition.

But Corinth was a Greek town, and there was an emancipation of women taking place in the Hellenistic culture. They were beginning to be given rights in matters of divorce and marriage that had been unknown before. They were developing their intellectual capacities and were sitting with their husbands at dinners discussing the art, literature, and philosophy of the day. Many of them had abandoned the traditional veil in their dress and had begun to experiment with different hair styles.

Paul's preaching on the freedom and oneness that we have in Christ may have contributed to the behavior. The principle that in Christ "there is neither Jew nor Greek, there is neither slave nor free, there is neither male nor female; for you are all one in Christ Jesus" (Gal. 3:28) had permeated Paul's preaching in Corinth. One of the most natural acts for new converts would have been to look upon the veiled woman as the symbol of the old age and the bare-headed woman as one who had been made free and equal in Christ. For those with a Jewish background, for a woman to speak in the worship service was an innovative thing and a stark contrast to worship in the synagogue. But for her to also be bare-headed was for many the final straw. This evidently was what was going on in the church and was the issue that Paul addressed.

We need to remember that Paul did not question the propriety of women praying aloud or prophesying in the worship services, although that represented a departure from tradition for many. His later admonition that a woman ought to keep silent in church (1 Cor. 14:35) was related to a particular problem of disorder in the worship service and not a general principle for all time. But Paul did tell the women that they should keep their heads covered as they participated in worship. We are in danger of missing what is really behind his suggestion.

Paul feels that when the church is dealing with things that relate to local customs or tradition, it is better to go along with them to the extent that the gospel is not compromised. To do so builds a beginning bridge of contact with the unbelieving world and to fail to do so could be offensive and create a barrier to the gospel of Christ. When a church (or individual Christians within the church) goes out of its way to flout the local customs, it forgets that the purpose of the church is to win persons to Christ and not to tell them about how Christians live. This very commonsense, wise approach to a very special problem is something we can use today.

The question that must be asked about this passage is: how much does Paul's rationale for his conclusion come from his adopting uncritically some of the traditional theology of his background? He supported his teaching with appeals to the order that God instituted in creation (v. 3), to social custom (vv. 4–6), to the presence of angels (v. 10), to nature (vv. 13–15), and to the prevailing practice in all of the churches (v. 16). Whatever Paul meant by submission, he intended for it to be mutual, as indicated in his letter to the Ephesians when he wrote, "Submit to one another in the fear of God" (Eph. 5:21). While the entire Bible continues to spell out different roles for men and women, Paul's statement in the Galatian letter that in Christ there is neither "male nor female" (Gal. 3:28) contains nothing of the notion of an inferior status with God or within society.

One of the basic principles for interpreting the Scriptures has been to interpret a passage in the light of the highest possible revelation on the subject. God seems to have revealed Himself in a progressive way to His children with the highest point of that self-revelation coming in Jesus Christ Himself. This seems to be the thesis of the author of Hebrews, who wrote, "God, who at various times and in different ways spoke in time past to the fathers by the prophets, has in these last days spoken to us by His Son, whom He has appointed heir of all things, through whom also He made the worlds" (Heb. 1:1–2). This means that when we deal with an individual in the Bible we take him at his point of highest understanding. Consequently, if we were discussing Simon Peter's teaching about the gospel as being shared with the Gentiles, we would not take his early attitude but the conclusions to which he came after God dealt with him at the house of Simon the tanner in Joppa. Up until then, even though he was a follower of Christ and one of the Apostles, he had still hung onto the more traditional Jewish attitude toward the Gentiles. It would be a mistake for the church to try to build a doctrine of racial exclusiveness on Peter's earlier attitudes toward other races even though they are preserved in the Bible, since we have recorded in the Scriptures a later account of his advocating that it was God's purpose for the church to share the gospel with the whole world.

This approach to interpreting the Scripture raises no questions about either the inspiration of the Scriptures or the authority of the Scriptures. But it does raise serious questions about the way in which a particular passage has been interpreted and applied. It is my belief that it is more consistent with Paul's later writing to conclude that in his effort to build a theological basis for women wearing veils in the church, he drew uncritically from the traditional Jewish interpretation of Genesis 2:18–25. Just as the Spirit of Christ continued to work with Simon Peter to develop his understanding of the universal nature of the gospel, just so that same Spirit worked with Paul to give him a more adequate understanding of the relationship of men and women within the church and within Christian marriage.

The ideal in marriage was to be mutual submission, as indicated in the first line of one of the great passages in the Scripture where Paul uses the relationship of the husband and wife as an analogy of the relationship between Christ and the church. He states that we are to "submit to one another in the fear of God" (Eph. 5:21). The ideal for the male-female relationship within the church is spelled out in his classic word to the church at Galatia: "For as many of you as were baptized into Christ have put on Christ. There is neither slave nor free, there is neither male nor female; for you are all one in Christ Jesus" (Gal. 3:27–28).

Both of these statements seem to mesh better with Christ's spirit and action concerning women. For Christ seemed to relate to women not so much as females but as persons, and He revealed God to them not as a male but as a person. There is nothing in anything Christ did or said that would suggest that He gave support to the traditional Jewish teaching about the natural inferiority of women. Consequently any interpretation of the Scriptures that would move us toward a superior-inferior distinction must be turned aside in favor of the interpretation that is in keeping with Christ who is God's highest revelation of Himself.

Don't Let Your Differences Undermine Your Worship

17 Now in giving these instructions I do not praise you, since you come together not for the better but for the worse.

18 For first of all, when you come together as a church, I hear that there are divisions among you, and in part I believe it.

19 For there must also be factions among you, that those who are approved may be recognized among you.

20 Therefore when you come together in one place, it is not to eat the Lord's Supper.

21 For in eating, each one takes his own supper ahead of others; and one is hungry and another is drunk.

22 What! Do you not have houses to eat and drink in? Or do you despise the church of God and shame those who have nothing? What shall I say to you? Shall I praise you in this? I do not praise you.

1 Cor. 11:17–22

Paul now switches from the behavior of women in the worship service to a problem related to an abuse of the observance of the

Lord's Supper. This problem was so bad that he suggested the meetings were actually "not for the better but for the worse" (v. 17). Since Holy Communion in the church today is usually in the context of a worship service in the sanctuary, it is hard for us to visualize the circumstances to which Paul was addressing himself. The early church had developed a very lovely tradition in connection with the observance of the Lord's Supper. They had a meal that was called a Love Feast to which each member brought what he or she was able to share. The resources were then pooled, and the whole church sat down to a common meal which provided a beautiful picture of the oneness they shared in Christ. It was a way of creating and developing real Christian fellowship in the church. Then, in connection with the meal, the Lord's Supper was celebrated. This had a certain naturalness to it since Christ had instituted the practice at the close of the Jewish Passover meal.

I hadn't realized the degree to which most churches have "sanitized" the ordinance until I attended a communion service that was conducted in our church on the Wednesday night before Thanksgiving. Instead of having it in the sanctuary it was held in the gym. Instead of having it at the conclusion of the morning worship service, we had it at the close of the Thanksgiving meal. Instead of having the beautiful silver trays with the glasses of juice and the silver plates with the unleavened bread, there was a pitcher of juice with some small plastic glasses and an unsliced loaf of bread covered by a napkin. As we came closer to the actual time for the observing of the memorial supper I looked at the tables with what was left of the meal—dirty plates, eating utensils, half empty tea glasses, spilled salad dressing, and crumpled napkins. My thought was: surely before we have the Lord's Supper served someone will come and clear away everything. I had this terrible feeling of the inappropriateness of acting out such a great event in such ordinary circumstances. Then I remembered that the supper itself was instituted at the conclusion of a meal and that Christ had used as the symbolic elements the bread and the wine that were left over from the meal. With this I realized and actually found myself discovering in this new context a larger dimension of joy in observing the Lord's Supper.

Several things had happened in the Corinthian church to take away from the Love Feast whatever love it had and to create a situation so bad that Paul rebuked them strongly. There were several problems. When they met, instead of being one family, they tended to divide up into separate groups. This could have been an extension of the divisions not along theological lines, but along social lines. This seems to be the case, because Paul mentioned how the richer members seemed to keep to themselves rather than share their food and have fellowship with those who were poor. Also, there were some people who were having so much to drink that they were becoming drunk. In this atmosphere where sharing had been forgotten, the church tried to celebrate the sacrifice God made in sharing His Son for our sins, and it was a mockery. To Paul it made no difference if the right words were spoken and the right actions were performed if the condition of the church's fellowship and the spirit of its members stood as a contradiction to the true meaning of the Lord's Supper.

Because the church today would never have abuses so primitive and so obvious, we might tend to think that there are none. This is a mistake. To bring into the worship services the divisions within the body of the church always diminishes the true meaning of worship. And to let social or cultural distinctions reflect themselves in fellowship of the church undermines the integrity of those events in which the church acts out Christ's sacrifice for the sins of the world. A fellowship of believers where some members have too much and some go hungry undermines the New Testament definition of love and of Christian fellowship.

I have but one memory of observing the Lord's Supper at the little rural church that licensed me to preach and the divisions that were created every time we observed it. The church had the policy that only those who were members of that local congregation could participate, so at the close of the worship everyone was dismissed with the instruction that the members should remain to observe the Lord's Supper. Mr. Croman, who was a wonderful Christian man but not a member of that congregation, would go outside and wait for his wife who was an official member of the church. This always upset Mr. Mullins, who was also a member of the church, so in protest that his friend was being excluded he always went out on the front steps with Mr. Croman during the observance. As the members went out from the church house, there were the two men sitting there as living reminders of the difference of opinion. This always served as a catalyst for another discussion of the church's policies, and the real purpose and intent of the ordinance was lost completely for most of those who participated.

REMEMBER WHAT THE LORD'S SUPPER REALLY IS

23 For I have received from the Lord that which I also delivered to you: that the Lord Jesus on the same night in which He was betrayed took bread;

24 and when He had given thanks, He broke it and said, "Take, eat; this is My body which is broken for you; do this in remembrance of Me."

25 In the same manner He also took the cup after supper, saying, "This cup is the new covenant in My blood. This do, as often as you drink it, in remembrance of Me."

26 For as often as you eat this bread and drink this cup, you proclaim the Lord's death till He comes.

27 Therefore whoever eats this bread or drinks this cup of the Lord in an unworthy manner will be guilty of the body and blood of the Lord.

28 But let a man examine himself, and so let him eat of that bread and drink of that cup.

29 For he who eats and drinks in an unworthy manner eats and drinks judgment to himself, not discerning the Lord's body.

30 For this reason many are weak and sick among you, and many sleep.

31 For if we would judge ourselves, we would not be judged.

32 But when we are judged, we are chastened by the Lord, that we may not be condemned with the world.

33 Therefore, my brethren, when you come together to eat, wait for one another.

34 But if anyone is hungry, let him eat at home, lest you come together for judgment. And the rest I will set in order when I come.

1 Cor. 11:23–34

Paul's method for correcting the abuse is to go back to the very beginning and to remind his readers of the Last Supper's institution and meaning. In four verses he reminds his readers how it all started and what its original purpose was. This represents the first written account of the origin of the Lord's Supper, preceding in time the writing of the gospels several years later. Paul had received the account as a part of the church's tradition, and had passed it along faithfully, and now he was reminding them again. In this brief account Paul makes at least six statements to remind them of its true meaning.

First, the Lord's Supper is rooted in history. It was a certain man, the Lord Jesus, and it was a certain night, *"the same night in which He was betrayed"* (v. 23), and it was a certain event in which He took real bread and wine and instituted the sacred rite. The Passover meal that had preceded the Lord's Supper looked back in Israel's history to the event by which God delivered Israel out of the bondage of Egypt. The Lord's Supper at the time of its beginning looked forward to an event of deliverance for all mankind, Christ's death on the cross and His resurrection. At the feast of the Passover it was traditional for a child to ask of his father, "Why is this night different from other nights?" and this would be the clue for the father to recount how God delivered Israel. Paul's explanation is an effort to remind the Corinthians of the historical roots of the sacred rite they were abusing.

Second, the Lord's Supper is about God's gift. We catch the work of sacrifice in Christ's words *"this is My body which is broken for you."* In this statement He is identifying Himself with the Paschal Lamb, the lamb that was sacrificed in connection with the Passover. But we make a mistake if we interpret the admonition to *"do this in remembrance of Me"* (v. 24) as a call to remember only His death. We are to remember that His death brings life. But we are to remember His life and His teaching, His resurrection and the hope that it brings, and we are to remember His purpose in the world.

For many years I found participating in the Lord's Supper to be depressing. I never told anyone about it for fear that they would misunderstand me, but I never looked forward to the services in which we observed communion. I had the same feeling about some of the Holy Week services. There seemed to be almost a morbid preoccupation with man's sinfulness and Christ's death. I just couldn't understand why Christ wanted me to do something as a part of my worship that left me so glum. Then I realized that in the observance Christ wanted me to remember everything about Him—His love for me, His forgiveness, His purpose, His hope, His presence, and His power. It was only when my thoughts and my prayers connected with communion began to reach out to remember everything that I began to find myself cleansed and renewed by my participation.

Third, the Lord's Supper celebrates a new covenant. The history of Israel was the story of a covenant that God initiated with them. It was a relationship in which He acted on their behalf and asked from them obedience in return. When Christ said, *"This cup is the new covenant"* (v. 25), He was announcing that He was entering into a relationship with those for whom He was to die upon the cross. We are more familiar in modern times with contracts than we are with covenants. Often when we buy a house or sell a house, borrow money, or take a job, we are asked to sign a contract. This means that we enter into an agreement according to the terms of the contract. Paul's reminder to his readers was that they had entered into a relationship with God through Jesus Christ that had demands connected with it.

Fourth, there is in the observing of the Lord's Supper a proclamation. Christ had said to them that every time they took communion they *"proclaim the Lord's death till He comes"* (v. 26). This is a word of evangelism and also a word of hope. In this Supper, Christ gave the church another way of preaching the gospel, a way for the eyes to see as well as for the ears to hear. One Sunday night I looked to the back of the sanctuary and saw a very large group of visitors who had come to the service from the International Seamen's Center located on the ship channel. Ships from all over the world docked there, and I realized that those who were visiting came from many different countries and in all probability were very limited in their understanding of English. To make matters even worse, it was the night on which a large part of the service was devoted to observing the Lord's Supper. Consequently, I was very surprised later when I received a letter from the chaplain who had brought them telling me how very meaningful the service had been to them. In the letter he told how their limited English had made it hard for them to understand my sermon, but that they were able to grasp clearly the symbolism of the Lord's Supper. As Christ had anticipated, they had followed the sermon with their eyes.

The message Paul gives in verses 27–34 is an effort to apply what he has said about the institution of the Lord's Supper to the abuses being practiced in the church. His main point was that the observance ought to cause everyone who participated to stop and examine himself or herself. The warning not to drink of the cup *"in an unworthy manner"* (v. 27) was not intended to introduce a new agenda to the discussion. It was a reference to the divisiveness, the selfishness, and the drunkenness that had crept into the observance. Paul was in effect saying, "Take a look at what you are doing. Do you think your activity is worthy of such a sacred rite?" I'm convinced that every Christian who heard Paul's letter understood exactly what he meant. Unfortunately, there are many today who misapply it to their lives and as a result create all sorts of anxiety in their minds and hearts as they come to take the Lord's Supper.

What does it mean to take the Supper "unworthily"? Does it mean that we are to be unworthy of such a sacrifice? Does it mean that those who do not have perfect lives should not participate? Does it mean that if we can think of any way in which we do not measure up that we should not participate? The answer to all these questions is "no." This is not a discussion of the character of the worshiper but the conduct of the worship. The Lord's Supper is a continuing reminder that there is forgiveness for the sinner and strength for the weak and weary. But the warning is not to come to it when we are insensitive to His presence, unloving to our fellow church members, or regretful for His great sacrifice on our behalf. If we truly enter into the spirit of the Supper we will have a heightened sense of our own unworthiness and of God's grace. This awareness of God's love for us ought to make it easier for us to love one another.

CHAPTER TWELVE

God's Gifts Unite the Church

1 Corinthians 12:1–31

Just when you think that Paul has run out of things which unite the church, he reaches back into his seemingly limitless resources and brings out yet another—the gifts God gives to the church members. This particular chapter can be of great help to Christians and churches today in their effort to build unity within the fellowship. We see all around us in the world the principle of which Paul speaks. We go to an athletic event where there are several players on one team. And while they have different positions to play and differing skills, that very fact is the source of their unity and the thing that makes it possible for them to play the game. The same is true when we go to the symphony. There is great variety in the instruments played and the skills required of the players, but all those instruments and all those different musicians create a musical unity as they give a concert.

But often in the church we have a tendency to seek unity in conformity. Rather than encouraging each person's uniqueness we often discourage it. In many churches this quest for uniformity is not satisfied with loyalty to the pastor and staff and faithfulness to all the activities, but often there is an effort to get all the members to think alike on all issues. While there is a certain short-term efficiency in any authoritarian approach to leadership, in the long run it is self-defeating because it does not recognize the giftedness of each member of the church. The kind of unity God wants comes from the exercising of those gifts. As Paul writes to the Corinthians about their gifts, we can learn from his letter valuable lessons for ourselves and for the church today.

EACH BELIEVER IS GIFTED

1 Now concerning spiritual gifts, brethren, I do not want you to be ignorant:

2 You know that you were Gentiles, carried away to these dumb idols, however you were led.

3 Therefore I make known to you that no one speaking by the Spirit of God calls Jesus accursed, and no one can say that Jesus is Lord except by the Holy Spirit.

4 Now there are diversities of gifts, but the same Spirit.

5 And there are differences of ministries, but the same Lord.

6 And there are diversities of activities, but it is the same God who works all in all.

7 But the manifestation of the Spirit is given to each one for the profit of all:

8 for to one is given the word of wisdom through the Spirit, to another the word of knowledge through the same Spirit,

9 to another faith by the same Spirit, to another gifts of healings by the same Spirit,

10 to another the working of miracles, to another prophecy, to another discerning of spirits, to another different kinds of tongues, to another the interpretation of tongues.

11 But one and the same Spirit works all these things, distributing to each one individually as He wills.

1 Cor. 12:1–11

There are few chapters in the Bible that have more potential for encouraging individual Christians or for strengthening the church in its life and work than this chapter with its emphasis upon the "gifts of the Spirit." But as strong as this emphasis is in the Scriptures, neither the church in which I was baptized nor the churches that were a part of the nurturing process as I grew spiritually called attention to this teaching.

As I reflect, I can better understand now why this was. The churches I grew up in were nervous about charismatic Christians and were not sure that a discussion on the gifts of the Spirit might not create problems. They were churches that were not really comfortable with the kind of diversity that this kind of emphasis affirms.

From time to time I heard an occasional doctrinal sermon on the Holy Spirit but the main emphasis, as I remember it, was the relationship of the Spirit to the Father and the Son in the Trinity and the importance of referring to the Holy Spirit as "He" and not "it." Never do I recall a preacher or a teacher telling me that when I became a Christian and the Spirit of God came into my life that He brought special gifts designed to enrich my life and make me more effective in God's work. Consequently, I was a young ministerial student before the truths in this chapter began to have an impact on my life.

The change took place when I heard Gordon Cosby deliver a series of lectures on the role of the church in identifying and developing the gifts of its members. He is pastor of The Church of the Saviour in Washington, D.C., a church that received national attention when Elizabeth O'Connor described its unusual life and ministry in *The Call to Commitment.*

He drew most of his illustrations out of the life of The Church of the Saviour, and he organized them around two theses. First, there is no gift the church needs that God has not given to one of the members. Second, the work of the church is to encourage the members in the discovery and use of these gifts. While some ignored what he said and others reacted to it, I found my life changed as he helped me to use what Paul wrote in this chapter to think differently about myself, about others, and about how the church can do its work in the world.

The idea of the gift of the Spirit goes all the way back to Simon Peter's sermon on the day of Pentecost when he closed with the fervent appeal for those who heard to repent and be baptized and promised that they would receive "the gift of the Holy Spirit" (Acts 2:38). Here he was referring to the Comforter that Christ promised to the Apostles and all believers in what is most often referred to as the "Upper Room Discourses" (John 13–17).

In this twelfth chapter of 1 Corinthians, Paul discusses how the Spirit operates in the life of the individual Christian in such a way that he or she discovers understandings and abilities not previously recognized. He calls them "gifts of the Spirit" (v. 1) and uses the word from which we get the term "charismatic," a word used broadly in society today to designate a specifically gifted individual. Paul doesn't describe here how this occurs, but merely states a fact.

One explanation that has seemed helpful to me is that God may have given to each person at birth all the gifts He wants each of us to have, and that sin causes us not to recognize or claim or use them to His glory. Our self-centeredness and our preoccupation with lesser things have a way of focusing our lives on things that are more temporal. Then when we become Christians, the Spirit comes to dwell within our lives and in the process begins to uncover valuable insights that have been buried beneath the clutter of our lives. He begins to open doors that we have nailed shut and to develop those parts of us that we have allowed to atrophy from disuse. To me this seems to describe better how He has worked in my life.

Either from the letter Paul had received from one of the church members or from some of the reports that had come to him, he knew certain problems existed in the church at Corinth which came from a misunderstanding of the gifts of the Spirit. And while the particular problems are not spelled out, a careful reading from verse 4 on gives pretty good indication of what they were.

But before looking at some of the problems, I want to refer briefly to a statement in verse 3. Many different students have made suggestions as to what would be the circumstances under which any church member would ever consider calling *"Jesus accursed."* There might have been Christians who were brought to trial and pressured to renounce Christ, or it could have been that some sort of pressure was exerted on Jewish converts coming from the synagogue. But since Paul is not discussing persecution but gifts, and since he closes this larger section with advice concerning ecstatic utterances, many feel that Paul is dealing with a misuse of one of the gifts that came out of their pagan background.

Most likely there were people who were so emotional that they went into a trance and said things that others heard but of which they themselves were not aware. Evidently someone said in some ecstatic utterance "a curse on Jesus." Because of their pagan background those who heard were likely to pay too much attention to what a person in a trance said. The Greeks tended to feel that before God spoke through a person He touched his mind and then spoke to others through the things which that person said. Paul reminds the Corinthians that since the confession of our faith is "Jesus is

Lord" (Rom. 10:9–10), anything contrary to this could not possibly be motivated by the Spirit of God.

While our science-oriented society long ago dropped the idea that God is trying to communicate with us through irrational statements of an individual who might be out of touch with reality or mentally ill, the church community continues to need to be encouraged to show more discernment when confronted by sincere people with bizarre ideas and plans that they introduce by saying "the Lord led me." In spite of the fact that we are warned to test the spirits to see whether or not they really are of God (1 John 4:1), among many believers there is a gullibility that has the possibility of discrediting that which is authentic in the church.

Each month I get several pieces of religious yellow journalism. The editors use their particular periodical and the United States mail to spread their view of what is going on in the religious world. With no concern for responsible research or the spirit of fair play, they attack individuals and institutions with whom they disagree. The first time I read one of the issues it seemed to me to be so irresponsible and one-sided that I could not conceive of anyone taking their writers seriously. That was because I overestimated the ability of many people to "test the spirits." It is sad to admit that many Christians will believe anything they read that is written by a person who claims to be a Christian.

This weakness leaves us open to the same dangers that confronted the early church, of doing and saying things that are diametrically opposed to our confession that "Jesus is Lord." When "the spirit" is used to manipulate people or to meet the ego needs of a leader or as a money-raising technique—then we need to run up a red flag.

In verse 4 Paul picks up on the problem that the church faced, created by the seeming disparity in the nature of the gifts. Some of the gifts were quite spectacular, and those who possessed them had a tendency to be proud. Those gifts that were exercised in the context of worship gave high visibility and prominence to those who possessed them, and it is easy to see, knowing the very human tendency to put self forward, how these individuals might begin to think that they were more important than the others. On the other hand, some of the members were given gifts that were exercised in less dramatic ways—in a servant role, for example—and it is easy to see how because of the quiet and unseen way in which they did their part they might wonder if their gift was important and if they were really needed in the church.

This is a continuing problem, even in the church today, which continues to try to make improper and invalid distinctions concerning gifts. There is still a tendency to treat the gifts of the clergy as being more important than the gifts of the laity, and within the clergy a pecking order has been established. Then within the laity a class system develops with men being thought to be more gifted than women and mid-adults to be more gifted than the youth or the elderly. Consequently, we have those with spectacular gifts who are tempted to be proud and those with gifts that seem less important and may cause the individual to demean himself or herself.

A third problem was present because there were those who despised their own gifts and coveted the gift of another. Paul's answer addressed all of these problems in a powerful and straightforward way. While Paul celebrated the diversity of gifts, of activities, and of ministries, he insisted that they had a common source and a common purpose. All the gifts were from the Holy Spirit and were for the purpose of building up the Body of Christ. Paul makes this great liberating truth in these verses by insisting that *every Christian is gifted* (v. 7). Each one is given an ability by God's grace, and no believer is left out. Each gift is a manifestation of the Holy Spirit.

It is truly a gift, not earned, lest we would be tempted to be proud. It may not be on the list Paul gives in this chapter or in Romans (12:3–8) or in Ephesians (4:7–11), because these lists were not meant to be exhaustive but to give examples of God's gifts. These needs may not be immediately recognized but in the context of prayer, Bible study, worship, and Christian fellowship they can be identified and claimed and developed.

It may be that some of the gifts don't surface until a need appears and we begin to pray about what to do. It is then we discover that God in His love and wisdom has already placed gifts within the church for dealing both with our problems and opportunities. Over the past decade I have watched one church over and over again call forth gifts from its members to meet new and challenging problems and opportunities. I am absolutely convinced that the church is merely touching the hem of the garment of God, mainly because there are still so many gifts undiscovered and so many gifted Christians whose gifts are not being used.

While the list isn't exhaustive, it is interesting to look with a little more depth at some of the gifts Paul mentioned in verses 8–10. The gift of the *"word of wisdom"* (v. 8) and the *"word of knowledge"* (v. 8) seem alike, but they are clearly distinguishable. The first is almost synonymous to revealed truth, that wisdom which is nothing less than the knowledge of God Himself. The second is specified by a different Greek word, one which has to do with making a practical application of wisdom to human life and to all of life's situations. It's easy to see how important both of these gifts would be to the church. As I write this I can put names and faces to these particular gifts. There is an actress in our church who has taught the Bible for years, a person of prayer who has the gift of understanding God's revelation. There is also a deacon who is a hospital administrator who has the gift of practical application that Paul mentions in these verses.

In verse 9 Paul mentions the gift of *"faith"* and the gift of *"healings."* By faith he means the ability to passionately believe in spiritual possibilities, that faith which turns the vision into reality.

It is an exciting experience to stand beside a person who has this kind of faith—the kind of faith that looks where nothing exists and sees what can be. When I was a college student, I went with one of the church's leaders to look at a ranch located in the foothills of the Sangre de Cristo mountains just a few miles east of Sante Fe, New Mexico. As I stood there looking at the dry hills covered by cedars and a few trees, I thought I could see why the rancher wanted to sell it. But my friend believed that he saw a great Christian assembly located on that very spot with thousands of youth and students and couples with children coming there to be drawn closer to God and to be better equipped for their work. I saw all the problems and obstacles but his gift of faith saw the possibilities. Today if you drive on the highway between Sante Fe and Las Vegas, New Mexico, you will see Glorieta Baptist Assembly located where the ranch was.

Those with the gift of *"healings"* were able in Jesus' name to heal certain physical diseases and illnesses. That this particular gift was present in the early church cannot be doubted, and there is evidence that this gift is still given to certain believers.

Four gifts are mentioned in verse 10: doing miracles, prophecy, spiritual discernment, and the ability to either speak with ecstatic utterance or to interpret the utterances. The gift of *"miracles"* probably covered wonderful works which were not healings, but most likely the ability to cast out demons, or exorcism. While this particular form of need is seen today primarily only on the mission field, the church continues to have people who have been given gifts with which to minister to troubled minds.

The gift of *"prophecy"* should probably be translated as the gift of preaching or communication. While the popular understanding of prophecy is that it is foretelling things which will happen, it more often means telling forth the word of God.

And there continue to be those individuals to whom God gives the gift of spiritual communication. While I was a student I heard the late great Andrew W. Blackwood, who had already retired as the preaching professor at Princeton Theological Seminary. He was a great student of worship and of preaching and gave much emphasis to the reading of Scripture in worship. He was with us for an entire week, and the high point of the day was when he stood to read from the Word of God. There was a sense in which even though he was reading a passage that I had read many times before, as he read it, God spoke in a fresh way to my mind and my heart. It takes nothing away from his study and planning and training to say that God had given him the gift of communication.

The *"discerning of spirits"* was very important to a church that did not yet have a New Testament as an objective reference and in a society in which the bizarre seemed normal. It was what God gave to serve as a check or balance to the gift of prophecy, to sort out that which was valid and real from that which was spurious. Though we have both the Bible and almost two thousand years of tradition in the church, we still need in every congregation those persons to whom the Spirit gives that intuitive discernment of spiritual things. There is wisdom that comes with age and insight that is born of experience, but there is also spiritual insight that God gives—a knowledge and wisdom and maturity of judgment that is a part of God's gifts.

Paul closes this section with the reminder that all the gifts are from one God, that they represent our hope for unity, and that they are distributed by God's sovereignty, or as Paul says, *"as He wills"* (v. 11). There is a hint here of the spirit expressed in the parable of the talents (Matt. 25), where the master gives to each of his servants varying amounts of money for which they are to be responsible. There is also the assumption that the road to fulfillment and effectiveness as a Christian comes when we accept God's gifts with joy, develop them with discipline, and dedicate them to God's purpose.

THE UNITY IS IN DIVERSITY

12 For as the body is one and has many members, but all the members of that one body, being many, are one body, so also is Christ.

13 For by one Spirit we were all baptized into one body—whether Jews or Greeks, whether slaves or free—and have all been made to drink into one Spirit.

14 For in fact the body is not one member but many.

15 If the foot should say, "Because I am not a hand, I am not of the body," is it therefore not of the body?

16 And if the ear should say, "Because I am not an eye, I am not of the body," is it therefore not of the body?

17 If the whole body were an eye, where would be the hearing? If the whole were hearing, where would be the smelling?

18 But now God has set the members, each one of them, in the body just as He pleased.

19 And if they were all one member, where would the body be?

20 But now indeed there are many members, yet one body.

21 And the eye cannot say to the hand, "I have no need of you"; nor again the head to the feet, "I have no need of you."

22 No, much rather, those members of the body which seem to be weaker are necessary.

23 And those members of the body which we think to be less honorable, on these we bestow greater honor; and our unpresentable parts have greater modesty,

24 but our presentable parts have no need. But God composed the body, having given greater honor to that part which lacks it,

25 that there should be no schism in the body, but that the members should have the same care for one another.

26 And if one member suffers, all the members suffer with it; or if one member is honored, all the members rejoice with it.

27 Now you are the body of Christ, and members individually.

28 And God has appointed these in the church: first apostles, second prophets, third teachers, after that miracles, then gifts of healings, helps, administrations, varieties of tongues.

29 Are all apostles? Are all prophets? Are all teachers? Are all workers of miracles?

30 Do all have gifts of healings? Do all speak with tongues? Do all interpret?

31 But earnestly desire the best gifts. And yet I show you a more excellent way.

1 Cor. 12:12–31

Paul is not yet through with the discussion of the gifts of the Spirit, but he now builds on what he has already said as he addresses the problems of divisions in the church and makes a case for unity. The continuing need for the church with all its diversity is to find a basis for oneness.

Paul has already argued for unity on the basis that all of our gifts have a common source, so now he seeks to strengthen his position by the use of a new analogy. Earlier, when he was trying to show the relationship of the different individuals who had worked in the church at Corinth, Paul said that the church is like a building or the church is like a field (1 Cor. 3). Later, in writing to the Ephesians, he will liken the church to a bride (Eph. 5). But here he uses one of the most interesting of all analogies in saying to the church, *"You are the body of Christ"* (v. 27).

Like the Apostle, I find myself looking for pictures of the church that show the essential unity behind all the diversity. In verses 12 and 13 he lays down the only lasting basis of unity: *"For by one Spirit we were all baptized into one body"* (v. 13). The only basis for being a member of the church was the confession "Jesus is Lord." In one of the beautiful descriptions of first-century baptism, the candidate is pictured laying aside his old clothes as a symbol of the putting off of the old nature; then he was immersed as a sign of belief in the death, burial, and resurrection of Christ. Afterwards, he was wrapped in a white garment as a reminder of the forgiveness of sin, and then received into the body of believers as one of them. As that particular member functioned within the life of the church, he would become increasingly aware of the diversity within the church and might even be tempted to forget the basis of the unity. In his letter Paul was reminding his readers of the essential unity built into the beginning.

Having established the picture of the church as a living body, Paul now draws some conclusions from that analogy. He uses a rational approach that draws upon everyone's knowledge of the human body. He likens the different members of the congregation to the different parts of a human body and shows in this way both its great diversity and its essential unity. The picture of a foot withdrawing from the body because it can't be a hand, or an ear resigning from the body if it can't be an eye, is so ridiculous that it is funny. The picture of a body made up of nothing but eyes or nothing but ears is ludicrous. The idea of the eye discussing with the hand its not being needed, or the head telling the feet, "You're not needed," simply compounds the folly. What Paul is describing are things that would never happen in a physical body but that were happening in the body of Christ.

Several important truths found in this analogy can be helpful to us today as we think about our relationship with the church. First, while we are not the same, each of us is important to the whole. Paul reminds the readers that in the body a part that may seem to be "weaker" or "less noble" may actually have a more important function than first thought. All of us have seen examples of this in the physical body.

When I was a freshman I met a student who had been destined to be one of the great fullbacks in college football. During his high school years, because of the combination of size, speed, and agility, he had broken all sorts of records and had been highly recruited by the major universities. Then on a summer job in a lumber camp, a job he had taken as much for the training aspects as for the income, he lost a part of his big toe in a freak accident, and it ended his career as an athlete. What he discovered was that the loss of his big toe lost him his fast starts and his agility. The church has a lot of "big toes" that are just taken for granted. We must be careful lest we forget how important they really are to the church.

Second, we desperately need each other. The fact that the different parts of the body need each other is obvious. When as a teenager I developed rheumatoid arthritis, I soon discovered that my sore knee needed the pituitary gland to stimulate the adrenal gland so that my body would produce its own version of cortisone, which would reduce the soreness in my knee.

But what is obvious for our bodies is not so apparent within the church. There is something in us that tries to make the Christian life a "Lone Ranger" kind of experience, but there is no such thing as isolation in the church. All the pictures of the church are group pictures. The more mature we become in Christ, the more we realize that throughout our entire life we will continue to need each other. We complement each other, challenge each other, comfort each other, and communicate with each other. Within this context we find our Christian identity, our ministry to one another, our growth, and our support. The church is the place where each of us is needed and each of us brings needs. This is what we all have in common and it gives us a basis for unity.

Finally, in the body, what affects one member is felt by all. One of the great insights into the nature of the church is shown in Paul's reflection that *"if one member suffers, all the members suffer . . . "* and also *"if one member is honored, all the members rejoice. . . . "* (v. 26). This happens automatically in the body. An infection in the hand spreads and the whole system feels the impact.

I have observed this same principle at work in the church body. When a prominent church strategist did an in-depth survey of our church leadership, one of the questions on a five-page questionnaire was, "If there were a crisis in your life or your family, do you think the church would be supportive to you?" After he scored the surveys, he came to me and said that without exception each person answered in the affirmative and most people wrote the word "absolutely." That response came because those people had learned the truth of what Paul wrote—in the church we share with each other both our joys and our sorrows. This ties us together into one body.

CHAPTER THIRTEEN

The Greatest Gift of All

1 Corinthians 13:1–13

At the conclusion of his chapter on the gifts of the Spirit, after having admonished his readers to "desire the best gifts," Paul then promises to show them the way that is superior to all others—love. While Paul does not call love a "gift," that is what is implied all the way through the chapter. It came as a surprise to me that the idea of a God who loved sinners was such a radical idea that it would cause people to have doubts as to whether or not Jesus was really the Son of God. I had missed the fact that when the Pharisees and scribes said of Jesus, "This man receives sinners and eats with them" (Luke 15:2), it was a criticism given in an effort to discredit Christ. But this is the context that gives us our best point from which to interpret the parables of the lost sheep (Luke 15:4–7), the lost coin (Luke 15:8–10) and the prodigal son and elder brother (Luke 15:11–32). The point of these three stories told by Christ was that His critics didn't really understand the nature of God if He loved only those who were righteous. These stories were meant to teach that at the very heart of God is a love that is not deserved nor earned, but a love that keeps on reaching out to those who are lost.

Just as it has been difficult for people to think of God as a loving and forgiving God, it has been equally difficult to think of love being of paramount importance in one's religion. In this famous chapter from 1 Corinthians Paul does for the significance of love in the Christian life what Jesus did in relating love to the nature of God. Just as God's love was not an abstract concept but one that was acted out in His revelation of Himself in Jesus Christ, so the love of which Paul writes is spelled out in concrete, do-able definitions.

1 Though I speak with the tongues of men and of angels, but have not love, I have become as sounding brass or a clanging cymbal.

2 And though I have the gift of prophecy, and understand all mysteries and all knowledge, and though I have all faith, so that I could remove mountains, but have not love, I am nothing.

3 And though I bestow all my goods to feed the poor, and though I give my body to be burned, but have not love, it profits me nothing.

4 Love suffers long and is kind; love does not envy; love does not parade itself, is not puffed up;

5 does not behave rudely, does not seek its own, is not provoked, thinks no evil;

6 does not rejoice in iniquity, but rejoices in the truth;

7 bears all things, believes all things, hopes all things, endures all things.

8 Love never fails. But whether there are prophecies, they will fail; whether there are tongues, they will cease; whether there is knowledge, it will vanish away.

9 For we know in part and we prophesy in part.

10 But when that which is perfect has come, then that which is in part will be done away.

11 When I was a child, I spoke as a child, I understood as a child, I thought as a child; but when I became a man, I put away childish things.

12 For now we see in a mirror, dimly, but then face to face. Now I know in part, but then I shall know just as I also am known.

13 And now abide faith, hope, love, these three; but the greatest of these is love.

1 Cor. 13:1–13

I have a friend who actually sings the Psalms in his private devotions. When discussing it one day he said to me, "they are hymns, and hymns need to be sung."

While 1 Corinthians 13 is not written in meter, it has so many of the characteristics of a hymn that when I'm reading it I feel it should be set to music. This segment of Paul's letter represents some of the grandest prose in the Bible. Evidently others feel the same way because I've heard the words set to music on several different occasions.

Paul does a very interesting thing with his use of the word "gift" in this chapter. In the previous chapter he treated gifts as the sovereign act of God and reprimanded those who coveted someone else's gift (1 Cor. 12:15–22). He closed the same chapter by urging them to "earnestly desire the best gifts" (1 Cor. 12:31). The early reference is to those gifts of the Spirit that are unique to each person and in their diversity make up the whole. Now he switches to a gift of the Spirit that God desires for every one of His children—the gift of love. When Paul wrote to the church at Galatia, he named love as the first fruit of the Spirit (Gal. 5:22–23). The author of 1 John stated plainly that the one sure way of knowing whether a person was really a Christian was that person's love for others. "Everyone who loves is born of God and knows God. He who does not love does not know God, for God is love" (1 John 4:7–8). In this chapter Paul switched his listeners from the gifts which had been the source of divisions to the supreme gift of all gifts, one which would unite them and make them one.

The Greek language has many different words for love, while in English we have just one. Consequently, before we look at the chapter in detail, we need to be sure we look at the word Paul used and the meaning he attached to it. *Eros* was the word the Greeks used for love when it defined intense physical desire. If you were to make a survey of the way the word "love" is used in the lyrics of popular songs or in the dialogue of soap operas, in most cases it would be what the Greeks meant by *eros*. But neither the verb nor noun form of *eros* is found in the New Testament. A Greek word for a more reciprocal kind of love appears in the Bible a number of times; that word is *philos*. (For an example of the ways in which it is used one has only to read such passages as Matt. 10:37 or John 11:36.) While *eros* was a kind of selfish passion and *philos* described a more brotherly love, neither was used consistently by the New Testament writers when discussing love.

The word that Paul used was *agapē*, a word used quite sparingly by the secular Greek writers, but used widely by Paul and the other writers of the New Testament books. There are those who feel that the seldom-used *agapē* was chosen in order to make it possible for them to give the word a Christian connotation much in the way Jesus took the phrase "Son of man" and filled it with Messianic meaning.

But what probably happened was that the Christians experienced a different kind of love in their relationship with God, and they used that new understanding to define *agapē* love. The love of which they spoke and wrote was not some abstract virtue out of Greek thought. Rather, it was a love that had been defined by God's action in sending Jesus Christ into the world. It was a love that reached out to those who did not deserve it; a love that put the interest of others first; a love that forgave people and started over with them; and a love that sacrificed itself for others. It means that caring, forgiving, spontaneous, redeeming love which is the essence of God's nature. Any different use of the word violates the Scripture's meaning.

In verses 1–3 Paul argues for the absolute necessity of love. In every religious controversy it is love that leaves first. This was certainly true in Corinth where they were fighting pro and con over the gift of tongues. In these verses Paul emphasizes that all the other gifts are gifts. He began with the gift they most prized—the gift of tongues—and suggested that to exercise this gift without love actually reduced the act of worship to little more than empty pagan rites. The *"tongues of men and of angels"* probably refers to ecstatic utterance, which Paul will discuss in the next chapter, but it could also have been a reference to oratory. In many of the temples there was hanging at the entrance a large cymbal. Often, as the would-be worshipers entered the temple, they struck it causing a loud noise. Some said the noise was for the purpose of rousing the gods. By the time Paul wrote this letter, the loud "gong" which was made from striking the cymbal had become the symbol for superficial oratory. With this picture in the background, Paul is saying that, without love, the finest oratory is nothing more than an empty pagan rite.

He next moves to the gift of prophecy, which he himself would consider superior to the gift of tongues. Prophecy, as used here, represents a revelation of God given to build up the church. To prophesy in the church meant to declare the word of God. In our day preaching is based on the Bible. Good preaching seeks to find in the Word of God a message for the people. But in Paul's day, because the only Scripture the church had was the Old Testament, prophesying in-

161

volved not just delivering a message from God, but also receiving by special revelation a word from God for the people. Connected with the gift of prophesying was the gift of faith. In the context of the chapter this probably means miracle-working power. But the summary Paul makes is that to have knowledge of mysteries and power for miracles without love reduces one to zero.

The Jews prized the giving of alms to the poor as a religious act, and the early Christians picked up the idea. Whether giving one's body to be burned (1 Cor. 13:3) meant to place oneself into slavery by having oneself branded or actually to sacrifice one's life in a fire is not certain. The point Paul makes is that if any of these are done without love, then it adds up to one big fat nothing. This had to be a severe blow to the readers who were all puffed up about their alms, but who did not love one another.

I have seen the absence of love negate the other gifts. Many years ago at a large meeting of ministers I shared the platform with a most outstanding speaker. He had an excellent education, and it was reflected in his understanding of the Bible and in his grasp of theology and church history. He had a perceptive understanding of today's world with its pressures, its values, its goals. He was a skilled communicator who knew how to work an audience, and his insights into human nature were keen. It seemed to me that he had every gift necessary for doing the job.

Later, when I read the evaluations that were done on all the program personalities, I was quite surprised to discover that there were few positive comments about his being on the program. In the light of that response, I decided to talk to some of the participants to find some clue. It came in the first conversation when a young minister said, "Quite frankly, everything he said was true. He said it well, but he spoke with a kind of anger. I didn't get the feeling that he loved any of us." This was just another way of saying that a speaker can proclaim God's word with great eloquence, but without love for the person being spoken to, the proclamation becomes an empty gesture.

I have also seen the way the presence of love both enhances all the other gifts and makes up even for inadequacies. In the community where I went to the seminary there was a pastor who had the reputation of being a dictator. He made no pretense of being a Biblical scholar and joked publicly about the number of years it had taken him to complete his studies. There was nothing polished about him. On the contrary, he seemed to work hard to preserve the image of himself as a "good old boy." Yet he was one of the most effective pastors in the community.

Once when I was a guest speaker at his church I was having lunch with one of the long-time members who knew and understood his pastor well. Over coffee we were discussing some of the excellent ministries the church had, and I asked my friend to share with me what he considered to be the clue as to why the church followed the pastor almost without question. He said, "There are really two reasons. First, there's never anything for himself in what he asks us to do. But the main reason we follow him is that we know he loves us." With this in mind we might paraphrase Paul's famous words and say, "I may not be eloquent, nor be able to work miracles, or do spectacular things, but because I love people I'm able to do wonderful and significant things."

Next Paul turns from the absolute necessity for love to a description of love. While it may be hard to define love, it is easy to recognize it by the way it acts.

In fifteen succinct phrases Paul defines this principle for relating to others which will utterly transform all human life. He is not describing a natural human kind of love but that love which was defined by God's gift of Himself in Jesus Christ. If we were to go through these four verses and everywhere the word "love" appears substitute the word "Christ," they would still be true because the kind of love being described is love that has its source in God. And as we look at each of the phrases it becomes obvious that we are defining a style of life that is beyond our reach at a human level—something absolutely impossible unless God's Spirit dwells within us and helps us.

It will help in looking at each of these characteristics of love to recognize that they were being described to some Christians who were fighting among themselves. Paul was making an effort to show them a better way. These same enriching characteristics apply to our lives today.

To all those who are impatient with others Paul wrote, *"Love suffers long"* (v. 4). It doesn't give way to bitterness and wrath when evil is done but is very slow to anger. The emphasis is not so much a call to patience with circumstances as to *patience with people.* The positive side is that love *"is kind"* (v. 4). It's not merely passive; it is actively engaged in doing good to others. It's the picture of a person who spontaneously seeks the good for others and shows it with friendly acts.

Love is the best antidote there is for jealousy in that it *"does not envy"* (v. 4). People who have learned to love don't begrudge others their earthly goods, their positions, or their spiritual gifts.

Love does not *"parade itself"* nor is it *"puffed up"* (v. 4). That is, love creates a self-effacing stance rather than giving in to the temptation to assume an air of superiority. It protects us from having an inflated view of our own importance.

Love creates that kind of charm and winsomeness that keeps persons from behaving *"rudely"* (v. 5). Instead of practicing self-assertiveness, love makes us more tactful and polite. Love has a way of making us more concerned for the real needs of others and less preoccupied with our own rights. Not to be *"provoked"* means that when we love people we are good-natured and don't have temper tantrums or "fly off the handle." This makes us easier to live with.

When we are able to love, we don't store up or keep a record of the wrongs that have been done to us. One of the most destructive things couples do to each other is to keep track of the injuries or supposed injuries. I met a couple who had been married almost forty years who destroyed their relationship by writing down every wrong with the pencil of memory but never taking any off with the eraser of forgiveness and love.

To *"think no evil"* does not mean that no mean thought will ever come into your mind, but that you will learn to forgive and to forget the slights or imagined slights. There are many of us who would be much happier if we were able to close out some of the accounts of wrongs we have been keeping for too long. Love has a way of keeping us from enjoying it when bad things happen to others. Something perverse in human nature seems to make many people more anxious to hear the bad news than the good news. But those who really love do not *"rejoice in iniquity"* (v. 6). Rather, they are happy when the truth is known and acted upon and they have no desire to veil the truth, cover it up, or to edit it. They honestly *"rejoice in the truth"* (v. 6). Rather than being glad about the bad, those who love have a way of excusing the faults of others.

To say that love *"believes all things"* (v. 7) does not mean that it is gullible or unrealistic. But it does call for us to ascribe the best of motives to others and create a spirit of trust. Even when things are not looking good, love has a way of looking to God's future and seeing a better day. True love keeps us from being discouraged. The picture of *"endures all things"* (v. 7) is much more than passive endurance. Love allows us to remain true in the most adverse circumstances and even to transform the situation by the enduring.

When I hold this list of the characteristics of love up before my life like a mirror, I am immediately shaken by the many ways in which I fall short of the perfect love that Christ modeled for me. But I also know that nothing will be more important to my life than letting God perfect the gift of love in me, not in some abstract theological way but by helping me learn to truly love every person as God loves me. These fifteen characteristics of God's kind of love would make a good outline for prayer, meditation, and study as we attempt to live the Christian life.

Having established that love was the most essential gift (vv. 1–3) and that it is superior to all other gifts, Paul concludes this chapter by reminding the readers that love is the most important ingredient in the relationship between a Christian and God.

Even of those things that abide forever, such as faith and hope, love is the greatest of all. When I am asked by parents to talk with their children about what God is like I usually limit myself to a discussion of four questions, all of which can be answered by a knowledge of John 3:16. How does God feel about me? He loves me. How has He shown His love? By sending His Son to die for me. What does He want me to do? He wants me to believe on Him. What will God bring to my life when I respond to His love? Life that never ends. But as Paul indicates in this passage, that is not an insight just for children—it is the most mature understanding we can come to.

When I perform a wedding and read the words "Love never fails," I am painfully aware that human affection can fail. When I busy myself studying the Scriptures for a sermon I realize that there will come a day when "prophecies will cease." But when I am learning to love another with that same unselfish love that God has poured out on me, then I am involved in doing something that will never end because God will never end. In a world that treats those things which are quite temporary as having such great value, the Christian comes and values love and is thought to be impractical. But when everything that seems permanent is gone—our buildings, our bureaucracies, our budgets, our books, and our programs—love will be as enduring as ever.

CHAPTER FOURTEEN

What Proclamation Does

1 Corinthians 14:1–40

For several years I tried to visit all of the children's Sunday school departments after they had begun coming to the worship services with their parents. The children called it "big church" and though they were usually very excited about the prospects of moving from the preschool division into the sanctuary, they tended to find certain aspects of the worship service somewhat baffling. So in my visits with them we would discuss each aspect of the worship in detail with my asking their opinions and their asking me questions. It was sometimes painful to look at everything through the watchful eyes of the children who had absolutely no reluctance to say what they thought or to ask what they wanted to know. But it was a profitable time and helped me to think a little more what the service ought to be and to make changes that made it more meaningful not just for the little children but for their parents.

In 1 Corinthians 14, Paul isolates two features of the worship service in Corinth and discusses their relative worth. In his comparison of tongues and prophecy, or ecstatic utterance and proclamation of the Word, Paul shows the latter to be superior and to be more beneficial for the church at every point. Many people, even those who have read this chapter many times, will be surprised to find that this is Paul's emphasis. Most of us have made the focus of our study not a comparison of prophecy with tongues but a study on the nature or validity of tongues. We need, if we are to catch Paul's original intention, to pick up on the positive teaching concerning what proclamation does.

THE WORD THAT BUILDS UP

1 Pursue love, and desire spiritual gifts, but especially that you may prophesy.

2 For he who speaks in a tongue does not speak
to men but to God, for no one understands him;
however, in the spirit he speaks mysteries.

3 But he who prophesies speaks edification and
exhortation and comfort to men.

4 He who speaks in a tongue edifies himself, but
he who prophesies edifies the church.

5 I wish you all spoke with tongues, but even more
that you prophesied; for he who prophesies is greater
than he who speaks with tongues, unless he interprets,
that the church may receive edification.

6 But now, brethren, if I come to you speaking
with tongues, what shall I profit you unless I speak
to you either by revelation, by knowledge, by
prophesying, or by teaching?

7 Even things without life, whether flute or harp,
when they make a sound, unless they make a
distinction in the sounds, how will it be known what
is piped or played?

8 For if the trumpet makes an uncertain sound,
who will prepare himself for battle?

9 So likewise you, unless you utter by the tongue
words easy to understand, how will it be known what
is spoken? For you will be speaking into the air.

10 There are, it may be, so many kinds of languages
in the world, and none of them is without significance.

11 Therefore, if I do not know the meaning of the
language, I shall be a foreigner to him who speaks,
and he who speaks will be a foreigner to me.

12 Even so you, since you are zealous for spiritual
gifts, let it be for the edification of the church that
you seek to excel.

13 Therefore let him who speaks in a tongue pray
that he may interpret.

14 For if I pray in a tongue, my spirit prays, but
my understanding is unfruitful.

15 What is the result then? I will pray with the
spirit, and I will also pray with the understanding. I
will sing with the spirit, and I will also sing with the
understanding.

16 Otherwise, if you bless with the spirit, how will
he who occupies the place of the uninformed say

"Amen" at your giving of thanks, since he does not understand what you say?

17 For you indeed give thanks well, but the other is not edified.

18 I thank my God I speak with tongues more than you all;

19 yet in the church I would rather speak five words with my understanding, that I may teach others also, than ten thousand words in a tongue.

20 Brethren, do not be children in understanding; however, in malice be babes, but in understanding be mature.

21 In the law it is written:

"With men of other tongues and other lips
I will speak to this people;
And yet, for all that, they will not hear Me,"

says the Lord.

22 Therefore tongues are for a sign, not to those who believe but to unbelievers; but prophesying is not for unbelievers but for those who believe.

23 Therefore if the whole church comes together in one place, and all speak with tongues, and there come in those who are uninformed or unbelievers, will they not say that you are out of your mind?

24 But if all prophesy, and an unbeliever or an uninformed person comes in he is convinced by all, he is judged by all.

25 And thus the secrets of his heart are revealed; and so, falling down on his face, he will worship God and report that God is truly among you.

1 Cor. 14:1-25

This fourteenth chapter of 1 Corinthians needs to be read as the conclusion of what begins in 1 Corinthians 12:1 when Paul writes "concerning spiritual gifts." In chapter 12 he urges his readers to celebrate the diversity of gifts in the church, but to see them as having a common source and a unifying purpose. In chapter 13 he writes of the superiority of the gift of love above all other gifts. But as the chapter develops, it becomes much more than a discussion of "unknown tongues." If we look carefully at the situation in the

Corinthian church and at Paul's suggestions, we'll find deep insights that will help us to think through ways in which the church today can make worship more meaningful for believers and more understandable to those who are not yet Christians.

While there is no clear understanding or agreement among students of the Bible as to what "a tongue" was, just from reading the text some things are obvious. First, it seems to have been common in the Corinthian church. Whether it was limited to that church or not isn't known, even though Paul does not mention "tongues" in the other letters he wrote. Second, the gift seemed to be supernaturally inspired. Third, it was a highly coveted gift.

From Paul's response we can conclude that there were people who suggested that it was actually superior to other gifts, creating the temptation of spiritual pride. Fourth, the way the gift was being exercised was not only creating tensions in the congregation but was causing confusion in the worship services. It was Paul's basic assumption, however, that when people exercised the gifts of the Spirit in a right way they never created problems in the fellowship nor confusion in the worship.

The temptation to divide a church over a misunderstanding of the gifts of the Spirit continues to this very day. When a fledgling congregation was formed on the west side of Houston, the newly licensed pastor came by to see me. He was bubbling with enthusiasm as he told me of the nucleus of people, of the loving spirit, of their wonderful gifts, and of the way they were going to be working together to reach others with the gospel of Christ. And when they moved toward a permanent place to meet, he called me to share the good news and to report on the rapid growth of the new congregation. Sensing something of the spirit of the group and knowing the potential of the neighborhood in which they were located, I fully expected that it was on its way to becoming one of the strongest congregations in the Houston area. But the next thing I heard was the sad news that almost half of the members had left. A tragic split had occurred because of a very intense disagreement over the exercise of the gift of tongues. Bitter strife had torn this church apart, causing it to lose its sense of mission and its attractiveness to unbelievers and Christians alike.

While both Paul and the congregation to which he was writing knew exactly what the phenomenon was to which he was referring, we do not. The Greek word used for "tongues" was *glōssa*, a word that referred to an ancient language or a rare expression. There are those who feel that Paul was referring to an ecstatic utterance. It is their feeling that the worshiper became so intense in his or her worship that he or she began to make sounds which seemed to be no known language. In support of this interpretation, reference is made to the words in 1 Corinthians 14:2: *"For he who speaks in a tongue does not speak to men but to God";* that the person speaking is not conscious of the meaning (1 Cor. 14:14); and that the reference to the tongues of "angels" (1 Cor. 13:1) is not to a foreign language, but to an ecstatic utterance.

Another interpretation is that this is a reference to speaking in a foreign language—that in a moment of extreme emotion the speakers would revert to another language, one which they did not use often though they could speak it and understand it. And, of course, this would create confusion for those who did not know that particular language or dialect.

Other interpreters of this passage feel that the Spirit inspired people to speak in an unlearned foreign tongue, a real language, which could be understood by those who knew it, but not by those who were speaking it. Their reasons for this interpretation are several. First, this is the most consistent use for the word "tongues" in the Bible. Second, if this experience is identical to that of Pentecost (Acts 2:1–11), this would strongly support the idea of a foreign language. Third, the word Paul used for "interpreter" and "interpretation" is most often used for one who translated a foreign language that was being spoken. Fourth, in the Old Testament passage Paul cites (Isa. 28:11–12) the reference is clearly to "languages." Finally, if all the gifts were for the purpose of proclaiming the gospel this would tend to favor the idea of foreign languages.

But whether the contemporary student of the Bible interprets it as ecstatic utterance or a foreign language does not change in any way Paul's counsel to the church. While he recognized tongues as a legitimate gift, he saw it as one that was very low on the scale compared to some others. The indication seems to be that while it might nurture private devotion, it was not as important as the gift of prophecy.

In making the contrast between the two gifts—prophecy and tongues—Paul reminds his readers of the purpose of all preaching and teaching. The purpose for "telling forth" the Word of God, which is what Paul meant by prophecy, was to build up and edify the church (1 Cor. 14:3).

The "prophet" in the early church received the gift of building up the knowledge of Christian truth and equipping people in living the Christian life. The prophet was to be the encourager who brought "comfort to men" (1 Cor. 14:3). Paul makes a very strong case for understanding in the worship service. It is essential that the ordinary person be able to join in (1 Cor. 14:16). In fact, Paul suggests that it was from the preaching of God's Word that people came convicted of sin, were brought under judgment, and came to "worship God" (1 Cor. 14:25).

When I read this passage in God's word, I am reminded of the importance of finding a balance between thought and feeling in a service of worship. Paul was addressing himself to a situation which prized frenzy and celebrated the "spiritual high," and he was seeking a corrective when he argued for understanding. It is well for us to remember that the church to which he wrote had no professional leadership as do our churches today. There was very little structure so natural spontaneity gave it the characteristics of a "happening." His counsel was intended to bring order and understanding. Congregations are still in existence today that major on feeling to the exclusion of understanding.

I have a close friend who attends a church that has as part of its heritage, worship services with lots of movement, where there is almost hypnotic repetition in the music, which takes a single phrase and repeats it over and over and over, where the preaching is a many-faceted dialogue between the preacher and the congregation, and where the sense of having worshiped God in a true fashion is measured by the noise level in the sanctuary and by the number who "faint in joy" in the service. He married a splendid Christian woman who had been reared in a church with an altogether different tradition, one with a paid quartet, with periods of quietness and reflection, and a sermon rich in content and related to life's needs, but delivered in a conversational manner to a congregation which listened intently. The first time she went to church with her husband she almost went into shock because what seemed like a high spiritual moment for her husband and his family seemed like bedlam to her. Finally, after trying in vain to shut out all the movement and talking from her consciousness so she could hear what the pastor was saying, she leaned over to her new husband and complained, "I can't understand a thing the pastor is saying." The husband's response explained the difference in their backgrounds when he said, "Sweetheart, this isn't understanding time. This is *feeling* time."

I am convinced that the heritage of both my friend and his wife need to be a part of authentic worship. There needs to be in our praise a balance between thought and feeling, because there is in our relationship with God both the need to use our minds and to express our emotions. My own background is more on the feeling side. To fathom all that God has done in Jesus Christ to save us challenges the best of our intellects, but to reflect upon that relationship creates a joy that must be expressed. Our faith has expressed both content and passion, and this needs to find balanced expression in our worship.

If Paul were writing the average congregation today, his advice would have to work the other side of the street. Rather than an unstructured spontaneity that creates bedlam he would be confronted with a well-regulated order of worship that often creates boredom. The smallest of churches often prints or mimeographs for its members a program of everything that is going to happen during the hour and the sequence in which it will take place, and once it has been printed it becomes a sacred thing to those who planned it. And the likelihood of the Spirit's leading anyone to say or do something that was not anticipated on Tuesday when the stencil was cut is very remote.

While the church does not need the disorder that comes from not planning, it does need to recognize the importance of using both human intellect and emotion in our expressions of gratitude to God for His love. It is a shame to waste all our tears on the plots of soap operas, all our shouting for a basketball game, and all our enthusiasm for the latest toy and then come into the presence of the Creator and sustainer of life without expressing our deep feelings of awe, of reverence, of unworthiness, and of thankfulness.

WORSHIP THAT BUILDS UP

26 How is it then, brethren? Whenever you come together, each of you has a psalm, has a teaching, has a tongue, has a revelation, has an interpretation. Let all things be done for edification.

27 If anyone speaks in a tongue, let there be two or at the most three, each in turn, and let one interpret.

28 But if there is no interpreter, let him keep silent in church, and let him speak to himself and to God.

29 Let two or three prophets speak, and let the others judge.

30 But if anything is revealed to another who sits by, let the first keep silent.

31 For you can all prophesy one by one, that all may learn and all may be encouraged.

32 And the spirits of the prophets are subject to the prophets.

33 For God is not the author of confusion but of peace, as in all the churches of the saints.

34 Let your women keep silent in the churches, for they are not permitted to speak; but they are to be submissive, as the law also says.

35 And if they want to learn something, let them ask their own husbands at home; for it is shameful for women to speak in church.

36 Or did the word of God come originally from you? Or was it you only that it reached?

37 If anyone thinks himself to be a prophet or spiritual, let him acknowledge that the things which I write to you are the commandments of the Lord.

38 But if anyone is ignorant, let him be ignorant.

39 Therefore, brethren, desire earnestly to prophesy, and do not forbid to speak with tongues.

40 Let all things be done decently and in order.

1 Cor. 14:26–40

In the process of dealing with the questions that had been raised about the gift of tongues, Paul has several insights into Christian worship that have application for Christians today.

The first principle is that of *participation*. His basic assumption was that when the congregation came together each person who had a gift ought to be able to exercise it but that it should not be competitive nor should it create disorder. Too often when we have studied these verses we have focused on the prohibition and missed altogether the affirmation: *"Whenever you come together, each of you has a psalm, has a teaching, has a tongue, has a revelation, has an interpretation"* (1 Cor. 14:26).

The obvious implication of this verse is that when we gather to worship God each of us needs to bring all of our gifts, our insights, and our experiences with God.

The contrast between the situation in our churches today and the one to which Paul addressed himself is so great that the idea frightens us. The church to which Paul wrote had no full-time staff, no history of worship, and very few models to copy. They did have an exciting experience with God to celebrate and a loving fellowship to nourish, and so their worship service was sort of a spiritual "covered dish" affair in which each person brought something to be shared by the group. Paul had no problem with the idea of each person participating. While Paul felt it was counterproductive for everyone to speak at once, he never questioned the need for each Christian to participate meaningfully in worship.

This is an emphasis that desperately needs to be recaptured, because in too many instances worship has become a "spectator" activity. For each person to be meaningfully involved would enrich both the lives of the people and the quality of worship. The church has been celebrating the Biblical teaching about the laity for a long time, but the implications of that emphasis in worship have not yet begun to be realized. A service can be planned and orderly and still have real participation in mind. If the needs and gifts and interests of the laity are kept in mind by those who plan, then the singing of the hymns, the reading of the Scriptures, the participation in the prayers, and even the involvement in the focus of the sermon can become an event that enriches all. While this requires sensitiveness to where the people are, openness to the diversity of gifts and needs, and great flexibility, it has such great potential that it is worth any effort.

The line between clergy and laity needs to be relaxed so that lay members of the church may exercise their gifts by leading in parts of the worship. What is needed is not a kind of tokenism in which on one Sunday each year the laity "take over the worship," but an honest effort to draw from the richness of the life of the congregation those individuals who can also lead.

Several years ago, when I was pastor of Houston's South Main Baptist Church, one of our most insightful members came to me with the suggestion that I use one of the church's deacons each Sunday to read the Scripture and lead the pastoral prayer. My first thought was that even to consider the idea was immediately to reduce the quality of that part of the worship service. I expressed to the man who had made the suggestion that preparing a pastoral prayer took a great deal of thought, awareness, and planning. He responded by asking me to do a teaching session with the deacons both on reading the Scriptures in worship and on how to prepare a pastoral prayer. I agreed to give it a try and was surprised at the attendance, the intelligent interest, and the seriousness with which they took the responsibility.

A different man or woman read the Scripture and led the pastoral prayer each Sunday for the remainder of my pastorate there, and both the staff and the congregation were amazed and blessed by the gifts of interest, experience, awareness, and concerns that became a part of the worship by the participation of the laity in the leadership. I am convinced that there is not a single aspect of the worship that could not be helped by involving more of the church members.

A second principle Paul writes about in this passage is that people, both the members and the unbelievers who may be present, need to be able to understand what is happening. This is reflected in his insistence that to make any sense at all, if a person speaks in a tongue then it is necessary to *"let one interpret"* (v. 27). But it is also the intent of his counsel that when one has a revelation from God, he should wait his turn to speak *"that all may learn and all may be encouraged"* (v. 31). While Paul is dealing with a very specific situation of one local congregation, I think the principle he espouses is one we need to hear today; people who come to worship should be able to understand what is sung and said and should feel that it makes sense in the world in which they live their lives.

While for the most part relatively few congregations today are involved with ecstatic utterance in worship, there is the potential for a great deal of confusion because of the use of a separate vocabulary for religion, a kind of "church talk" that requires special definitions and knowledge of technical phrases. So the "unknown tongues" in many churches may be found in lyrics of many of the hymns, the translations of the Scriptures, traditional phrases of the prayers, and the oftentimes irrelevant perspective of the sermon. If God's people gather to worship and do not find help for their lives for this week, then the service could just as easily have been done in a different language. Too often this is the case.

One of the classroom experiences I used as a professor of evangelism was to have a student stand and explain the meaning of John 3:16 to me as though I were a sixteen-year-old who was interested but who had no background in church. After the first student tried it, I would ask the class to list all the words or phrases they had heard that would have had no meaning to a person who had never been to church. I wrote them all on the chalkboard. Then we discussed in great detail what reality we were trying to communicate about God and what would be a better way to communicate it. Before the class was over, almost everyone realized that without really being aware of it, they had developed a kind of "religious jargon" that was hard for people to understand and to relate to life.

Paul also urged that worship have order. From time to time I want to quote his advice, *"let all things be done decently and in order"* (v. 40), when I find myself in a religious service that resembles a three-ring circus more than a sanctuary of God. Paul had an interesting insight into the disorder of Corinth. He felt that it was created by selfishness, by each person thinking more about his or her part than about the needs of the whole church. There is a sense in which people who want every part of the service to meet only their needs create a problem, and the person who realizes that the church has many different people with different needs lays the foundation for a kind of order that honors God.

When I became pastor after years of teaching, one of the first problems I faced in planning worship had to do with the kind of music I wanted. From talking to the minister of music I learned that the church's interests and tastes in music ran the gamut from heavy anthems to gospel choruses, from pipe organ to classical guitar, and from Handel's stately "Messiah" to the Gaithers' popular song "The King Is Coming." Together we decided that the music needed to reflect the richness of variety in the church and that we would have to find our *order* by reflecting our diversity and by counting on the people to think not just of themselves but of the needs of others. This sample principle needs to be reflected in all the parts of worship.

CHAPTER FIFTEEN

The Living Christ

1 Corinthians 15:1–58

The central fact of the Christian religion is the resurrection of Jesus Christ from the dead. Had it all ended on the cross there would have been no good news to share, no bold church to bear witness, no New Testament to teach and preach, and no hope for real life here or in the hereafter. It is impossible to overestimate the importance of the resurrection to our faith.

Since I have read the church's account of the resurrection in the Gospels from childhood, it had not occurred to me that for a long period of time after Christ had been raised from the grave that the word was proclaimed but not written down. But in one of the first survey courses on the New Testament that I ever attended, I was really surprised to learn that Paul was the first New Testament writer to record what had been preached about the resurrection for years, and that this account precedes by almost fifteen years the accounts in the earliest Gospel. Those of us who have had access to the full story for our whole Christian lives cannot possibly realize what it must have been like during that first century for those early believers.

While we do not have the precise question which prompted Paul to include this portion of Christ's history in his letter to the Corinthians, we do know that it had grown out of someone's questioning the resurrection. Paul's rather extensive answer gathered up the teachings concerning the resurrection and elaborated on its significance to the faith and the hope of those who asked the question.

In the first part of chapter 15 (vv. 1–38) Paul dwells on the fact that the resurrection of Christ actually took place, and in the last part of the chapter (vv. 39–58) he makes an introductory statement concerning the nature of resurrection life. It is truly one of the great chapters in the Bible and one that will bring stability and hope to any who study it with seriousness.

GOSPEL BASED ON HISTORICAL EVENT

1 Moreover, brethren, I declare to you the gospel which I preached to you, which also you have received and in which you stand,

2 by which also you are saved, if you hold fast that word which I preached to you—unless you believed in vain.

3 For I delivered to you first of all that which I also received: that Christ died for our sins according to the Scriptures,

4 and that He was buried, and that He rose again the third day according to the Scriptures,

5 and that He was seen by Cephas, then by the twelve.

6 After that He was seen by over five hundred brethren at once, of whom the greater part remain to the present, but some have fallen asleep.

7 After that He was seen by James, then by all the apostles.

8 Then last of all He was seen by me also, as by one born out of due time.

9 For I am the least of the apostles, who am not worthy to be called an apostle, because I persecuted the church of God.

10 But by the grace of God I am what I am, and His grace toward me was not in vain; but I labored more abundantly than they all, yet not I, but the grace of God which was with me.

11 Therefore, whether it was I or they, so we preach and so you believed.

1 Cor. 15:1–11

Paul has packed so much into these first eleven verses that volumes could be written elaborating on the implications of the themes introduced.

First, Paul reminds the Corinthians how they had come to hear the gospel and the difference it had made in their lives. Paul had been that human instrument in bringing the gospel to them. It was by the reception of that word that they had been saved (v. 2) and had taken their stand in the world as believers (v. 1). Paul had wanted them to realize how precious this word was, and he urged them to *"hold fast that word which I preached to you"* (v. 2).

Then Paul reminded them that when the gospel is reduced to its essence, it is an event in history. It was not something which was enacted in another place, like the activities of the Greek gods, but a happening that can be given date and place and person. Paul summarizes God's activity in three statements: Christ died for our sins, was buried, and He rose again (vv. 3–4). Many feel the words of verses 3 and 4 may have been used as a confession by believers at the time of their baptism. In a very condensed form Paul focused on the significance of the cross in salvation, the reality of His death on our behalf, and our hope in the resurrection. But his reminding them of what the gospel was and what it meant in their lives was really leading up to the main point of the chapter—that the resurrection of Jesus Christ was an event that really took place and whose implications were enormous.

Paul's main argument was that there were still eyewitnesses to the resurrection. That Christ died and was really raised from the dead was a fact that could be corroborated by individuals who were still living at the time 1 Corinthians was being written. While acknowledging that some who had been eyewitnesses had died, Paul estimated that there were approximately five hundred persons living at the time he wrote who could verify the fact of the resurrection. He identifies Cephas and the Twelve (v. 5), James and all the apostles (v. 7), and himself. While Paul confessed his unworthiness for having *"persecuted the church"* (v. 9) and that his meeting with Christ came later, he made no distinction between the Christ who was seen by Cephas and the Christ who appeared to him on the road to Damascus. These are all powerful witnesses.

Every year in the process of preparing sermons for the Easter season I go back and study again these earliest documents concerning the cross and resurrection. One thing becomes clear from even a casual reading of the text: the disciples did not expect the resurrection to take place. The things that Christ said to them about it beforehand somehow did not register. At first they saw nothing but crushing defeat in the cross. They were confused, fearful, disorganized, and whipped.

Then we read that when reports that Jesus had risen first came to them, they did not believe the news. Though Christ had said that He would rise again, they somehow missed His point and did not expect it to happen. It wasn't just Thomas but all of the disciples who had to be convinced by Christ's personal presence in their lives. These are not gullible witnesses who are testifying to what they had hoped would happen. Rather, they had to be convinced by the hard evidence.

That the gospel is based upon a historical event is of great importance to Christians today. Years ago, as a part of my devotional life during the Easter season, I read each day a chapter from a devotional book written by one of the ministers who was prominent around the turn of the century. The book focused on the events of Holy Week, and I timed my reading so I could read the chapter on the crucifixion on Good Friday and the one on the resurrection on Easter Eve. It has been years since this happened, but I can still remember how let down I felt from reading the last chapter in that book. The author did not believe the resurrection took place. He felt that the accounts of the resurrection in the Scriptures were nothing but faith's expression of what the disciples had wanted to happen. The author had imagined an upper room scene in which they were all lamenting that one who had loved so freely should have died as the object of such hatred, that one whose teaching had such authority should be silenced so young. Then, in the scenario he was imagining, he had one of the disciples jump to his feet and shout, "We will not let Him die. The way He lived, we will live. The things He taught, we will teach. The mission He had will become our mission. We will not let Him die." The plain inference was that the church had created the resurrection, but the exact opposite is true. It was the risen Christ, and nothing else, that transformed that defeated band of followers into witnesses so bold that they turned their world upside down.

THE RESURRECTION, OUR ONLY HOPE

12 Now if Christ is preached that He has been raised from the dead, how do some among you say that there is no resurrection of the dead?

13 But if there is no resurrection of the dead, then Christ is not risen.

14 And if Christ is not risen, then our preaching is vain and your faith is also vain.

15 Yes, and we are found false witnesses of God, because we have testified of God that He raised up Christ, whom He did not raise up—if in fact the dead do not rise.

16 For if the dead do not rise, then Christ is not risen.

17 And if Christ is not risen, your faith is futile; you are still in your sins!

18 Then also those who have fallen asleep in Christ have perished.

19 If in this life only we have hope in Christ, we are of all men the most pitiable.

20 But now Christ is risen from the dead, and has become the firstfruits of those who have fallen asleep.

21 For since by man came death, by Man also came the resurrection of the dead.

22 For as in Adam all die, even so in Christ all shall be made alive.

23 But each one in his own order: Christ the firstfruits, afterward those who are Christ's at His coming.

24 Then comes the end, when He delivers the kingdom to God the Father, when He puts an end to all rule and all authority and power.

25 For He must reign till He has put all enemies under His feet.

26 The last enemy that will be destroyed is death.

27 For *"He has put all things under His feet."* But when He says "all things are put under Him," it is evident that He who put all things under Him is excepted.

28 Now when all things are made subject to Him, then the Son Himself will also be subject to Him who put all things under Him, that God may be all in all.

29 Otherwise, what will they do who are baptized for the dead, if the dead do not rise at all? Why then are they baptized for the dead?

30 And why do we stand in jeopardy every hour?

31 I affirm, by the boasting in you which I have in Christ Jesus our Lord, I die daily.

32 If, in the manner of men, I have fought with beasts at Ephesus, what advantage is it to me? If the dead do not rise, *"Let us eat and drink, for tomorrow we die."*

33 Do not be deceived: "Evil company corrupts good habits."

34 Awake to righteousness, and do not sin; for some do not have the knowledge of God. I speak this to your shame.

1 Cor. 15:12–34

The Corinthian question surfaces in verse 12: *"How do some among you say that there is no resurrection of the dead?"* In all likelihood they had not questioned Christ's resurrection, but whether or not Christians who died would be raised. Something had happened, perhaps a death in the church, that had served as a catalyst for discussion. Had they had the New Testament, they could have read the comforting words "I am the resurrection and the life. He who believes in Me, though he may die, he shall live" (John 11:25).

The Corinthian question could have had several sources. Buried deep in the thinking of all those reared in the Greek culture was the idea that the body was a prison in which the soul was incarcerated and that in death the soul that is good is freed. To a person with this kind of background, the idea of any bodily resurrection would have been offensive. There may have been a reaction to a popular Jewish idea of the day that resurrection meant that the present physical life would start all over again. But today's questions about the resurrection are more apt to come out of narrow humanism that has been created by our scientific culture—a position that insists that this life is all there is.

Paul answered the question by pointing out the ridiculous conclusions that would follow if there were no resurrection of the dead. The first conclusion was that *"if there is no resurrection of the dead, then Christ is not risen"* (v. 13). There were those who were willing to believe that Christ had risen from the grave but doubted that others would. Paul reminds them that Christ was a human being, too, and that if people are not raised from the dead then Christ wasn't raised either. All the other conclusions flow from this, and Paul paints a very dark picture of what it would be like to live in a world without resurrection. All preaching would be empty or even false witnessing. There would be no forgiveness of sin. We would all face death without hope, and even now we would be tortured by the thought that those we love who have already died have perished forever.

I remember hearing a person say once that even if Christ had not been raised from the dead, he thought he would continue to live the Christian life because "it would still be the best way to live." But I wonder if he didn't say that because he could not conceive what it would be like to live in a world without the hope of the resurrection. The Christian life is only the best life if it is based upon truth, and Paul is right in stating, *"If in this life only we have hope in Christ, we are of all men the most pitiable"* (v. 19).

When I was a teenager, someone gave me a pamphlet written by Luther Burbank, a rather famous man who was an agnostic. He was an expert in the field of agronomy, but in the pamphlet he was trying to speak with authority in the area of religion. The gist of the pamphlet was that it wasn't really necessary to believe in Christ's divinity or in His resurrection in order to admire Him for His good life and for His teachings.

I was young and inexperienced and lacked the ability to properly weigh his argument, but I was impressed that this great man had some nice things to say about Jesus. At the time I was living with my Uncle Walter and Aunt Bertie, so I decided to try the man's idea out on Aunt Bertie, who, though she lacked formal training, had an excellent knowledge of the Bible and a profound faith in God. I took the pamphlet into the kitchen where she was cooking supper on an old wood-burning stove. She was making gravy in a large cast-iron skillet and was stirring it with a wooden spoon to keep it from sticking.

After I read the pamphlet out loud to her, I asked what she thought of the idea. Without looking up or even interrupting her stirring of the gravy she said, "Jesus was either the Son of God or one big liar. If He didn't rise from the dead the whole thing's a hoax." She hadn't met Christ on the road to Damascus as Paul had, but she had met Him and she knew how much was riding on the fact that He was alive.

But Paul does not stop with the "what if" paragraph. He throws those ideas aside and makes them totally irrelevant with the affirmation, *"But now Christ is risen from the dead"* (v. 20). He mixes two very popular analogies as he moves to show the effects of the resurrection of Christ: the firstfruits of the harvest and the contrast between Adam and Christ. When the harvest was over before grain could be sold in the markets or could be used by the people, the firstfruits of the harvest had to be offered to God. From a general field the grain was harvested and specially prepared and then offered to God. Only then could the grain be used.

Building on that picture, Paul said that until God had raised Christ from the dead, no one had any hope. But His resurrection became like the grain that had been offered to God: it opened the way for everyone to have hope. He made Adam the symbol of the old earthly order and Christ the symbol of the new order and the new age.

Paul felt that the great hope of the resurrection was that it gave promise of the ultimate victory of God in all things. When God raised Christ from the dead He took sides: for the truth and against lies; for the good and against evil; for love instead of hate; for life rather than death.

I once heard a very popular philosopher-lecturer-writer discuss death. He drew applause from the audience when he scolded those who still felt death was the enemy and urged them to think of themselves as leaves on a tree which "must turn loose and fall to the ground and become mulch in order to make room for the new leaves." That may be a very stimulating and sophisticated idea to try on a formally dressed, well-educated group who had just had a large meal and felt good about everything. But my vocation forces me too often to be a witness to what death does to those same gifted, exciting personalities. I still think that death is our one unconquered enemy and that there is nothing that makes the resurrection better news than that *"the last enemy that will be destroyed is death"* (v. 26).

When I preside at the graveside funeral service, I always read the same Scripture passage, Revelation 21:1–8. I never come to the words in verse 4 without my heart skipping a beat! "And God will wipe away every tear from their eyes; there shall be no more death, nor sorrow, nor crying; and there shall be no more pain, for the former things have passed away." After reading the entire passage and concluding the service, I get into my car to leave. But starting the engine I look around the cemetery at all the tombstones and say out loud, "Death—you are not the final word." Then I drive from the cemetery with the certain knowledge that as surely as God raised Jesus from the grave that there will come a day when death will die.

THE RESURRECTION LIFE

35 But someone will say, "How are the dead raised up? And with what body do they come?"

36 Foolish one, what you sow is not made alive unless it dies.

37 And what you sow, you do not sow that body that shall be, but mere grain—perhaps wheat or some other grain.

38 But God gives it a body as He pleases, and to each seed its own body.

39 All flesh is not the same flesh, but there is one kind of flesh of men, another flesh of beasts, another of fish, and another of birds.

40 There are also celestial bodies and terrestrial bodies; but the glory of the celestial is one, and the glory of the terrestrial is another.

41 There is one glory of the sun, another glory of the moon, and another glory of the stars; for one star differs from another star in glory.

42 So also is the resurrection of the dead. The body is sown in corruption, it is raised in incorruption.

43 It is sown in dishonor, it is raised in glory. It is sown in weakness, it is raised in power.

44 It is sown a natural body, it is raised a spiritual body. There is a natural body, and there is a spiritual body.

45 And so it is written, *"The first man Adam became a living being."* The last Adam became a life-giving spirit.

46 However, the spiritual is not first, but the natural, and afterward the spiritual.

47 The first man was of the earth, made of dust; the second Man is the Lord from heaven.

48 As was the man of dust, so also are those who are made of dust; and as is the heavenly Man, so also are those who are heavenly.

49 And as we have borne the image of the man of dust, we shall also bear the image of the heavenly Man.

50 Now this I say, brethren, that flesh and blood

cannot inherit the kingdom of God; nor does corruption
inherit incorruption.

51 Behold, I tell you a mystery: We shall not all
sleep, but we shall all be changed—

52 in a moment, in the twinkling of an eye, at the
last trumpet. For the trumpet will sound, and the dead
will be raised incorruptible, and we shall be changed.

53 For this corruptible must put on incorruption,
and this mortal must put on immortality.

54 So when this corruptible has put on incorruption,
and this mortal has put on immortality, then shall be
brought to pass the saying that is written: *"Death is
swallowed up in victory."*

55 *"O death, where is your sting?*
O Hades, where is your victory?"

56 The sting of death is sin, and the strength of
sin is the law.

57 But thanks be to God, who gives us the victory
through our Lord Jesus Christ.

58 Therefore, my beloved brethren, be steadfast,
immovable, always abounding in the work of the Lord,
knowing that your labor is not in vain in the Lord.

1 Cor. 15:35–58

The second part of the chapter reflects Paul's answer to a second
question: what kind of a body will a resurrected person have? While
the Bible is very clear about the fact of the resurrection, the accounts
of the post-resurrection appearances of Jesus leave lots of questions
unanswered. Since His disciples and friends didn't always recognize
Him immediately indicates that He was different in appearance,
though He was the same person. The stories of His appearing suddenly
in the room where the disciples were meeting, even when the doors
were closed, caused people to wonder how the resurrection body
related to material things. Then, too, it seemed that Christ no longer
needed physical nourishment, as our bodies do, but John tells of
His eating fish with His disciples after the resurrection (John 21). It
is hard for us, with our knowledge of the parts of the body and
their functions, to imagine what a person would be like with any

other kind of body. But Paul's word to the Corinthians has some helpful insight for us.

Paul's first illustration comes from nature. He compares a person's dying to the planting of a seed in the ground where it germinates, and he compares the resurrection body with the new plant that comes up (vv. 36–38). As is true of all illustrations, this should not be pressed too far but we should seek to understand its basic truth.

I would draw from Paul's analogy two truths: first, it is not possible to tell from the appearance of a seed exactly what the plant will look like when it is grown. A person with no gardening experience could look at a tiny tomato seed and never dream that it would become a tall green plant with yellow blossoms that develop into huge tomatoes. In the same way, we cannot look at our present bodies and know exactly what the resurrection body will be like. By saying of the different grains that *"God gives it a body as He pleases, and to each seed its own body"* (v. 38), Paul reminds us that God in His sovereignty will give us the body that we need and that pleases Him.

But the main teaching of the analogy from nature is that death and resurrection is a transition to a higher life. Nothing in the background of either the Greek or Jewish members of the church would have prepared them for the idea that the life beyond the grave would be superior to this life. The Greek culture looked upon the best position in the land of the dead as inferior to the lowest position in the world. Even the Old Testament painted a very unattractive picture of the land beyond death. The lament of the Psalmist that "in death there is no remembrance of You" (Ps. 6:5), and "The dead do not praise the Lord, Nor any who go down into silence" (Ps. 115:17) stands in stark contrast to the statement which Paul would later write to the Philippians: "To live is Christ, to die is gain" (Phil. 1:21).

While Paul's illustration leaves many questions unanswered, it does address itself to the fact of future self. While young people today may ask their Bible teacher, "What's it like in heaven?" what they really would rather know is, does my individuality survive death? There is in the back of our minds the vague fear that all we have been promised is that we will be sort of a "generic soul," without distinction. Paul's analogy between the seed and the plant promises that there is some kind of continuity of person and personality. He shows the superiority of the resurrection life by a series of contrasts between the body which is planted in death and the resurrection body. We're planted in corruption, dishonor, and weakness and raised in incorruption, glory and in power (vv. 42–43).

Paul's second analogy contrasts what he calls the "natural body" with the "spiritual body" (v. 44). Again he picks up the comparison of Adam and Christ, calling them the first and second Adams (v. 45). He relates the first Adam to the original creation and the second Adam to the new creation of God through the living Christ (v. 47). The basic teaching is the same as with the seed and the plant. We are not to be disembodied spirits floating around in eternity. We are to have some bodily form for the expressing of the personality. While in the "natural body" we are controlled by our lower nature, in the new "spiritual body" we will be controlled by the life-giving spirit.

The concluding nine verses of this chapter redefine the death of a Christian in the light of Christ's resurrection as a victory and not a defeat. He is so sure of that day when death will be *"swallowed up in victory"* (v. 54) that he taunts death with: *"O death, where is your sting? O Hades, where is your victory?"* (v. 55). Then he answers the question with the statement of thanks to God for *"the victory through our Lord Jesus Christ."*

It's interesting how Paul was able, in the midst of a world in which death seemed to rule, to sound a note of celebration of victory. I know many people who have that same sense of ultimate triumph, and I have it, too. It is because the Christ who appeared to Cephas, and to the Twelve, and even to Paul, has come into my life, also. And the longer I know and serve this living Christ the more I can begin to understand Paul's writing to his friends in Philippi and describing death not so much as the end of the journey but as the beginning. He wrote about death in terms of having a desire to "depart and be with Christ" (Phil. 1:23). The word used for "depart" was a word used for taking down the tent and beginning a journey or for untying the ship from the dock and setting sail on an adventure. This hope is born only from a relationship with the risen Christ.

When I went back into the pastorate from the classroom, I began conducting funerals again, and I was surprised by how many of these memorial services were conducted in the chapels of the funeral homes instead of the sanctuary of the church. One day as I rode back from the cemetery with the funeral director I asked about this trend. He assured me that eventually all the memorial services would be conducted away from the church because, in his words, "People don't like to go to church and be reminded of death." Although I did not outwardly react to his remark, I determined in my mind that I was going to do what I could to reverse the trend because I believe that people should be buried from the place where they made their profession of faith in the living Christ and where they met to worship God and celebrate the resurrection of Christ from the dead.

Some of the high religious moments in the life of the church have been when we have gathered as the people of God in the context of loss and pain and grief to mark the death of a believer. Besides the Scriptures and prayers and eulogy there is usually a congregational hymn. And in that hymn we try to sing the hope that Paul celebrated in this chapter of 1 Corinthians. I recall the service for an outstanding young mother who had died. The sanctuary was so packed with members and guests that the immediate family was forced to sit on the front pew, and there were still guests who had to stand. For the close of the memorial service the congregation sang the very strong hymn "How Firm a Foundation." When we came to the last stanza the teenage daughter of the woman stood, and the family and congregation followed suit and as one we sang:

> The soul that on Jesus hath leaned for repose
> I will not, I will not desert to his foes;
> That soul, though all hell should endeavor to shake,
> I'll never, no, never, no, never forsake!

This is our only hope.

CHAPTER SIXTEEN

A Final Word

1 Corinthians 16:1–24

Paul's first letter to the Corinthians reached its highest peak with his discussion of the hope of life beyond the grave and of the nature of resurrection life. He had spoken to them of his concerns and had replied to their questions, bringing it all together in a hymn of victory. In this closing chapter the mood changes and he attends to what would be called today a few "housekeeping matters" and a formal goodbye. There was the reminder of an offering (vv. 13–18), and formal greetings and farewell (vv. 19–24).

1 Now concerning the collection for the saints, as I have given orders to the churches of Galatia, so you must do also:

2 On the first day of the week let each one of you lay something aside, storing up as he may prosper, that there be no collections when I come.

3 And when I come, whomever you approve by your letters, I will send to bear your gift to Jerusalem.

4 But if it is fitting that I go also, they will go with me.

5 Now I will come to you when I pass through Macedonia (for I am passing through Macedonia).

6 But it may be that I will remain, or even spend the winter with you, that you may send me on my journey, wherever I go.

7 For I do not wish to see you now on the way; but I hope to stay a while with you, if the Lord permits.

8 But I will tarry in Ephesus until Pentecost.

9 For a great and effective door has opened to me, and there are many adversaries.

10 Now if Timothy comes, see that he may be with you without fear; for he does the work of the Lord, as I also do.

11 Therefore let no one despise him. But send him on his journey in peace, that he may come to me; for I am waiting for him with the brethren.

12 Now concerning our brother Apollos, I strongly urged him to come to you with the brethren, but he was quite unwilling to come at this time; however, he will come when he has a convenient time.

13 Watch, stand fast in the faith, be brave, be strong.

14 Let all that you do be done with love.

15 I urge you, brethren—you know the household of Stephanas, that it is the firstfruits of Achaia, and that they have devoted themselves to the ministry of the saints—

16 that you also submit to such, and to everyone who works and labors with us.

17 I am glad about the coming of Stephanas, Fortunatus, and Achaius, for what was lacking on your part they have supplied.

18 For they have refreshed my spirit and yours; therefore acknowledge such men.

19 The churches of Asia greet you. Aquila and Priscilla greet you heartily in the Lord, with the church that is in their house.

20 All the brethren greet you. Greet one another with a holy kiss.

21 The salutation with my own hand—Paul.

22 If anyone does not love the Lord Jesus Christ, let him be accursed. O Lord, come!

23 The grace of our Lord Jesus Christ be with you.

24 My love be with you all in Christ Jesus. Amen.

1 Cor. 16:1–24

The word about the *"collection for the saints"* at Jerusalem reveals a lot about the Apostle Paul. That he would put his discussion of the resurrection of Jesus Christ from the dead and the offering for the impoverished Christians in Jerusalem so close together without any sense of inappropriateness gives an index to the wholeness of the man. Paul was a genius at communication. He could write prose about the nature of love which inspired musicians to put it to music; or he could soar with the eagles as he thought of the better existence God was preparing for us beyond the grave, and, just as naturally, he could discuss the practical details of gathering a love offering for some fellow Christians. There has always been an unhealthy tendency in the church to create a dichotomy between theology and practical helpfulness, but Paul's wedding of the theological basis of life and its practical application is a healthy corrective to this tendency.

In Galatians 2:10 Paul said that when he had been in Jerusalem the apostles asked him to remember in his travels the needs of his fellow Christians in Jerusalem. And he had given careful attention to comply with their needs by urging the churches everywhere to participate in a special offering. Paul had several reasons for giving such a high priority to that kind of project. He had natural ties to his fellow Jews, and it is quite likely he had many friends and acquaintances among those who were suffering. But the thing of utmost importance about this offering was that it had the potential for drawing the gentile and Jewish Christians closer together. Paul was constantly aware of the fact that the Jewish Christians were nervous about many of the things that were happening in the new churches out in the Greek world. And Paul felt that participating in the offering, either as a giver or a recipient, would create a bond.

The principle is a sound one, and I have seen it demonstrated over and over in the church. People who give to the cause of missions grow in their love for the cause to which they give. I watched this happen with a group of laymen in Mississippi several years ago. Owen Cooper wanted to get some of the men of his state more interested in world missions. They made their living with large commercial chicken-raising operations, and though they were active in the church, they had little interest outside their own community. Owen shared with the men the fact that in some of the countries in Africa, it was impossible for the people to produce sufficient protein to support life, and he got them interested in equipping and training African nationals in the raising of chickens as a source of high protein. The men not only gave of their money but of their time and experience. In the process of bringing the project to completion the men learned more and more about all the needs of those who live in underdeveloped countries and their eyes were opened to Christian missions. Not only was the effort a success, but one of its valuable by-products was a group of men in Mississippi who now have a much larger interest in the needs of their fellow human beings around the world.

I worked closely on one occasion with a dozen fellow pastors as we each led the laity of our churches to give money to build a retreat center for all the churches. While there were a number of pastors and churches who did not participate at all, those of us who did reaped a harvest of blessings that we had not anticipated. Our interest grew because we were more informed and more involved, but most of all our churches drew closer to each other. I'm convinced that nothing would bring a spirit of unity among churches quicker than involving ourselves in helping each other.

While two chapters in 2 Corinthians (8 and 9) are devoted to expanding Paul's thoughts on the importance of the offerings, these four brief verses that are dropped in only as a reminder leave us with a wonderful pattern for giving, both for special offerings and for the meeting of ongoing needs. While these are not rules or commandments to be adhered to with legalistic rigidity, they contain great wisdom and insight on the matter of Christian charity. Everyone should be involved in the offering whether they had little or much to give. The system Paul suggested was that each week as they met to worship, they add to the offering. This giving should reflect each member's own circumstances. He closed his brief reminder by saying that there should be careful administration of the money that was raised. During the years I have been involved in the church both as a staff member and as a part of the laity, I have seen many different approaches made to raising money for the church's work. Paul's simple formula seems to be an excellent way for God's people to give.

In verses 5–12, Paul shares with his readers his personal plans. He tells them of his plans to visit them, but rather than go directly by boat, he plans to take the overland route and visit the churches in Macedonia on the way. This will allow him to have a longer visit with them, and considering all the matters he has discussed in this letter, Paul feels that a longer visit will be more enjoyable and profitable.

Then, in verse 9, he explains his reason for tarrying in Ephesus: *"For a great and effective door has opened to me, and there are many adversaries."* This was his way of saying that new opportunities of ministry and service were open to him.

Paul also mentions the plans of Timothy and Apollos. Timothy would probably be coming to Corinth, and Paul wanted them to receive him with respect and understanding. Timothy was younger and less experienced and did not have the status Paul had, so Paul was paving the way for him. Through the years so many persons have played this role in my life and have made the work more enjoyable. Now I am having the privilege of playing the role of "Paul" to the "Timothies" whom God sends. Paul also told them that Apollos did not feel that the circumstances were right to come to Corinth.

The final exhortation and greetings give us a beautiful picture of the warmth of Paul, and of the relationships which had been built with those who were a part of the work in the churches. After mentioning again those whom he had baptized, and those who had come from Corinth to bring messages and to ask questions, and those who were his fellow workers, Paul took the manuscript from his secretary and signed his name. Then he personally wrote a reminder of his feelings for those to whom he had written so much: *"My love be with you all in Christ Jesus. Amen"* (v. 24).

Recently I said goodbye to a congregation I had served for more than a decade. With these people I had shared life with all its variety of experiences—joy and sadness, anger and forgiveness, praise and prayer, work and play. At the end of that last service of worship I looked at those who were there and sought some appropriate last word. There were so many words that would have been appropriate, but because of the deep emotions of the hour I found it almost impossible to speak. All I could finally say was, "You know of my love." That summed it up, and that was enough.

Introduction to 2 Corinthians

Although the second letter to the Corinthians is full of profound theological truths, it is one of the least studied books that Paul wrote. One reason is that, in contrast to 1 Corinthians, which has been referred to as the "layman's charter," this book seems to be dominated by the discussion of Paul's ministry and his authority—a sort of "preacher's discussion."

Second Corinthians is also difficult to understand because, in its function as a letter, it alludes to people and events with which the readers were quite familiar, but which we know little or nothing about. Paul also makes assumptions about the knowledge of his readers, often leaving us in the dark. For instance, it is likely that nearly everyone who read this letter knew about Paul's "thorn in the flesh" (2 Cor. 12:7). But the many different theories that scholars have advanced concerning it are proof that *we* do not know what it was.

In addition, there is a defensiveness in the letter that seems uncharacteristic of Paul. His approach was dictated by the accusations he was answering. But as we read the letter, it becomes quite clear that even Paul himself was not entirely comfortable with some of the things he was called upon to say. In a real sense this letter is Paul's self-portrait. It is more intimate, less reserved, and more revealing of Paul's own feelings than anything else in the New Testament. But theology wrapped in autobiography is often difficult to understand and relate to our lives today.

The Recipients of the Letter

The discussion found on pages 17–19 in the first section of this volume applies equally to 2 Corinthians, except where the first letter is specifically designated. To avoid repetition, that discussion is not reprinted here.

The Occasion of the Letter

The difference in the tone of this letter is to be found in the occasion that precipitated it. There seems to have been a resurgence of antagonism toward Paul's leadership. 2 Corinthians was written primarily to deal with that problem.

The letter has three fairly obvious divisions: in chapters 1–7 Paul defines his ministry; in chapters 8–9 he promotes the offering for the impoverished Christians in Jerusalem; and in chapters 10–13 he strongly defends his apostolic authority.

At the time of the writing of this letter Paul was in Macedonia (2:12). Since 1 Corinthians is often dated in the spring of A.D. 55, many feel that this letter was probably written in the fall of the same year. It is so obviously from the pen of Paul and reflects his experiences that there are no serious questions among scholars about its authorship.

For many years the only interest in 2 Corinthians was in the profound theological truths to be found there. But in recent years scholars have also become interested in putting together the sequence of events in order to reach a better understanding of Paul's total relationship with the church at Corinth. While the nature of this commentary does not lend itself to an exhaustive study of this relationship, some discussion of the situation will add to an understanding of the various parts of the letter.

From Paul's own writing it is clear that he wrote four letters to the church at Corinth. The first, which preceded what we call 1 Corinthians, was a warning that Christians should not relate to believers who were careless with their lives. Paul refers to the fact of the letter and to its content in 1 Corinthians 5:9–10. The second letter Paul wrote was what we have in the Bible as 1 Corinthians. The third letter is often called the "severe letter" and is referred to in 2 Corinthians 7:8–9. Evidently after Paul wrote 1 Corinthians, the situation in the church deteriorated and Paul made a quick visit which was not pleasant or successful (2 Cor. 2:4). Most scholars think that the "severe letter" was written following the fast visit and before he wrote 2 Corinthians.

The natural question is, "If Paul wrote four times to the church, where are the other two letters?" Most people feel that the first one was not preserved. Their thinking is that it was addressed to a specific church on a specific problem that did not seem to have broad application to the other churches and that it was thus not saved. The real question about the unity of 2 Corinthians has arisen over what happened to the "severe letter." There are many who feel that it probably shared the same fate as the first letter and was not preserved. But a rather large group of scholars have suggested that the church may have saved the letter and attached it to the end of 2 Corinthians as what we now call chapters 10–13. There are convincing arguments for each interpretation.

While the interpretation and application are not affected by taking either position, to see the last four chapters as the "severe letter" would help our understanding of the change in tone between that section and the tone of the first nine chapters. But whether what we have is a letter or letters does not really matter as much as the fact that we have them and that they still speak to us today as God's word to God's people.

An Outline of 2 Corinthians

CHAPTER ONE

Leadership with Integrity

2 Corinthians 1:1–24

THE FELLOWSHIP OF SUFFERING

1 Paul, an apostle of Jesus Christ by the will of God, and Timothy our brother,

To the church of God which is at Corinth, with all the saints who are in all Achaia:

2 Grace to you and peace from God our Father and the Lord Jesus Christ.

3 Blessed be the God and Father of our Lord Jesus Christ, the Father of mercies and God of all comfort,

4 who comforts us in all our tribulation, that we may be able to comfort those who are in any trouble, with the comfort with which we ourselves are comforted by God.

5 For as the sufferings of Christ abound in us, so our consolation also abounds through Christ.

6 Now if we are afflicted, it is for your consolation and salvation, which is effective for enduring the same sufferings which we also suffer. Or if we are comforted, it is for your consolation and salvation.

7 And our hope for you is steadfast, because we know that as you are partakers of the sufferings, so also you will partake of the consolation.

8 For we do not want you to be ignorant, brethren, of our trouble which came to us in Asia: that we were burdened beyond measure, above strength, so that we despaired even of life.

9 Yes, we had the sentence of death in ourselves,

that we should not trust in ourselves but in God who
raises the dead,

10 who delivered us from so great a death, and does
deliver us; in whom we trust that He will still deliver
us,

11 you also helping together in prayer for us, that
thanks may be given by many persons on our behalf
for the gift granted to us through many.

2 Cor. 1:1–11

While this second letter to the Corinthians begins with the traditional Pauline greeting, it continues in a more autobiographical style
than Paul's other writings. Here, rather than recounting a series of
acts or events in chronological order, Paul opens his heart to his
readers and allows us to share his deepest concerns.

Titus had returned and reported on the reception of the first letter
(2 Cor. 7:7). It seems that while many of the members had accepted
Paul's counsel and acted upon it, others had questioned Paul's authority, and still others were suspicious of his motives. Some even doubted
the validity of his ministry.

Paul was no different from any other minister in that there was
never a time when *everyone* held him or his ministry in the highest
esteem. Ordinarily he would have ignored the criticism, but it was
so widespread and damaging that Paul must have decided he should
defend himself and his actions. He did so in this letter, and we and
the church through all the ages are the benefactors because of its
great insight into the riches of the Christian life. It is a classic example
of the way in which God in His sovereignty takes a bad situation
and redeems it and creates a blessing for others.

In reading the Bible, most of us tend to skip over the words of
the salutation of a book in the same way we run past the greetings
in a personal letter in our hurry to get to the content. But to do
that is to miss a great deal of profound religious truth. I once heard
a great New Testament scholar make an hour-long explanation of
Paul's traditional greeting, *"Grace to you and peace,"* and what it
means to be able to give such a greeting from the heart.

When we look closely at Paul's greeting here, we see that there
is rich truth to be found in his identification of the author and the
primary recipients of the letter. In identifying himself as an "apostle

THE FELLOWSHIP OF SUFFERING

of Jesus Christ," Paul is saying that he is a messenger sent from God. That is what the word "apostle" means. There was a technical sense in which the word was limited to the original twelve plus some whom God had added, such as Paul. It is interesting to note that in the greeting Paul refers to his close friend and colleague Timothy as a "brother," not an apostle.

But in a broader sense, every believer is a messenger sent from God, and we in the church need to rediscover this truth. One of the first times my wife and I visited little St. Paul's Lutheran Church in the farm community where we were vacationing, I was surprised and delighted to see this idea reflected in the printed order of worship. At the top of the bulletin beneath the name of the pastor was a category entitled "Ministers of the Church." This wording intrigued me because it was obvious the church was too small to need or support more than one pastor. But then "light dawned" as I looked at who the ministers were and read, "All the Members of the Church."

Any first-century Christian would have read Paul's statement *"To the church of God which is at Corinth,"* and wondered at the contradiction. In a city whose name was a byword for godlessness, how could there be a church made up of godly people? So often we give in to the notion that it is impossible for God's work to gain a foothold where evil is strong. But there is no place where evil is so aggressive or persuasive that we won't find people whose lives have been changed by the touch of God.

Christian visitors to the Soviet Union are always surprised to discover groups of devout Christians. And I recall my reaction on a trip to Las Vegas, Nevada, to conduct a school of evangelism for ministers for Dr. Billy Graham. I was at first overwhelmed by the way in which this city seemed so totally given over to the love of pleasure. I wondered how the people of God could exist in such an atmosphere. Then I had dinner with Don and Anne, friends from college days. Don was the pastor of one of the sponsoring churches for the crusade. They helped me see how God was at work creating a "people for Himself" right in the midst of the casinos and bright neon lights.

It was Paul's custom to follow the formal greetings in his letters with words of thanksgiving in which he expressed his appreciation to God for those to whom he was writing. But this time Paul writes about the blessings for which he is thankful in his own life.

Verses 3–11 give us a magnificent statement about both divine comfort (vv. 3–7) and divine deliverance (vv. 8–11). There is a lot of practical insight in this passage. First, we see that even the most devout of God's people can become discouraged. Paul had experienced outstanding success in his ministry in Ephesus, but that was followed by a time of great pain. Since Paul doesn't give us any details, there has been much speculation among scholars as to the nature of the trouble. Theories range from a severe illness to violent persecution or to Paul's reaction to the criticism from the Corinthians. But Paul did state that its effect on him caused him to feel that "this is the end." He was so completely overwhelmed by this problem that he compared it to experiencing death.

When I read about Paul and his trials it makes me wonder about those within the church who suggest that Christians who are trying to live within the will of God won't have trouble. They have somehow come to a mistaken notion that in Christ's death on the cross provision was not only made for the forgiveness of sin but for health, wealth, and undisturbed happiness.

I know firsthand of a church where the peace of the midweek prayer service was shattered by an argument over this very thing. One of the members who had been to a seminar on prayer said anyone who ended a prayer for those in the hospital by saying "Not my will but thine be done" was not exercising real faith. This person had come to the conclusion that it was God's will for every Christian to be healthy, wealthy, and happy.

But Paul's approach to his troubles was not to try to construct a theology that denied the reality of suffering for the Christian. Rather, he wants his readers to set their theology in the context of Christ's suffering and Christ's consolation. He doesn't try to send us on a "guilt trip," but he tries to help us understand how what we may be suffering is related to Christ's suffering. While Paul never intended to teach that the suffering of Christians had any atoning quality, he did feel that Christians share the kind of experiences Christ had. We live in the same kind of world in which He lived and face the same forces of evil He faced, and if we are faithful to Christ we will get the same reaction He received. This is a truth that is easy for us to accept intellectually, but on the emotional level we are still surprised when trouble comes. We wonder what we have done wrong, what God is trying to say to us, and we have doubts about our relationship with Him.

But all who share Christ's trials can also tap the resources of comfort that were His. In verses 3 and 4 of this first chapter, Paul reminds all of us that true comfort always has a divine source. He uses the word for "comfort" which is also used for the Holy Spirit, *paraklētos* ("paraclete"), "one who stands alongside and helps."

Very often I have experienced this God-sent comfort in my own life. It comes in different ways, sometimes as I read the Scriptures. Many times when I am troubled I get up early in the morning, find a quiet place, and read the Psalms. So many of the Psalms were written when the writer was experiencing stress.

I remember so well one morning when I was feeling especially low. Turning to Psalm 107, I found words of thanksgiving to God for great acts of deliverance. In between the Psalm's introduction and conclusion, there is the story of four different persons who came to the "end of their rope" in terms of spiritual resources. In each case they "cried out to the Lord in their trouble and He delivered them out of their distresses" (Ps. 107:6, 13, 19, 28).

At other times comfort comes from God through one of His children. And this may not come through words spoken but through a person's presence or expressed concern. When my father lay dying in a hospital room in Illinois, I was amazed at the comfort I received through the interest of Christian friends who called or wrote or visited. I have long forgotten the details of what was said, but I will never forget the way in which God used their interest and concern to comfort and prepare me to turn loose of my father without feeling that I had been abandoned by the Heavenly Father.

But we also get a clue here to the truth that even as we receive comfort from God, we are to share that comfort with others. He reminded his readers that one of God's ultimate purposes as He encourages us is *"that we may be able to comfort those who are in any trouble, with the comfort with which we ourselves are comforted by God"* (2 Cor. 1:4). I do not subscribe to the notion that in order really to identify with what a person is going through we have to have experienced it ourselves. But I do know that there is a special ability to bring comfort to another when we have walked down that road ourselves.

When the young son of missionary friends died while he was still in college, I watched those families in our church who had experienced a similar loss minister to this couple with a depth of understanding that was not possible for many of us.

When teenagers whose lives are being torn apart by the divorce of parents comes for help, they look to me for comfort because I was a teenager when my parents divorced. And in the same way the church's most effective visitors of cancer patients are those who themselves have cancer and have found resources within their faith to cope with their illness. There is almost a cyclical process that God creates, when those who have experienced God's comfort in times of difficulty reach out to comfort others and find a new and deeper comfort for themselves.

Finally, Paul reminds his readers that the God who comforts can also deliver. Paul knew what it was to be stripped of all confidence in his own strength. He stated that in our difficult times we learn that we *"should not trust in ourselves but in God"* (2 Cor. 1:9). He sticks with the analogy of death and identifies the God he is talking about as the one who *"raises the dead"* (2 Cor. 1:9). Here he is undoubtedly referring to the resurrection of Jesus Christ from the dead, but he suggests that the same God who could raise Christ from the dead could resurrect him (Paul) from his *"sentence of death"* (2 Cor. 1:9). There are many different kinds of death besides physical death, and everywhere that there is death the living Christ comes to create life. This is a marvelous analogy and a beautiful picture of the Spirit's ministry to us in our times of trouble and extreme discouragement. Paul's trouble was like Calvary and God's rescue was like Easter Sunday morning.

While I do not know the exact details of Paul's trouble and how God delivered him, I do know enough about God's help to identify personally with Paul's experience. There was a period in my life when I experienced so much pain, loss, grief, and betrayal in just a few months' time that I wondered if I would survive. But even as I struck bottom and seriously questioned my ability to manage my life, I began to experience a wonderful sense of God's presence and peace and purpose. My friends who were aware of the difficulty but did not know what was happening to my spirit would call and ask, "Kenneth, how are you?" When I told them I was fine, they apparently felt I was covering up, and would say, "I know that you've been through a lot this year and I've been worrying about you."

In each case I was able to assure them that all was well and that I had never had a stronger sense of God's presence and power in my life. Then they would ask, "How do you explain it?" To me the explanation was found in that event which was at the heart of the gospel, and I would reply, "After the cross comes Easter." The grand good news is that the Spirit of God who raises the dead can and will resurrect our comatose spirits.

MAKING CLEAR WHERE YOU STAND

12 For our boasting is this: the testimony of our conscience that we conducted ourselves in the world in simplicity and godly sincerity, not with fleshly wisdom but by the grace of God, and more abundantly toward you.

13 For we are not writing any other things to you than what you read or understand. Now I trust you will understand, even to the end

14 (as also you have understood us in part), that we are your boast as you also are ours, in the day of the Lord Jesus.

15 And in this confidence I intended to come to you before, that you might have a second benefit—

16 to pass by way of you to Macedonia, to come again from Macedonia to you, and be helped by you on my way to Judea.

17 Therefore, when I was planning this, did I do it lightly? Or the things I plan, do I plan according to the flesh, that with me there should be Yes, Yes and No, No?

18 But as God is faithful, our word to you was not Yes and No.

19 For the Son of God, Jesus Christ, who was preached among you by us—by me, Silvanus, and Timothy—was not Yes and No, but in Him was Yes.

20 For all the promises of God in Him are Yes, and in Him Amen, to the glory of God through us.

21 Now He who establishes us with you in Christ and has anointed us is God,

22 who also has sealed us and given us the Spirit in our hearts as a deposit.

23 Moreover I call God as witness against my soul, that to spare you I came no more to Corinth.

24 Not that we have dominion over your faith, but
are fellow workers for your joy; for by faith you stand.

2 Cor. 1:12–24

When you think about the criticisms that had been leveled at Paul
in Corinth, they seem quite trivial. First they picked at him for changing his travel route. In his first letter he had mentioned that it was
his plan to come by land through Macedonia and then to visit them.
Evidently they had understood that he was coming to them first,
and were upset at what seemed to them a change of plans. In their
childlikeness they had completely forgotten that Paul had qualified
his plans with the words "if the Lord permits" (1 Cor. 16:7). When
Paul's plans called for a delay, this caused some to say that Paul
took too lightly his promises to the church. I'm aware that when
people have a contentious spirit they don't need much excuse to
find fault, but it still bothers me to think of the petty criticism the
great Apostle was subject to and the questions that were raised about
the authority and integrity of his ministry.

Paul's answer to the criticism creates for us a priceless picture of
what it means to have integrity in our ministry, and the description
of his ministry with these new Christians can serve as a model for
all of us.

Paul begins by insisting that he is sincere and that his conscience
is clear and untroubled. He wasn't suggesting that he hadn't made
any mistakes in his relationship with them, because to live without
any regrets would be almost impossible. But he was affirming that
the relationship had been open and above-board, and he gave two
illustrations to substantiate the claim.

First, he reminds them they don't have to read between the lines
"for we are not writing any other things to you than what you read or understand"
(v. 13). Paul certainly wasn't guilty of double talk.

When I was a seminary student a joke was making the rounds
about a professor who had been asked to write a letter of reference
for one of the students. The professor really didn't have much confidence in the student, but he didn't want to ruin the young man's
chances for the appointment. At the same time he didn't want to
lie to the pastoral committee, so he wrote, "If you knew him the
way I know him you would feel about him the way I do." While I
have not become cynical, I have learned since then that all too often

there is a tendency, even in the Lord's service, to write or say one thing when something else is really meant. This has only caused me to admire and respect the Apostle's integrity.

Paul's integrity was based on his practice of always letting people know exactly where he stood on all matters. He had not been vacillating, contradictory, or unreliable in dealing with the Corinthians. Rather, there had been a certain transparency, a consistency, and a steadfastness in all his relationships. In verses 17 and 18 he uses a fascinating play on the words "yes" and "no." While Paul takes no prideful credit for his integrity, he insists that its source is in a God whose "yes" never turns to "no."

Think of all the profound questions to which God says "yes": Do you love me? Am I forgiven? Am I secure in your love? Is there purpose for my life? Is there life beyond the grave? To all of these questions God answers an everlasting "yes." Paul's question was, "How can a person who preaches a gospel of 'yes' that never becomes 'no' even consider becoming a 'yes-and-no person'?"

As witnesses to the power of the gospel, it is important for people around us to know where we stand. They must feel confident that today's "yes" will not become tomorrow's "no." Too many people are afraid to reveal where they stand on an issue without first conducting a poll on the question. Insecurity makes some people keep all communications vague in order not to upset people, and personal ambition causes others to take stands that will most advance their cause. An opportunist may appear to be successful, but he or she is building causes where "yes" sometimes becomes "no." Ultimately this approach brings failure!

CHAPTER TWO

The Sweet Smell of Victory

2 Corinthians 2:1–17

WHEN THINGS GO FROM BAD TO WORSE

1 But I determined this within myself, that I would not come again to you in sorrow.

2 For if I make you sorrowful, then who is he who makes me glad but the one who is made sorrowful by me?

3 And I wrote this very thing to you, lest, when I came, I should have sorrow over those from whom I ought to have joy, having confidence in you all that my joy is the joy of you all.

4 For out of much affliction and anguish of heart I wrote to you, with many tears, not that you should be grieved, but that you might know the love which I have so abundantly for you.

2 Cor. 2:1–4

Sometimes when I have been at ministers' meetings and the "successful pastors" are telling how smoothly everything is going in their work, I've been tempted to wonder why I have problems and whether something is wrong with me. But then I turn to the Bible and discover that even the Apostle Paul had moments in his relationship with the church and with people when things were less than ideal.

Paul begins this second chapter of his letter by completing his answer as to why he had not come to Corinth. While scholars may never agree entirely on the sequence of Paul's visits to the church at Corinth, there is a great deal of agreement that the following sequence occurred: Even after Paul wrote 1 Corinthians the situation

212

in the church and its problems persisted. Then because of deteriorating conditions there Paul apparently made a hurried visit.

Evidently, though, things got worse instead of better. He then wrote a very severe letter to the church that some think may have been incorporated into what we call 2 Corinthians. In the light of the painful visit and the severe letter, Paul wisely had delayed his promised visit out of a love for the church. Now he sits down to write again. The fact that Paul had problems to deal with ought to keep the rest of us from thinking we're the only ones whose leadership has been ignored. And the way in which Paul dealt with the problem gives us a model for our ministry with people and the church.

That Paul was a strong individual who had been given a great deal of authority by God is undeniable. Few people in the history of the church have been looked to for the final word as Paul was. Yet it is interesting, and a bit comforting, to see that when it came to rebuking others he did so with great restraint. He found no joy in painful confrontation.

LEARNING TO FORGIVE AND RESTORE

5 But if anyone has caused grief, he has not grieved me, but all of you to some extent—not to be too severe.

6 This punishment which was inflicted by the majority is sufficient for such a man,

7 so that, on the contrary, you ought rather to forgive and comfort him, lest perhaps such a one be swallowed up with too much sorrow.

8 Therefore I urge you to reaffirm your love to him.

9 For to this end I also wrote, that I might put you to the test, whether you are obedient in all things.

10 Now whom you forgive anything, I also forgive. For if indeed I have forgiven anything, I have forgiven that one for your sakes in the presence of Christ,

11 lest Satan should take advantage of us; for we are not ignorant of his devices.

2 Cor. 2:5–11

It is always easier to preach the gospel of forgiveness than it is to forgive people, and it is often more difficult to forgive a person who has hurt someone you love than it is to forgive those who hurt you. In these verses Paul asks the church to forgive an unnamed person and to restore him to the fellowship.

Some students of Scripture have thought this is a reference to the man who had committed incest with his father's wife (1 Cor. 5:1–8). It was assumed that the discipline had resulted in repentance and a change of lifestyle and that Paul was here pleading with the church to take him back. It is more likely, though, that this is a reference to the person who had opposed Paul when he had made his hurried visit and who as a result of Paul's "severe letter" had been disciplined. Paul's wording would indicate that the person had in some way insulted him and that the offender had been disciplined at Paul's request. But evidently, in view of the person's response to the discipline, Paul thinks he should be forgiven and restored to the fellowship.

Even though we don't know a great deal about what was going on we do get some insights into how ministers and congregations should handle certain problems. First, we need to deal forthrightly with anyone who attempts to undermine the leadership. I'm not suggesting here a kind of blind, unthinking, superficial conformity to whatever is being promoted by the leader. But there are times when individuals in the church are off-base in their spirit and in the things they say and do and this poisons the spirit of the church and lessens the ability of those who are trying to give leadership. Often even those fellow members who disagree strongly with the critic remain silent. This fear of the tensions created by honest disagreement is at its heart self-centered and unhealthy. It does not serve the best interest of the individuals involved nor the church. The pain of confrontation is to be preferred to the sin of silence.

Second, anyone who is in a leadership role needs to develop a style for dealing with critics. While I was a student at seminary I took courses in Bible, theology, missions, evangelism, and preaching, but for many years I wished a course had been given on "dealing with those who reject your leadership." Later, though, I came to realize that if I had paid close attention to my New Testament studies—especially these verses—I would have recognized that Paul has modeled for us some excellent principles.

First, Paul didn't take criticism or opposition personally. When any of us take ourselves more seriously than we take God's work, then any question about our leadership, no matter how innocent, is considered a personal attack. It is important that we become secure enough to look at the content of criticism in proper perspective.

Second, Paul's call for discipline was for correction, not vengeance. There was none of the punitive attitude of "he hurt me, and I'll hurt him back." Paul felt that the person's action was more against the church than against him personally, and he felt discipline should benefit both parties.

Third, there was a desire not to be so severe that the heart would be taken out of the person. Paul never lost sight of God's continuing purpose for the person. There is a healthy and redeeming dynamic to how he dealt with his critics.

Paul then asserted that restoration needs to follow forgiveness, and he made two suggestions. In verse 7 Paul writes that the person needed to be comforted, encouraged, and strengthened. When we become Christians God does not stop with forgiving our sins; He brings us back into fellowship with Him and sends His Spirit to help us. The church was to act out its forgiveness of the offending brother in this same way. Then Paul went on to suggest that he should be reaffirmed (v. 8). Here he is asking for an act of restoration that was as formal and as public as the act of discipline had been. While on the surface it may have appeared the rite of restoration was cruel, it was needed to accomplish real restoration.

I sat at lunch one day with a man who had suffered a failure in his marriage. By his own admission the divorce was his fault. Not only had he turned his back on his family, but he left the church as well.

After he had come to himself, he had asked God's forgiveness and began that slow and painful process of rebuilding his life. While we were eating he said, "Kenneth, I've been back in the church for more than a decade but somehow I still don't feel quite right about it. I know that God has forgiven me, but I need a place or some service of closure in which the church formally recognizes that I have been forgiven and am restored back to the fellowship." Had my friend been a member of the church in Corinth, he might have found it, because Paul taught them the importance of "reaffirming" those who had found forgiveness.

LEARNING TO LIVE WITH A SENSE OF WINNING

12 Furthermore, when I came to Troas to preach Christ's gospel, and a door was opened to me by the Lord,

13 I had no rest in my spirit, because I did not find Titus my brother; but taking my leave of them, I departed for Macedonia.

14 Now thanks be to God who always leads us in triumph in Christ, and through us diffuses the fragrance of His knowledge in every place.

15 For we are to God the fragrance of Christ among those who are being saved and among those who are perishing.

16 To the one we are the aroma of death to death, and to the other the aroma of life to life. And who is sufficient for these things?

17 For we are not, as so many, peddling the word of God; but as of sincerity, but as from God, we speak in the sight of God in Christ.

2 Cor. 2:12–17

The section of 2 Corinthians beginning here and going to the middle of the sixth chapter deals with the Christian ministry. While Paul was defining and defending his work in Corinth, he was giving us a measuring stick for all ministry done in the church, whether by laity or by clergy. There are those who feel this section may be a digression. But I feel it is possible this is Paul's reaction to those who have raised grave questions about the integrity of his ministry. We have therefore been presented in this section of his second letter with one of the Scripture's grandest pictures of the ministry of all Christians.

The section begins with a description of Paul's feeling as he waited for a report on how the church had responded to his first letter to the Corinthians. Possibly most of us have experienced "no rest of spirit" as we've waited for a reply to a crucial letter.

But whatever the cause, in verse 14 Paul's spirit is lifted and he breaks into a doxology of praise to God. Possibly Titus had arrived at that point with good news. We don't know what caused him to be "up," but whatever it was sets the context of a hymn of triumph for the whole discussion of his ministry. It became his point of reference for all things. It's remarkable that with all the pressure, persecution, and opposition he had experienced that Paul would think of his ministry in terms of triumph and not defeat. This vision of the ultimate triumph of God and of the gospel gave him a platform from which to view in a different light all that was involved in his work.

Recently I was asked to speak to an important group of ministers preceding their national meeting, and I knew these people would be confronted for several days with hard questions that might well cause them tremendous concern, so I decided to speak on the subject "An Encouraging Word." Most people realize that church members need to be encouraged. How often as I have looked at the individuals in the congregation and realized the loads they were carrying, I have prayed to God, "Please let me be a source of encouragement to them today." But those who lead churches also need encouragement. They live in the same pressure-cooker world with everyone else and when they feel their confidence eroded they can lose sight of their goals.

As I spoke to the leaders that day, I tried to encourage them about the gospel they were called to share, about the churches in which they had been called to minister, and about the way in which God could use their individual gifts. Their appreciation for my message confirmed to me that all of us need to be reminded of the ultimate victory we shall experience in Christ.

Paul's analogy of triumph was taken from one of the great Roman spectacles, the picture of a victorious general leading a procession through the streets of Rome. Since Paul had not yet been to Rome, he hadn't seen with his own eyes what he was describing, but Philippi was full of retired high-ranking officers from the Roman legion. Paul had most likely heard a number of eyewitness accounts of such a "triumph," as they were called.

For a general to qualify for a "triumph" celebration, he had to have been a field commander in a victorious campaign where at least five thousand of the enemy had fallen in battle. But it couldn't be just any battle—it had to be a battle where the conquered country was occupied and stabilized to become a part of the vast Roman Empire. The story of the conquest was told in the order of the procession: first the senators and state officials, then the spoils taken from the conquered lands, then pictures of the conquered lands, followed by a white bull which would afterward be sacrificed. Then captives followed who later would be put into prison or executed; then musicians and priests with their incense; and finally the conquering general riding in a chariot pulled by four horses, followed by his family and then his conquering soldiers. The streets were lined with excited, shouting people. Anyone who chanced to witness such a grand spectacle would never forget it.

In giving this account Paul mixed his metaphors, as he often did, but the basic meaning is still very clear. Instead of a Roman general he saw Christ as the universal conqueror. Paul saw Christ winning the victory and all of us who are a part of His work as being in His victory procession. This was the vision that transformed all the circumstances of his life and kept adversity from weighing him down and temporary setbacks from depressing him. It is the loss of this vision of the victorious Christ that creates a defeated ministry and a church wringing its hands.

Though Paul in other places refers to Christians as "slaves," it is not known whether he was trying to press that analogy in this passage. In the Roman procession the captives were usually humiliated and then killed. He could have been saying, as some think, that to be Christ's slaves is better than to be Rome's conquerors. But he probably was saying that just as there were those who shared in the great victory of the general, so we who are "in Christ" shall share in his ultimate victory.

In verses 15 and 16 Paul picked up the picture of the incense that was a part of the procession to say something fascinating about the gospel and about the influence of Christians. He refers to the sharing of the gospel as the diffusing of *"the fragrance of His knowledge in every place."* He pictures the priests walking in the Triumph procession, as sweet odors were released into the street from the burning of the spices.

This vivid metaphor is a marvelous sharing of the gospel of Christ in the world.

CHAPTER THREE

The Religion of the Spirit

2 Corinthians 3:1–18

BASED ON SUPERIOR CREDENTIALS

1 Do we begin again to commend ourselves? Or do we need, as some others, epistles of commendation to you or letters of commendation from you?

2 You are our epistle written in our hearts, known and read by all men;

3 you are manifestly an epistle of Christ, ministered by us, written not with ink but by the Spirit of the living God, not on tablets of stone but on tablets of flesh, that is, of the heart.

4 And we have such trust through Christ toward God.

5 Not that we are sufficient of ourselves to think of anything as being from ourselves, but our sufficiency is from God,

6 who also made us sufficient as ministers of the new covenant, not of the letter but of the Spirit; for the letter kills, but the Spirit gives life.

2 Cor. 3:1–6

Hardly a week goes by without my being asked to write a letter of recommendation for someone. A couple wants to adopt a baby, and the agency asks if they are Christians, if they are active in the church, what their values are, how strong is their marriage, and would I commend them to be considered as potential parents.

A young woman applied for a job in New York City and gave my name as a character reference. The personnel manager wants to know if she is the kind of person who gets along well with others, if she is disciplined, and if she can be trusted.

I feel a deep sense of responsibility when writing letters of recommendation for someone or when writing a letter of introduction. Such letters were especially important in the days of the early church. This was the only way fledgling congregations had of knowing whether a new prophet or teacher who appeared on the scene had the right credentials and could be trusted. The book of Philemon was such a letter, and frequently at the close of his epistles Paul had a habit of commending certain people, and in other cases warning against them.

But apparently there was a breakdown of some kind, because some strangers had shown up in Corinth with an impressive letter of introduction from someone in Jerusalem and had been received into the confidence of the church on the basis of the letter. After ingratiating themselves with the members, they had begun to be critical of Paul and his ministry and had even asked the church if Paul had come to them with a letter of introduction such as they had, implying that Paul was a man without proper credentials.

In reality, their implications were outrageous because when Paul first arrived in Corinth, there was no church. He founded it and it was the product of his ministry. But then as now, the most spurious accusation will usually find some shallow soil in which to germinate, and the word got back to Paul that there were now members of the church who were questioning his authority because he hadn't carried a letter of introduction when he first came to them.

Paul's immediate response was, "I don't need a letter of introduction," and he claimed the Corinthian Christians as the only credentials he needed. Then he began to compare and contrast his credentials, the church members themselves, with the letter the strangers had brought with them.

Paul pointed out to them that his critics came with a letter written by human beings but that his authority was their witness as epistles of Christ (vv. 1–2). And in verse 3 he points out that the introduction his critics had carried was written on a scroll or a tablet, but that his authority was impressed by the Spirit of God on human hearts. But one senses that even as Paul was making the comparison, he is fearful that he is taking too much credit for himself. With this in mind he disclaims any sufficiency in himself and explains *"our sufficiency is from God"* (v. 5). He was making the point that the real change in the lives of the Corinthian Christians had been the work of God rather than of himself, and that God had merely allowed him to be the minister through whom it had all happened. In other words, Paul is insisting that in his case the existence of a community of believers in Corinth is all the accreditation that he needs.

As I read this passage I have wondered what I would claim as credentials if someone questioned the validity of my ministry. There would be a natural temptation to show my certificate of ordination or my seminary diploma. And, of course, I could list the books I've written, the positions I've held, or the honors that have been bestowed on me. But I doubt whether any of this sort of thing will be worth mentioning when we stand before God to give an account of ourselves. Rather, at that time our "recommendation" will be those persons who have experienced God's love and His healing through our ministry and witness.

It was Paul's contrast here between what was written on tablets of stone and what the Spirit had written on human hearts that stressed the difference between the Jewish religion and Christianity, between the Old Covenant and the New Covenant. Both Old Testament and New Testament were covenant religions, a two-way relationship between God and persons which God had initiated. In both there was a revelation and a response.

Paul's early life had been devoted to trying to keep every aspect of the written code and it had heightened the knowledge of his own inadequacy without any hope of deliverance. But after his Damascus Road experience everything was changed because the New Covenant was written in his heart by the Spirit of God. When he wrote, *"The letter kills, but the Spirit gives life"* (v. 6), he was making an autobiographical statement.

Based on a Superior Covenant

7 But if the ministry of death, written and engraved
on stones, was glorious, so that the children of Israel
could not look steadily at the face of Moses because
of the glory of his countenance, which glory was
passing away,

8 how will the ministry of the Spirit not be more glorious?

9 For if the ministry of condemnation had glory, the ministry of righteousness exceeds much more in glory.

10 For even what was made glorious had no glory in this respect, because of the glory that excels.

11 For if what is passing away was glorious, what remains is much more glorious.

12 Therefore since we have such hope, we use great boldness of speech—

13 unlike Moses, who put a veil over his face so that the children of Israel could not look steadily at the end of what was passing away.

14 But their minds were hardened. For until this day the same veil remains unlifted in the reading of the Old Testament, because the veil is taken away in Christ.

15 But even to this day, when Moses is read, a veil lies on their heart.

16 Nevertheless when one turns to the Lord, the veil is taken away.

17 Now the Lord is the Spirit; and where the Spirit of the Lord is, there is liberty.

18 But we all, with unveiled face, beholding as in a mirror the glory of the Lord, are being transformed into the same image from glory to glory, just as by the Spirit of the Lord.

2 Cor. 3:7–18

Modern-day Bible students who come to one of the passages in the Scriptures where Paul is contrasting the religion of the Law with the reign of grace have a tendency to skip lightly over it as just another quarrel between Paul and the Judaizers who were always trying to undermine his work. It is true that Paul wrote these words in response to those who had come from Jerusalem to Corinth with a form of Christianity that insisted people should adopt Jewish customs before becoming Christians. But the underlying issue of the difference between a religion of freedom through the Spirit and a religion of bondage through the Law is still very relevant today. What most of us need to discover today is the superiority of spiritual religion over legalistic religion.

As Paul wrote about how the words of the Old Covenant had been written down and had become rigid laws binding all those who sought life by attempting to keep them, he had no way of knowing that there would come a day when sincere Christians would take the things which he wrote and create out of them the very kind of legalistic Christianity to which he was so opposed. As we read his words about the inadequacy of Old Testament legalism, we need to see that his argument against all forms of legalism, even that which we face today, is still valid.

The spirit of these twelve verses can be summarized by Paul's words in 2 Corinthians 3:17, *"where the Spirit of the Lord is, there is liberty."* Paul always preached a liberating gospel—those who were "in Christ" (Paul's favorite description of a Christian) were free from the penalty and power of sin in their lives, and ultimately would be free also from its very presence. In the resurrection they were free from the fear of death and in the circle of God's love they were secure from anything that could happen. Within the church, that liberating community which the Spirit of God had created, they had been made free—free to love everyone, free to celebrate their own unique gifts, and free to minister in unselfish ways to one another. In this liberty there was a sense of joy and celebration and love that captured the attention of all who came in touch with it and which made it attractive to even the most jaded.

While Paul recognized a special experience in the giving and the receiving of the Law, he felt that the "ministry of the Spirit" was superior (v. 8). He saw every effort to mix certain elements of the Old Covenant with the New Covenant as a prostituting of the gospel and an undermining of the work of the Spirit. Instead of freedom and liberty he felt that this introduced *"death"* (v. 7) and *"condemnation"* (v. 9). The Old Covenant became the religion of struggling to impress God with one's goodness, of endless rules and regulations governing every conceivable area of one's life, of outward conformity and worrying about appearance, and of spiritual pride and competitiveness. In this form of religion Paul insisted that he outperformed them all and found in it death and not life. In these verses he gives some of the reasons for the superiority of spiritual religion.

His arguments would be better understood by the Jewish Christians in Corinth than the Gentiles because he tied them to a story with which all of them would have been very familiar, the story of the giving of the Law on Mount Sinai. His first argument was that *the religion of the Spirit is more permanent.* He reminds his readers of the true reasons for Moses' putting a veil over his face after coming down the mountain from the presence of the Lord. Many people have erroneously felt that the veil was to protect the Israelites from the glow of God's presence. But Paul reminds us all that the veil was put on after he had spoken *"so that the children of Israel could not look steadily at the end of what was passing away"* (2 Cor. 3:13). The veil was to keep the Israelites from realizing that the glory was fading.

Paul uses the well-known story to illustrate the fact that *there is always a temporariness to legalistic religion.* Legalists are always busy working out new sets of rules for new places, new circumstances, and new generations. The religion that is based upon a list of things Christians do or don't do will usually fade into insignificant irrelevance. In a world where millions are starving each year, rules about whether it's a sin to shop for food on Sunday seem out of order. Where nations continue to use vast resources on weapons of destruction, arguing over beards or hairstyles for Christians seems irrelevant. In a world in which medical advances are causing doctors to turn to religious leaders for difficult ethical guidelines and a world in which an irresponsible leader could push the wrong button and begin nuclear holocaust, all the little questions of "right or wrong" which legalistic Christians have asked in the past seem to fade away like the glow on Moses' face.

Paul also used Moses' veil to suggest that *legalistic religion lacks an understanding heart.* We sometimes forget that in the first century both the Jewish synagogue and the Christian church used the same Scriptures. Paul pointed out that in the Jewish worship *"a veil lies on their heart"* (v. 15). He felt that when the Spirit of Christ came into a life the *"veil is taken away"* (v. 16), and he or she is able to understand God's message with his or her heart. When Isaiah 53 was read in the Corinthian church, every believer knew that it was speaking of Christ's sacrifice for the sins of the world, but when those same words were read in the synagogue there was no such understanding.

There has always been something in legalism which causes people to miss the heart of things and become fascinated with the surface and the superficial. After all, before Paul became a Christian he was a man who loved the Scriptures, worshiped God, defended orthodoxy, and lived a good life by the definition of his religion. But he so missed the meaning of God that he orchestrated the death and imprisonment of Christians. His heart had been so veiled by legalism that he could not understand the religion of the Spirit.

Paul also used the veil of Moses as an illustration in which the religion of the Old Covenant was mediated through Moses while the New Covenant had more of a direct face-to-face contact with God. While the Bible is the final written authority for every believer, it is the Living Word, Jesus Christ, who is the ultimate authority. While the community of believers is a visible force in the life of a believer as it nurtures and supports, it is the Spirit of the Living God who administers His grace and forgiveness. There is always the danger of legalism for each of us. We are tempted to love the Bible and not the God to whom it witnesses. We can join the church, whatever the process, without entering into a personal relationship with Jesus Christ. Often an individual will conform to what is called a "Christian lifestyle" and never have his or her heart changed. Consequently, there is always the danger that one would have all the trappings of religion and not know the love and joy and freedom that is in Christ.

CHAPTER FOUR

The Unconquerable Spirit

2 Corinthians 4:1–18

THE GOSPEL WE SHARE

1 Therefore, since we have this ministry, as we have received mercy, we do not lose heart.

2 But we have renounced the hidden things of shame, not walking in craftiness nor handling the word of God deceitfully, but by manifestation of the truth commending ourselves to every man's conscience in the sight of God.

3 But even if our gospel is veiled, it is veiled to those who are perishing,

4 whose minds the god of this age has blinded, who do not believe, lest the light of the gospel of the glory of Christ, who is the image of God, should shine on them.

5 For we do not preach ourselves, but Christ Jesus the Lord, and ourselves your servants for Jesus' sake.

6 For it is the God who commanded light to shine out of darkness who has shone in our hearts to give the light of the knowledge of the glory of God in the face of Jesus Christ.

2 Cor. 4:1–6

Any of us who try to serve God in any way often have reasons for being discouraged. The awareness of our human limitation and the awareness of our imperfection gnaw at our self-confidence. Then, too, the indifference of people to whom we try to witness and share the gospel makes us wonder sometimes if it's really such good news.

It is easy to feel discouraged when we see the aggressiveness of evil in our world. And the disunity in the church and the lack of love among so many Christians certainly take the edge off of our witness.

But when we read the Scriptures and the story of the lives of the early Christians, we discover that it has always been this way. Paul experienced this and yet wrote to his friends that in spite of everything, *"we do not lose heart"* (v. 1). And in the first six verses of the fourth chapter, he introduces the reasons for his encouragement.

Paul felt that God had given him a ministry. There is a sense in which when he said, *"we have this ministry"* (v. 1), he was referring to the calling that had come to him out of God's new purpose for his life. Before he met Christ his life was not without a purpose. After all, he had been a man obsessed with a mission, but it was a mission full of hatred and violence and destruction. Then when Christ captured his heart He made him a servant and gave him a ministry of love, of reconciliation, and of service. This is the pattern God has for all of us. He gives each of us a specific ministry—something we can do and that He wants done. Each life undirected has the potential to drift into an aimless, self-seeking, purposeless existence. But God comes to each one who trusts Him and gives something that needs to be done, and in the doing of it we find encouragement about ourselves and about life.

My Aunt Orphea is a classic example of the way in which being given a ministry keeps our spirits up, keeps us encouraged. This isn't to say that there isn't a whole lot in Aunt Orphea's life that couldn't get her down. She's in her seventies, has been a widow for years, has all sorts of problems with her health, and is trying to support herself in a time of high inflation on a small fixed income. There are just a lot of things in her life that could give her ample reasons for complaint. But the truth is that she is a very happy woman, and when we spend time with her, it is easy to see why she has a happy disposition.

Her little church has made her responsible for the small children's Bible study time on Sunday morning and she loves it. Each Saturday evening she has preparations to make: a gift to wrap, a song to learn, a game to plan, or a verse to copy. She has to be there early so she can greet the children and see that her room is the way she feels it ought to be. It was obvious that this "ministry" that she has been given is not only blessing all those with whom she works, but it is giving her life meaning as well. She feels needed and wanted and useful. Those Christians who do not have a ministry have missed God's purpose for their lives.

The Apostle Paul was also encouraged by the gospel that he had been given to share. In verse 2 he has several things to say about the way in which he has shared the gospel. His wording suggests that he is answering some criticism which has been aimed at the gospel he preached. He contrasts himself with the methods of his critics.

The gospel he preached did not include what he called "craftiness" (v. 2). The word translated "craftiness" here is translated "knavery" in other places and means the "readiness to do anything." Paul was suggesting that his critics would stop at nothing in their efforts.

Then Paul's claim to not *"handling the word of God deceitfully"* (v. 2) comes from a word which refers to a doctor adulterating medicines. His critics had accused Paul of adulterating the gospel, probably by not requiring persons to observe Jewish laws in order to become Christians.

But Paul claimed that he would rest his case with *"every man's conscience in the sight of God"* (v. 2).

I think that the temptation to tamper with the gospel will always be with us. And every time we try to be clever or add something to it or take something away from it we empty the gospel of its power and our witness and ministry of its effectiveness.

One rather prevalent temptation is to attempt to make the gospel more intellectually respectable. We are to love God with all our minds and to use our minds as we seek to communicate the gospel, but there has always been something in the very nature of the gospel that seems "foolish," and people are often tempted to try to remove that stumbling block.

There is also the temptation to try to make the gospel more acceptable. When this happens, repentance, the cost of discipleship, and the Lordship of Christ are played down so it will be easy for people to respond. What Bonhoeffer referred to as "cheap grace" becomes acceptable.

Still others use the gospel to support worldly values that are actually in conflict with the true Christian life. All the God-wants-you-to-be-rich messages that are heard so much today are nothing but a form of religious materialism. They ignore the extreme poverty of many early Christians and the fact that in many areas of the world today Christians pay a very high price for their faith in terms of material things. The temptation to "craftiness" and "deceitful" use of the gospel is one every Christian needs to continue to resist.

We read in verse 5 that Paul was also encouraged by the fact that the gospel that he had been given to share centered in a person: *"We do not preach ourselves, but Christ Jesus the Lord."* Two words—Jesus Christ—epitomized the message of the early church. The Apostles and evangelists didn't preach a book, a ritual, an institution, or a set of teachings, but a person. To them world evangelization was the sharing of Jesus Christ with the whole world.

While the Gospels record many of the acts and teachings of Christ's ministry, they were meant to point a person to the living Christ. Though the Apostle Paul did a great deal of writing about the atoning work of Christ, it was not a theory of atonement that he preached, but a person who could forgive sins. It is this aspect of the gospel that makes it possible for all Christians to become witnesses. Evangelism in its most wholesome form is one believer introducing someone else to the person of Jesus Christ.

Then again, Paul was encouraged by the fact that the gospel did not have to be accepted by everyone to remain valid. I have often shared Christ with people and they have acted absolutely indifferent to what I was talking about.

I remember once when I was a very young minister I became quite discouraged because everyone didn't respond. I commented to an older member of the church that "they seem to shed the gospel the way a duck sheds water." Sensing my discouragement he said, "Kenneth, you need to remember that it's not the water's fault." Paul had understood from the beginning that sin had created a veil over man's understanding (v. 3) and that people who are lost are suffering from a kind of spiritual blindness. This is why the Holy Spirit is so important to the work of sharing the gospel—He can lift the veil and open our spiritual eyes.

The first time I heard Dr. Billy Graham say to an audience, "You have two sets of ears—your physical ears with which you hear what I'm saying to you right now, and your spiritual ears with which you hear what God says to you," I wondered about it. But I think he is right. When the gospel is preached in all of its power, God uses it to shine a light where before there was only darkness.

THE UNCONQUERABLE LIFE

7 But we have this treasure in earthen vessels, that the excellence of the power may be of God and not of us.

8 We are hard pressed on every side, yet not crushed; we are perplexed, but not in despair;

9 persecuted, but not forsaken; struck down, but not destroyed—

10 always carrying about in the body the dying of the Lord Jesus, that the life of Jesus also may be manifested in our body.

11 For we who live are always delivered to death for Jesus' sake, that the life of Jesus may also be manifested in our mortal flesh.

12 So then death is working in us, but life in you.

13 But since we have the same spirit of faith, according to what is written, *"I believed and therefore I spoke,"* we also believe and therefore speak,

14 knowing that He who raised up the Lord Jesus will also raise us up with Jesus, and will present us with you.

15 For all things are for your sakes, that grace, having spread through the many, may cause thanksgiving to abound to the glory of God.

16 Therefore we do not lose heart. But though our outward man is perishing, yet the inward man is being renewed day by day.

17 For our light affliction, which is but for a moment, is working for us a far more exceeding and eternal weight of glory,

18 while we do not look at the things which are seen, but at the things which are not seen. For the things which are seen are temporary, but the things which are not seen are eternal.

2 Cor. 4:7–18

In these twelve verses Paul gives several reasons why in the midst of great difficulty he never loses heart. Each one of those reasons is applicable to us.

First, Paul knew that the real treasure was Christ and that he, Paul, was merely the vessel that carried it. There is no more beautiful description of the Christian life than *"we have this treasure in earthen vessels"* (v. 7).

It is still the custom in some places in the world to hide valuables such as money or jewels in an ordinary clay pot. After all, who would think anything of value would be hidden in an inexpensive clay pot?

I have a teapot that was given to me by friends years ago, and I brew tea in it for my breakfast each morning. The outside glaze is cracked from the many trips through the dishwasher. The spout is chipped, and the lid was broken long ago and has been replaced by a lid of a different color from another pot. Sometimes I look at the teapot and am reminded that I'm an earthen vessel much like it. In places my skin is scarred and wrinkled. There are some "chipped places" from the mistakes I've made, and there are many things in my life that don't match. But the most amazing thing is that the treasure I bear is not diminished by the vessel; rather, the vessel is made valuable by the treasure it contains.

Second, Paul was encouraged because life had not thrown more at him than he could handle. When we read verses 7–10 we are likely to catch only the bad things that had happened to him and to notice the words *"hard pressed," "perplexed," "persecuted," "struck down,"* and *"always carrying about in the body the dying of the Lord Jesus"* (v. 10). If Paul had told us all the bad things that had happened to him as a servant of the Lord, we would have felt that he would be justified in being bitter, leaving the ministry, or having a nervous breakdown. But we need to go back and pick up the other end of the sentence where he talked of being *"not crushed . . . not in despair . . . not forsaken . . . not destroyed,"* and of the *"life of Jesus"* being manifest in his body. If we read carefully what he has written, we hear the note of celebration that even though life had knocked him down, it had not knocked him out; he was still functioning.

As God's people, we are a lot tougher than we sometimes think, and it's encouraging for us to realize that we can cope with a great deal with the strength that Christ gives. During my years as a pastor I have seen Christians deal realistically and triumphantly with calamity, sorrow, tragedy, illness, death, and losses of every sort. I've stood by them during times of almost unbelievable stress with the assurance they would not be abandoned by Christ. And with time and patience and encouragement from Christian friends, I've seen them bounce back with renewed faith and confidence.

Third, Paul was encouraged by God's ability to renew his spirit when circumstances got him down. Though he was confronted by both the aging process and the possibility of death, he could still write, *"Though our outward man is perishing, yet the inward man is being renewed day by day"* (v. 16).

Paul's strenuous and arduous schedule had taken its toll on his body and his spirit, but he said that through God's Spirit he daily experienced renewal. This helped him to face life now and gave him hope even about death. When after a long winter I begin to see the early flowers that announce the coming of spring, I think how our spirits grow cold and seem as barren as winter and how we need for God to come and "bring back the springtime to our souls." Through all the years those who have come really to know God have been encouraged by the fact that He is constantly restoring and reviving and renewing our spirits.

Fourth, Paul was encouraged about his ministry when he set what he was doing into the larger context of things. In verses 17 and 18 he put the "moment" in the context of "eternity" and the "visible" in the context of the "invisible," and it gave him a different perspective. Often when people get a little discouraged about what they are getting done, it helps them to step back and get a broader perspective. We have become too spiritually nearsighted, and living in a world of "instant everything" has robbed us of the perspective of time. Time has a way of reversing judgments, and eternity has a way of telling us what was valuable and what was permanent and exposing that which was temporary and useless.

Woven through all of Paul's encouragement are the beginnings of a discussion of death and a celebration of the hope that we have in the resurrection. When he wrote in his first letter, "If in this life only we have hope in Christ, we are of all men the most pitiable" (1 Cor. 15:19), many early Christians felt they would still be alive at the time of Christ's second coming. In these verses there is the awakening of the feeling that physical death might come to some before Christ's second coming. It is encouraging that Paul's unconquerable faith was spelled out against this backdrop and that he felt that the same God whose Spirit was renewing him day by day was the one who had raised up Christ and who will *"also raise us up with Jesus, and will present us with you"* (v. 14).

CHAPTER FIVE

The Hope That Motivates

2 Corinthians 5:1–21

LOOKING AT LIFE AFTER DEATH

1 For we know that if our earthly house, this tent, is destroyed, we have a building from God, a house not made with hands, eternal in the heavens.

2 For in this we groan, earnestly desiring to be clothed with our habitation which is from heaven,

3 if indeed, having been clothed, we shall not be found naked.

4 For we who are in this tent groan, being burdened, not because we want to be unclothed, but further clothed, that mortality may be swallowed up by life.

5 Now He who has prepared us for this very thing is God, who also has given us the Spirit as a guarantee.

6 Therefore we are always confident, knowing that while we are at home in the body we are absent from the Lord.

7 For we walk by faith, not by sight.

8 We are confident, yes, well pleased rather to be absent from the body and to be present with the Lord.

9 Therefore we make it our aim, whether present or absent, to be well pleasing to Him.

10 For we must all appear before the judgment seat of Christ, that each one may receive the things done in the body, according to what he has done, whether good or bad.

11 Knowing, therefore, the terror of the Lord, we

persuade men; but we are well-known to God, and I
also trust are well-known in your consciences.

2 Cor. 5:1–11

Most people are not able to discuss the possibility of their own
death, although they may think about death and dying often. When
this fact was introduced to me as a college student I was surprised.
To take care of my expenses for books, room and board, and tuition
I applied for a position with a sales team that was developing one
of the first modern cemeteries in Albuquerque, New Mexico. I was
trained by the sales manager whom I knew at church, and he taught
me everything he felt I needed to know about making the presentation, getting an affirmative response, and closing the deal.

An important part of my training centered on how to handle the
various objections that might be given. And even today I still remember one suggestion that came as quite a surprise to me at the time:
"If they say that they need some time to discuss it, just ask them
how long it's been since they had a serious talk in the family about
death. Their answer to that question will prove that although death
is one of the inescapable realities of our existence most people never
discuss it." My brief experience with that company and my years
as a minister have shown me that he was right.

Fortunately the Apostle Paul was not afraid to think about death
or to talk about it, and we are the richer for it. In these verses in 2
Corinthians 5, written at a time when illness, violent persecution,
and the aging process were constant factors in his consciousness,
Paul writes with the assumption that possibly he and many who
would read this letter might face death before Christ's return. Then,
later, writing to the church at Philippi from a prison and facing the
possibility of execution, he spoke of physical death not just as a
possibility but as being preferable: "For me a desire to depart and
be with Christ, which is far better" (Phil. 1:21, 23). And to show
that his attitude was not one of tired resignation to a reality he could
not stop, he used a Greek word for "depart" which meant the striking
of a tent in preparation for a journey or the loosing of a ship's lines
from the dock so the sails could be raised and the journey begun.
All of Paul's discussions of life and death are permeated with the
idea that for the Christian, death is not the end but a new beginning.

As Paul writes about the possibility of his death, his tone exudes a spirit of confidence. He begins with a *"we know"* (v. 1), and he twice speaks of his absolute confidence in life after death (vv. 6, 8). He was convinced that death would lead to a closer and more meaningful relationship with Christ as indicated by His Word. *"While we are at home in the body we are absent from the Lord. . . . rather to be absent from the body and to be present with the Lord"* (vv. 6, 8).

I used to wonder at the source of Paul's confidence until I met some of today's Christians who had the same ability to look death in the face with no fear of loss. During my first year back in the pastorate after several years of teaching, I went to visit one of our church members who had just been told by her doctor that she was terminally ill with cancer. As her pastor, I wanted to be a comfort to her, but I was so obviously ill at ease that she noticed it and commented on it. Somewhat embarrassed, I confessed to her that I had been told what the doctors had said and that I was really at a loss as to what to say to her under the circumstances. It is one thing to sit in a New Testament class as a student and listen to a profound lecture on the hope of the resurrection, and an entirely different thing to sit by the bedside of a vital human being who has a family and friends, who enjoys life, who is gifted but is dying. She reached out, took my hand, and held it between her two hands and said, "Pastor, I know what's about to happen, and I want to assure you that I have resources in Christ and my family and my Christian friends to face whatever happens." Like Paul, she had known and served Christ a long time and there was in her words that same confident attitude displayed by Paul.

Often when Jesus was trying to communicate an idea that was not easy to grasp He would begin an illustration with the words, "It is like a . . . ." Paul does that here when he compares living in this world and in the world to come with the difference between living in a tent and in a house. While he didn't need to explain the illustration for his readers, the tent symbolized a temporary living place while the house was obviously more permanent. His words, *"If our earthly house, this tent, is destroyed"* (v. 1) is his way of saying, "When we die." And his words, *"we have a building from God, a house not made with hands, eternal in the heavens"* (v. 1) meant that dying is not "leaving home" but "going home."

Paul did not believe that death was the place of extinction, or that in death we are absorbed up into the divine being, or that we become some disembodied spirit floating around in eternity. Rather, he believed that in death God gives us a new body and that we will be able to love and serve God better then than now. He felt that this was the way that those who walked *"by faith, not by sight"* (v. 7) could look at death. For Paul it was never a question of "does the person survive death?" but rather he insisted "the life beyond the grave is better."

After using the analogy of the tent and the house Paul introduced a second picture, that of clothing. While the Greek world tended to look upon the body as a tomb for the soul and death as an escape, the Jews thought of their bodies as clothing for the person. The body was what made contact and communication with others possible. To them the death of the body deprived them of everything which meant being a person; it was being unclothed or naked. It was this fear that made them want to go directly from this life to the resurrection life without experiencing death. But the promise of God was, whether we are alive when He comes or have died, that *"we shall not be found naked"* (v. 3).

We don't know whether Paul was saying that at the moment of death God gives us a new body, or that the hope was so very real that they shouldn't worry about the time in between. Some feel that the reference is to the fact that physical death does not make us lose our relationship within the body of Christ. Bible scholars and theologians will continue to discuss those possibilities for years to come. But there is general agreement on the idea that death, rather than lessening the person or the relationship, actually creates a greater potential for growth and service.

Frequently, when I've been invited to speak to a young people's group, I have asked what they would like for me to speak on. Their response has often been, "Tell us about heaven—where it is and what it is like." Because I have never been convinced that their request represents what they are really interested in, I usually question them further to find out what they *really* want to know. In almost every case their question isn't "Will I be in heaven?" but "Will I *be?*" Upon reflection I've come to believe that is everyone's question who has thought about death. And the answer from the Word of God is an everlasting "yes."

Then in verses 9–11 Paul reinforces the idea that there is continuity between this world and the next by reminding his readers that *"we must all appear before the judgment seat of Christ"* (v. 10). He wanted to remind them and us that we are responsible to God for our thoughts and our actions, both in this life and in the world to come. Ours is a generation that has reacted to the ideal of the judgment of God, but it has missed Paul's point. He was comforted in that the very Christ whom we serve here is the One before whom we shall stand in judgment. That everything will eventually be known will not strike fear in the hearts of those who have discovered His love and forgiveness.

The Motive for Ministry

12 For we do not commend ourselves again to you, but give you opportunity to glory on our behalf, that you may have something to answer those who glory in appearance and not in heart.

13 For if we are beside ourselves, it is for God; or if we are of sound mind, it is for you.

14 For the love of Christ constrains us, because we judge thus: that if One died for all, then all died;

15 and He died for all, that those who live should live no longer for themselves, but for Him who died for them and rose again.

16 Therefore, from now on, we know no one according to the flesh. Even though we have known Christ according to the flesh, yet now we know Him thus no longer.

17 Therefore, if anyone is in Christ, he is a new creation; old things have passed away; behold, all things have become new.

18 Now all things are of God, who has reconciled us to Himself through Jesus Christ, and has given us the ministry of reconciliation,

19 that is, that God was in Christ reconciling the world to Himself, not imputing their trespasses to them, and has committed to us the word of reconciliation.

20 Therefore we are ambassadors for Christ, as
though God were pleading through us: we implore
you on Christ's behalf, be reconciled to God.

21 For He made Him who knew no sin to be sin
for us, that we might become the righteousness of God
in Him.

2 Cor. 5:12–21

There are verses in this passage of Scripture which for practically
all of my Christian life have inspired and challenged me. And it
continues to amaze me that so magnificent a passage of the Bible
was written by the Apostle Paul in answer to his critics and in defense
of his ministry. Paul, who is fixed in our minds as the significant
human instrument for the spread of the gospel in the first century,
was guided by the Holy Spirit in writing a good portion of the New
Testament. Consequently, it is difficult for us to imagine that there
was a time when he was accused of being a crazy, self-appointed
peddler of the gospel. Enough people took the criticism seriously
that Paul felt it necessary to defend himself. However, we also remember that there was a time when Jesus' immediate family wondered
if He might be crazy. But as a result of Paul's defense, we have these
classic statements about his motive for ministry (v. 20).

For Paul the reason for doing something was as important as what
was done. Christ also stressed this principle in the Sermon on the
Mount where He criticized those who did good things—like fasting,
praying, or giving—for the wrong reasons (Matt. 6:1–18). Paul was
reared in a religious world that glorified the deed and ignored the
motive. But in his relationship with Jesus Christ he came to realize
that fear or guilt or a sense of duty or a desire to impress God or
others were woefully inadequate as a reason for sharing the gospel.
In verses 14 and 15 he opens his heart and reveals the secret that
drove him to spend his life the way he did. These six words, *"the
love of Christ constrains us"* (v. 14), say it all. This was the truth and
this was what above all else Paul wanted the Corinthians to believe
about him.

The primary focus was on Christ's love for us and not our love
for him. The belief that on the cross Christ acted on behalf of the
whole human race became the foundation of Paul's thinking and

action. When the implication of the statement, *"He died for all"* (v. 15), began to get hold of Paul, it changed permanently his feeling about every person in the world. The fact that every person he met was the object of God's eternal love and was one for whom Christ died defined the nature of his ministry. This is why Paul's evangelism never exploited or manipulated people. He had come to love them the way Christ did.

But Paul saw more in Christ's death than a way to feel about persons. He believed that on the cross sinful humanity had at least in principle been destroyed and that "in Christ" a new humanity was being created. As he moved out boldly into the cities of the then-known world to proclaim this gospel of love, there was a note of victory already won, a feeling that he already knew the ultimate outcome. It was true, of course, that sin was still present in the world and the forces of evil were very powerful, but Paul had seen in God's action by Christ's death and resurrection a clue concerning the end, and this awareness gave him great confidence.

It is this note of confidence that seems to be absent from the church and from Christians in so much of the world today. I sat one day in a national gathering and listened to a noted leader spell out the sad plight of the church in an increasingly urban society. The facts he shared could not be argued with, for they were heavily documented with the hard statistics and the insights of sociological analysis. As the meeting progressed, one could feel a deep pessimism moving through the group and a kind of desperation to come up with some strategy for reversing the trends. The last thing that particular group needed was for some theological Pollyanna to stand ignoring every reality and announce that everything was fine. But I had the feeling that the way of dealing with the problem might have been trans- formed had we been able to remember that the ultimate outcome— who is going to win—was settled a long time ago by Christ on the cross.

There are few words in the Scripture filled with more hope than those from Paul in verse 17 of this chapter: *"If anyone is in Christ, he is a new creation; old things have passed away; behold, all things have become new."* In this verse Paul relates his feeling about growing older and about the age to come. He felt that this world, as we know it, had "had" it and that the new order that would last forever had already begun. His gospel was that when any person became a Christian then God made him a part of that new creation. The church is often tempted to make something less of conversion than this.

At a meeting I once heard Professor Peter Wagner bring a lecture on church growth. He said, "When I use the word *Christian* I am referring to someone who is committed to the person of Christ, the body of Christ, and to the work of Christ."

One of the young participants in the meeting came to me afterwards and said that he did not agree with Dr. Wagner's definition. When I pressed him for his definition, he quoted this passage and said, "All you have to be is *in Christ.*"

It had apparently never occurred to him that there was no essential difference in what Professor Wagner said and what Paul meant. Paul was *not* discussing a newness that was merely cosmetic, like a new hairdo or new clothes. Rather, he was talking about an inner change that only God could make. It was a newness that ties together our past, our present, and our future. It was a newness that, while not seen immediately, would eventually reflect itself in every area of life. Christ's coming into our lives creates a new unity, a new direction, new goals, and a new commitment.

Eleven years ago I had a class of children who had made personal commitments to Christ, and I spent several sessions with them prior to their baptism. We talked about what it means to become a Christian, what it means to be a member of the church, and about growing as new believers. In one of the meetings I tried to explain all of the things that Christ's presence in their lives would make different: school work, family, dating, career choices, lifestyle in general.

Their parents were in this particular session, and I could sense a certain skepticism about the changes God was making in their children. But now, more than a decade later, these same children are finishing college, entering careers, getting married, and assuming places of responsibility in the community, and they are different. Christ has given them different friends, different priorities, different ways of thinking about life, different values. He has truly made them a part of His new creation.

There is no more beautiful description of the work that God has given Christians to do in the world than is found in Paul's statement that Christ has *"given us the ministry of reconciliation"* (v. 18). Authentic religion is always interested in the nature of man's relationship with

God. In the sense that every child has some kind of relationship with his or her parent, whether good or bad, every person lives in some kind of relationship with God. It was God's intention from the beginning for people to live in a relationship of trust and obedience. But sin entered the world and created a hostility to God's will and an estrangement from Him. Then God's action through Christ was a reaching out in love to reestablish the relationship. When Paul had to define his ministry and ours, he took a phrase from the world of politics, *"We are ambassadors for Christ"* (v. 20). In Paul's world this metaphor would be clearly understood as describing the act of representing Christ in the Roman Empire. And here he is relating this to our role. We play that same role for the Kingdom of God.

CHAPTER SIX

The Consistent Life

2 Corinthians 6:1–18

THE HIGH COST OF MINISTRY

1 We then, as workers together with Him, also plead with you not to receive the grace of God in vain.

2 For He says:

> *"In an acceptable time I have heard you,*
> *And in the day of salvation I have helped you."*

Behold, now is the accepted time; behold, now is the day of salvation.

3 We give no offense in anything, that our ministry may not be blamed.

4 But in all things we commend ourselves as ministers of God: in much patience, in tribulations, in needs, in distresses,

5 in stripes, in imprisonments, in tumults, in labors, in sleeplessness, in fastings;

6 by purity, by knowledge, by longsuffering, by kindness, by the Holy Spirit, by sincere love,

7 by the word of truth, by the power of God, by the armor of righteousness on the right hand and on the left,

8 by honor and dishonor, by evil report and good report; as deceivers, and yet true;

9 as unknown, and yet well-known; as dying, and behold we live; as chastened, and yet not killed;

10 as sorrowful, yet always rejoicing; as poor, yet making many rich; as having nothing, and yet possessing all things.

11 O Corinthians! We have spoken openly to you, our heart is wide open.

12 You are not restricted by us, but you are restricted by your own affections.

13 Now in return for the same (I speak as to children), you also be open.

2 Cor. 6:1–13

The student of 2 Corinthians has to keep remembering that this is a letter and not an essay. In a manner quite natural for a letter, Paul keeps coming back to subjects he had written about earlier, either to repeat what he said or to make some additional comment.

In this sixth chapter, the first two verses are a carryover from chapter 5 and conclude his discussion of our task as ambassadors. Then in verses 3–9 Paul returns to the theme he mentioned in 2 Corinthians 5:12. My first reaction to this repetition was to wonder why he couldn't just drop the subject once he had made his point. But then I was reminded that his commission had been questioned, his motive disparaged, and his conduct impugned. Even more hurtful, though, was that some of those whom he had led to Christ had believed all the charges were true.

My own service for the Lord has been relatively free of the type of abuse which Paul suffered, but in different ways I believe I've experienced some of the feelings he had at that time. I well recall one particular occasion when I was under attack for certain of my views. Some of those who disagreed with me began to spread the word that I didn't believe the Bible.

I paid little attention to the accusations. But then one day one of the ladies of the church appeared at my study and asked, "Pastor, I've come to see if you believe the Bible."

When I asked what had prompted her question, I was told that she had been attending a Bible study in another church, and when the leader had found that she was from the church where I was the pastor had asked, "How can you stay in a church where the pastor doesn't believe the Bible?"

She had been a member of the church for over six years and had heard me preach and teach the Scriptures on a fairly regular basis. So I asked her, "In all the years you have listened to me, have you ever heard me say anything that would raise the slightest doubt concerning the Bible's inspiration or authority?" Without a moment's hesitation she said, "No, I haven't, but he seemed like such a spiritual man I couldn't imagine his saying something that wasn't true." My emotions ranged from being angry at that "spiritual man" who attempted to undermine confidence in me and a feeling of sadness for the woman who in her immaturity and gullibility was so easily taken in by irresponsible criticism.

In these verses Paul doesn't merely go back and repeat himself, but he plows new ground that gives insight into the costs of his ministry. He argues in verses 4–5 that the trials he had endured gave witness to the genuineness of his ministry. In these two verses he paints a word picture of the price he had paid to share the gospel. Some parts of the price were general in nature—such as tribulations, distresses, and tumults. Other parts were inflicted by other people— stripes and imprisonments. Some of the cost was self-imposed—waiting, sleeplessness, and fastings. Then in further reaction, Paul seems to be saying here, "If I'm the self-seeking person that people have said I am, how do you explain what I have gone through on your behalf?" The price a person is willing to pay is a very powerful argument for his or her sincerity.

I vividly recall a seminar for ministers and lay people on the theme of "The Ministering Congregation." I had just shared a description of the many and varied ministries being carried on by a certain church. Some were ministering to international students, others were working in a free medical clinic for the indigents in the neighborhood. Another group was involved in doing immigration counseling with people who lacked adequate documentation. And other people loved ministering on a one-to-one basis with out-of-town cancer patients in Houston's M. D. Anderson Hospital.

At discussion time one of the first questions asked was, "With all of these exciting and fulfilling ministries, isn't there a lot of jockeying for positions in them?" The question caught me completely off guard because in all the years we had been involved in those programs what he had suggested had never been a problem. But then I began to see why this was true. People quite naturally vie for positions of honor, but there is never competition for the servant roles.

Next Paul lists those spiritual qualities he had endeavored to cultivate in his ministry—those qualities of the mind and heart and those God-given attributes that equipped him for preaching the gospel (vv. 6–7). In verses 8–10 these are followed by a restatement of the position in which the faithful servant is placed. To illustrate his point Paul points up two opposite assessments of him and his ministry.

In looking over these opposite viewpoints we can't help wondering how one person could be seen so differently by different people. To some Paul was a poor, sorrowful, unknown, dying imposter without honor. To others he was a spiritually rich, alive, honorable, well-thought-of servant of God whose ministry enriched others.

Obviously, the difference was not in Paul but in the different ways people saw him—evaluating him by worldly standards or by spiritual ones. While most Christians don't like to admit it, the world in which they live and minister and witness has a very stereotyped view of them. A secular society may at times make nice gestures toward certain Christian values, but at heart it has a very patronizing attitude toward Christians. Also, it is still true that two sincere Christians may take opposing views of a ministry. Paul deals very realistically in verses 8–10 with these conflicting attitudes. In verses 11–13 he goes on to ask his Christian friends to take the divine assessment of his work.

The Separated Life

14 Do not be unequally yoked together with unbelievers. For what fellowship has righteousness with lawlessness? And what communion has light with darkness?

15 And what accord has Christ with Belial? Or what part has a believer with an unbeliever?

16 And what agreement has the temple of God with idols? For you are the temple of the living God. As God has said:

"I will dwell in them
And walk among them.
I will be their God,
And they shall be My people."

17 Therefore

"Come out from among them
And be separate, says the Lord.
Do not touch what is unclean,
And I will receive you."
18 *"I will be a Father to you,*
And you shall be My sons and daughters,
Says the LORD Almighty."

2 Cor. 6:14–18

There are times when something Paul writes doesn't seem to fit in with either what has gone before or what follows. This is certainly true of these five verses. Some feel this may be the short letter referred to in 1 Corinthians 5:9 where Paul said, "I wrote to you in my epistle not to keep company with sexually immoral people." Others explain it by suggesting that Paul had interrupted his dictation and then come back to it with this specific concern on his mind. But whatever may have been the circumstances of its writing and preservation, it is a valuable part of God's Word, and through it Paul makes a strong and helpful statement about the importance of Christians living a different kind of life. This thought certainly ties in to the teachings of Jesus on Matthew 7:15–20 where he stressed that people who have God in their heart need to give evidence of His presence by their fruits, by the kinds of lives they live.

The theme of these verses is that a Christian should avoid close contact with the pagan world. This came from the idea that the church was a separate community of people who had been chosen by God for a special purpose.

This picture of the nature and calling of the church is reflected in the salutation in Paul's letter: "To the church of God which is at Corinth, to those who are called to be saints" (1 Cor. 1:2). Paul was realistic enough to realize that it would be impossible for Christians to live totally without contact with unbelievers. This was reflected in his first letter when he was making a distinction between how they were to treat the member they were disciplining and how they were to treat unbelievers. "I wrote to you in my epistle not to keep company with sexually immoral people. Yet I certainly did not mean with the sexually immoral people of this world, or with the covetous, or extortioners, or idolaters, since then you would need to go out of the world" (1 Cor. 5:9–10). Paul was not calling for withdrawal from the secular world. He was pleading with the church members not to put themselves into relationships with either pagan persons or pagan institutions that would water down or undermine their Christian values. He makes his point concerning the incompatibility of Christian and pagan values with five rhetorical questions (vv. 14–16), all of which assume "none" as the answer.

It will be a serious mistake if we assume that Paul was addressing a first-century problem that has no relevance for today. While contemporary paganism may be more sophisticated than that from which the Corinthians had come, it can be just as deadly in compromising the Christian and turning him away from his calling.

For example, I have two close friends who are on the staff of a major daily newspaper. Their marriage is good; they have wonderful children; and the whole family is involved in the church. They are sensitive and articulate people and have often talked to me about the pressures they feel at work because of their Christian values. The rejection that they felt was not a reaction to a superficial piety. But the tension grew out of a very real and serious conflict of values. And sad as it may seem, this will increasingly be the situation for Christians who live in this world.

The ongoing question that confronts every Christian is: do we take seriously the call of Scripture to *"come out from among them and be separate"* (2 Cor. 6:17)? Of course, the call to holy living needs to be taken seriously, but we also need to be aware of the temptation to settle for a cheap imitation.

The church of my childhood defined holy living as not doing worldly things. And along with that definition came a very precise list of things good Christians didn't do. This attitude shaped my earliest concept of what was meant by the separated life. It was many years before I realized that the list didn't include a single thing that would have been a violation of any one of the Ten Commandments. It is tragic but true that each generation and each culture produces its own list as a guide to living holy lives, but sometimes the tendency is to produce Pharisees instead of healthy Christians.

The effort to define the church in terms of a haven from the world has an element of truth in it, but it also offers all sorts of danger. It can produce a kind of "enclave" mentality in the church. In this environment the church is not a fellowship in which we are equipped to function with integrity in the world, but a place where we do everything we can to hide from the world.

There is no doubt that it is intimidating to try to live a Christian life in an un-Christian world. At the same time I think it is a serious mistake for people to try to satisfy all of their recreational, social, and intellectual needs within the spiritual environment of the church. This sort of person epitomizes the old cliché that says that it is possible to be so heavenly minded we're of no earthly good. It is irresponsible to live and make a living in the world and never be involved in the solving of its problems because of being submerged in church activities alone. It is true that we all benefit from close Christian fellowship, but Jesus laid great emphasis on the importance of Christians being salt and light in the world (Matt. 5:13–16).

There are several things the church can and ought to do to help Christians live more separated lives. First, the church in its worship and its study needs to articulate Christian ideals as they relate to all of life and to put them into today's context. These ideals need to relate to sex, marriage, material possessions, how people are to be treated, war and power.

I believe it is a mistake to assume that everyone knows what the Biblical ideals are and how they relate to all of life. Fresh guidance is needed in confronting the new ethical questions posed by high technology, by genetic engineering, and by organ transplants. We Christians need to find insight within our faith for giving and receiving guidance. This is an exercise that needs to be constantly going on, and our failure to do it is what has often left the church providing answers for questions that are no longer being asked. It is as we find help in the church in clarifying the goals and values of Christ for our lives and receive practical insight into how to apply what we've learned that we will be better equipped to live separated lives.

A close friend of mine exemplifies this point. Although he is a very successful builder and developer, he is also a serious Christian who tries to work in the church and to blend into the way he does business the best insights of the Christian life. He is not satisfied to build a wall between the world of business and the world of church and have a different standard for each.

Because of his serious and practical approach to the Christian life he often finds himself in interesting situations in which he must take stands that could be quite costly. For instance, a group of overseas investors wanted to go into a joint venture with him to build a chain of hotels throughout the nation. It was a multi-million-dollar deal that had great potential for profit for everyone involved. The negotiations had not been underway long before their value systems clashed head on. It seems that the investors came out of a background with a very different business ethic. For example, this clash surfaced in one instance by the way in which they were going to keep the letter of a deal but violate its spirit—in order to save a little money. In response to that my friend risked his partnership in the whole deal when he said, "There's lots of money in this deal for everyone without our having to be dishonest. If you want me to stay in, let's agree right now that we'll go by the book."

It is important for the church to give guidance to its members in their effort to judge worldly ways in the light of Christian commitments. One way of doing this is to encourage those who work in similar professions to get together and help each other gain insights into how they should conduct themselves in their work as Christians.

Another friend of mine is an outstanding attorney who is a partner in a prestigious firm, and he is also a serious, sensitive, growing Christian. In his effort to find a legitimate difference for his life as a Christian attorney he has organized breakfasts and luncheons for men and women in his church who are lawyers. The agenda is very simple as they confront this question: What are the issues we face as attorneys where the fact that we are followers of Jesus Christ ought to make a real difference? I have sat at some of these meetings and felt among them, in the midst of vigorous thought and a diversity of opinions, a deep seriousness. These are people who have heard the call for a separate life and are trying to live it.

CHAPTER SEVEN

When Pain Produces Joy

2 Corinthians 7:1–16

1 Therefore, having these promises, beloved, let us cleanse ourselves from all filthiness of the flesh and spirit, perfecting holiness in the fear of God.

2 Open your hearts to us. We have wronged no one, we have corrupted no one, we have defrauded no one.

3 I do not say this to condemn you; for I have said before that you are in our hearts, to die together and to live together.

4 Great is my boldness of speech toward you, great is my boasting on your behalf. I am filled with comfort. I am exceedingly joyful in all our tribulation.

5 For indeed, when we came to Macedonia, our flesh had no rest, but we were troubled on every side. Outside were conflicts, inside were fears.

6 Nevertheless God, who comforts the downcast, comforted us by the coming of Titus,

7 and not only by his coming, but also by the consolation with which he was comforted in you, when he told us of your earnest desire, your mourning, your zeal for me, so that I rejoiced even more.

8 For even if I made you sorry with my letter, I do not regret it; though I did regret it. For I perceive that the same epistle made you sorry, though only for a while.

9 Now I rejoice, not that you were made sorry, but that your sorrow led to repentance. For you were made sorry in a godly manner, that you might suffer loss from us in nothing.

10 For godly sorrow produces repentance to salvation, not to be regretted; but the sorrow of the world produces death.

11 For observe this very thing, that you sorrowed in a godly manner: What diligence it produced in you, what clearing of yourselves, what indignation, what fear, what vehement desire, what zeal, what vindication! In all things you proved yourselves to be clear in this matter.

12 Therefore, although I wrote to you, I did not do it for the sake of him who had done the wrong, nor for the sake of him who suffered wrong, but that our care for you in the sight of God might appear to you.

13 Therefore we have been comforted in your comfort. And we rejoiced exceedingly more for the joy of Titus, because his spirit has been refreshed by you all.

14 For if in anything I have boasted to him about you, I am not ashamed. But as we spoke all things to you in truth, even so our boasting to Titus was found true.

15 And his affections are greater for you as he remembers the obedience of you all, how with fear and trembling you received him.

16 Therefore I rejoice that I have confidence in you in everything.

2 Cor. 7:1–16

In my first class in Christian ethics, the professor, Dr. T. B. Maston, introduced me to his philosophy of leadership. Because he dealt constantly with the field of applied Christianity, his teachings and writings often created strong reaction from the students and tensions within the Christian community. The tension was created because many of us had made commitments to Christ without ever exploring what the implications of that commitment were in every area of our lives. He said that leading your people to go where they need to go on an idea or an issue is like trying to pull a heavy object with a large rubber band. If the band is not stretched at all the people stay where they are, and if it is stretched too much the band breaks

251

and the people still stay where they are. The secret of good leadership, he said, was to keep the band tight enough that the people were moving toward the goal but not pulling it so tightly that it broke and you lost completely the ability to lead. Christ illustrated this principle as He taught the people. He always had a "stretching point" to the things He said.

When the Apostle Paul arrived in Macedonia, he was concerned that possibly he had stretched the band so tightly in his relationship with the church in Corinth that it had broken and his leadership role had been jeopardized.

When, after writing his first letter, the spiritual condition in the church deteriorated, Paul then made a hurried visit to Corinth, but rather than correcting the situation it had gotten worse. Then in yet another effort to stabilize the situation and resume his proper spiritual role, he wrote them a very strong letter and sent it by Titus. And, earlier in 2 Corinthians, Paul had expressed in poignant language the deep concern and anxiety he felt over their reactions to his strongly worded letter. "For out of much affliction and anguish of heart I wrote to you, with many tears, not that you should be grieved, but that you might know the love which I have so abundantly for you" (2 Cor. 2:4). Now again he writes, *"Our flesh had no rest, but we were troubled on every side. Outside were conflicts, inside were fears"* (2 Cor. 7:5). It is impossible to read those words without feeling the heart throb of emotion that flows through them. Most of us can identify with Paul's anxiety as we remember those times when we've waited for a reassuring word.

But before we look at the whole dynamic of confrontation in which Paul engaged and its possible implication for our own leadership, we need to skip over to the last verses of the chapter and celebrate with him. Here we see that the coldness is gone, with its tears and anxiety, and in its place there is comfort, rejoicing, and joy. Even though he was still physically separated from the Corinthians, Paul sensed in the report of Titus that there had been a complete reconciliation, for he says, *"Therefore I rejoice that I have confidence in you in everything"* (v. 16).

Everyone who has ever experienced the joy that comes when a broken relationship was healed will understand Paul's response to Titus's report. I'm sure Paul questioned Titus again and again about every little detail of his visit. On the basis of the good news Titus brought Paul, he began to go back and interpret his actions with the Corinthians. That's what we have in 2 Corinthians 7:8–12, and there is something to be learned about brave and redemptive leadership from this painful experience which eventually turned to joy.

I believe we learn from this experience of Paul's that there are circumstances in which honest confrontation, with all of its pain, must occur. This is true in marriage, in parent-child relationships, in friendships, and in our church life.

At an early age I learned that sometimes we have to endure something painful for healing to take place. I remember so well the summer I spent with my Aunt Ida. A boil erupted on my leg. It was red and swollen and caused so much pain up and down my leg that I couldn't stand for anything to touch it. When it was ready to be lanced, my aunt appeared with a large needle and some disinfectant. I tried to resist, but she responded, "Kenneth, there are times when you have to inflict a little pain in order to relieve a lot of pain, and this is one of those times."

She was so right, but when it comes to my interpersonal relationships, I still want to shy away from the pain and risk of confrontation. Both in the family in which I was reared and in the world in which I live now, I have been exposed to the philosophy that when confronted with a bad situation, the best thing to do is to ignore it and maybe it will go away. Such philosophy suggests that the ultimate sin in the church is to "rock the boat."

This fear of confrontation is often covered up with such clever and spiritual platitudes as "I'm a lover and not a fighter." Not only is there a natural reluctance to deal head on with critical problems; there is often a resentment of those who act differently. Early in my ministry I invited an outstanding woman to speak in our church. She and her husband had served as medical missionaries in South America, and since returning to the United States, she had done quite a bit of speaking and writing on the role of women in the church. The topic on which she spoke to us was "Growth Through Confrontation," and to illustrate her point she shared with us some of the anger and frustration that she was feeling as a Christian woman in the church. And while her message was disturbing and disquieting to nearly everyone, she illustrated quite readily the truth that the church cannot always be a spiritual massage parlor where everyone leaves feeling good about themselves.

There are times in our Christian relationships and service when we need to faithfully confront issues as a means of correcting wrong. And these times can be very painful. Of course, it is natural for us to want to avoid them. But if the ongoing integrity of our witness is to be maintained, there will undoubtedly be times when we must take the risk and take our stand.

In taking a stand, though, we are to do it with the same attitude Paul had toward the Corinthians. His deepest feeling for them was love, and this love was not just a slogan that he used as a salutation. It was a deep love whose source was God Himself. Paul described it in his first letter: "Love suffers long and is kind; love does not envy; love does not parade itself, is not puffed up; does not behave rudely, does not seek its own, is not provoked, thinks no evil; does not rejoice in iniquity, but rejoices in the truth; bears all things, believes all things, hopes all things, endures all things" (1 Cor. 13:4–7). This wasn't just one of Paul's favorite sermons but was the way he lived his life. He loved the Corinthian Christians and they knew it.

Several years ago I went to hear a much-publicized young preacher who was conducting a series of services in a nearby community. I soon realized that I was listening to a very gifted speaker with a compelling sense of presence. But at the same time I had a haunting feeling that for me at least, something was wrong in his manner and sound. As he expounded on the text, "Whatever a man sows, that he will also reap," I felt a spirit of anger, not love. His words were all right, but it was the emotion that seemed to be seething below the surface of those words that troubled me. But with Paul and the Corinthian church it was just the opposite. Paul's words were strong, but the church could sense his feeling of love.

I'm certainly not suggesting that all it takes to turn a painful situation into one of joy is for a strong word to be spoken in love. Not at all. It was the right response of the Corinthians to Paul's words that give this a happy ending. A wrong and defensive response from them would have filled Paul with sadness. After all, they could have responded in anger. Or they could have denied that anything was wrong and, in turn, could have attacked Paul. I'm aware that a variety of responses can be made.

If any confrontation is to produce redemptive results, everyone's attitude must be open and not defensive. During my senior year in high school I developed a warm friendship with a girl who served with me on the student council. It was a genuine friendship without romantic overtones.

One day after school we were sitting on the steps of the administration building, and I said, "Mary Lou, we're good friends, so I think I can ask you this question and you'll answer me honestly. Tell me some ways in which I can improve myself."

She was reluctant to respond, but I kept insisting, so finally she mentioned several specific things. And even though I had asked for criticism, I was floored by her response and it put a real strain on our friendship. I learned the hard way how difficult it is sometimes to hear the truth.

Just as God was in Paul's letter to his friends in Corinth, He must have been in their response. The letter created not only a godly sorrow in them but a change of mind and attitude that led to the restoration of their relationship with Paul as their spiritual leader. And as Paul reflects on their response, he draws the distinction between godly sorrow that leads to repentance and worldly grief that leads to death. It was worldly grief without repentance that drove Judas to suicide after his infamous betrayal of Jesus. By contrast, though, it was godly sorrow or grief that, through repentance, restored Peter to the circle after his betrayal of Jesus in the courtyard of the high priest. And we know from Paul's comments, *"In all things you proved yourselves to be clear in this matter"* (2 Cor. 7:11), that it was indeed godly grief in the hearts of the Corinthian Christians which brought healing and hope.

Like every reflective person, from time to time I look back over my life and think of things I would do differently. This is not just a whimsical game of "what if" for me. Rather it helps me work through new and creative attitudes and life responses for the days ahead. One of the things I regret not having learned to do earlier and more effectively is to bring to the surface and deal with certain potentially destructive situations more directly and openly and lovingly. The principle Paul models for us here can be applied to our marriages, our friendships, our work, and to every area of life.

CHAPTER EIGHT

Learning to Enjoy Giving

2 Corinthians 8:1–24

Few people are more attractive or more contagious than those individuals who find happiness in generosity. It is unfortunate that so many of us seem to find it hard to associate the two words "enjoyment" and "giving." The words seem to them to be mutually exclusive. Because ours is a society that is preoccupied with "getting," we often fail to experience personally the truth of Christ's saying, "It is more blessed to give than to receive" (Acts 20:35).

In 2 Corinthians 8 and 9, Paul picks up an agenda item that had been introduced almost a year before—the offering for the impoverished Christians in Jerusalem. He was concerned not only about the plight of the Jerusalem Christians who were in desperate need, but for the Corinthian Christians. He knew they needed to feel the responsibility for their brothers and sisters in Christ if they were to grow spiritually. So, in these two chapters, the Apostle Paul, who was the early church's missionary to the gentile world, church planter, theologian, and pastor, takes on the role of a fund-raiser. He saw no basic conflict in all of this. As a matter of fact, he has given us in these two chapters the Bible's finest insight into both the motivation for and method of giving that can be joyful. It is obvious that in Paul's mind there is nothing unspiritual about promoting an offering, and I'm sure that if he could be with us in today's church, he would emphasize the importance of budgets and good stewardship.

As we read these verses it is apparent that the members of the mother church in Jerusalem were suffering from extreme poverty. The exact cause is not known, but it could have come from a number of sources: a drought, persecution by their employers because of their faith, or even from the brief experiment in which the members all sold their property and put it into a common warehouse (Acts 2:44–45). But whatever the cause, the need was very real.

We all need to work hard to present this larger interest in the needs of our fellow Christians. While at a convention, I visited with several pastors and one of them dominated the conversation with his concern that a number of his best members were giving very generously to a certain world hunger program that they had only read about in one of the denomination's publications. What had him upset was that in an effort to completely refurbish and redecorate the church parlor, he had set up a special committee, preached a sermon, and written articles for the bulletin, and the project had not even gotten off the ground. While I didn't comment on his dilemma, in my mind I could see how much more attractive I would find it to furnish grain for planting or eating for people who were starving than it would be to buy a new carpet or new drapes for the church parlor. When we give to others whose needs are real we feel fulfilled because we are reflecting God's priorities.

But Paul also knew that the gentile Christians in Corinth needed to experience the joy that comes from helping others—especially their Jewish brethren. Consequently, when the church in Jerusalem asked him to remember the "poor saints in Jerusalem," he gladly responded and began a campaign to involve every gentile church in an offering. He saw this as an opportunity to meet a real need—to give new Christians a chance to put their faith into action—and as a means of drawing these two distinct parts of the church into a closer bond of fellowship.

Earlier Paul had mentioned the offering (1 Cor. 16:1–4) and there had been an eager response, but then that enthusiasm had waned, probably as the church's relationship with Paul had been strained. But now Paul, having heard the good word from Titus about their response to his letter, seeks to revive their interest in the offering.

LEARNING FROM THE GIVING OF OTHERS

1 Moreover, brethren, we make known to you the grace of God bestowed on the churches of Macedonia:
2 that in a great trial of affliction the abundance of their joy and their deep poverty abounded in the riches of their liberality.

3 For I bear witness that according to their ability, yes, and beyond their ability, they were freely willing,

4 imploring us with much urgency that we would receive the gift and the fellowship of the ministering to the saints.

5 And this they did, not as we had hoped, but first gave themselves to the Lord, and then to us by the will of God.

6 So we urged Titus, that as he had begun, so he would also complete this grace in you as well.

7 But as you abound in everything—in faith, in speech, in knowledge, in all diligence, and in your love for us—see that you abound in this grace also.

8 I speak not by commandment, but I am testing the sincerity of your love by the diligence of others.

9 For you know the grace of our Lord Jesus Christ, that though He was rich, yet for your sakes He became poor, that you through His poverty might become rich.

10 And in this I give my advice: It is to your advantage not only to be doing what you began and were desiring to do a year ago;

11 but now also complete the doing of it; that as there was a readiness to desire it, so there also may be a completion out of what you have.

12 For if there is first a willing mind, it is accepted according to what one has, and not according to what he does not have.

13 For I do not mean that others should be eased and you burdened;

14 but by an equality, that now at this time your abundance may supply their lack, that their abundance also may supply your lack—that there may be equality.

15 As it is written, *"He who gathered much had nothing left over, and he who gathered little had no lack."*

2 Cor. 8:1–15

In order to revive the interest of the Corinthian Christians in the offering Paul reminded them of the example set by their fellow gentile Christians (vv. 1–7) and of the example of Christ (vv. 8–15). And in doing this Paul very wisely appeals to their emotions. This is why a scholarly article on world hunger doesn't have the impact of a photograph of one three-year-old child whose stomach is swollen with hunger. And it is equally true that when we see generosity acted out in the life of another person it is easier for us to understand it and identify with it. The presence of Mother Teresa in a group speaks volumes because of her own example. As Paul refers in these verses to the Macedonian churches who have given so freely—probably Philippi, Thessalonica, and Berea—he gives us several principles of Christian giving that are valid for Christians of all ages.

First, giving is more a matter of the heart than of circumstances. Everything about the circumstances in the Macedonian churches would have suggested that, because of their own needs, this was not a good time for them to worry about the needs of others. They were experiencing both deep poverty and *"a great trial of affliction"* (v. 2), and yet they participated liberally and joyfully in the offering.

Poverty does not automatically create unselfishness nor does persecution automatically produce giving. Those who insist they were much happier when they had less need to remember that it isn't what we have or don't have that promotes happiness or generosity. The difference, according to Paul, is the *"grace of God"* (v. 1) which creates an open and generous heart. Anyone within the church community who feels that the raising of money is nothing more than finding a way to pay the bills will profit by carefully reading Paul's words, *"As you abound in everything—in faith, in speech, in knowledge, in all diligence, and in your love for us—see that you abound in this grace also"* (v. 7). These words stress the truth that learning to be generous with material things is a matter of spiritual growth and maturity.

It has always been inspiring to know people of quite limited financial resource who are exceptionally generous in their giving to the church because of the richness of their relationship with God. The church where I served as pastor for more than ten years had a very active international ministry with Chinese, Koreans, Cambodians and Hispanics. For the most part, though, these people were well-educated middle- and upper-middle-class persons. But when we started to work with the Cambodian refugees who moved to our city, the situation was entirely different. These refugees had lost everything in their escape from Communist persecution. In vivid contrast to the other international groups they were quite limited in education, in skills, and in experience. But as more and more of them were introduced to Jesus Christ, we discovered one way in which the Cambodians were richer than all the other groups. God had developed in them the "grace of generosity." In the midst of their displacement, difficulty, and poverty, their gifts to the Lord far exceeded their financial means. Their example inspired the rest of the church, especially those who had so much to give but who still lacked that grace of generosity.

Another principle Paul mentions here is paradoxical—giving becomes a joy when it comes out of sacrifice. Paul's model for sacrificial giving was Christ Himself, *"Though He was rich, yet for your sakes He became poor, that you through His poverty might become rich"* (v. 9). The Macedonian Christians had taken Christ's model, and in total disregard for their present needs or future requirements, they gave *"beyond their ability"* (v. 3). Theirs was a sacrificial offering and it became an inspiration for Christians everywhere.

By contrast, I sometimes feel there is little sacrifice in much of our giving. At Christmas time our tendency is to spend more on presents for ourselves and family than we give to the Lord. And it has been estimated that the personal budget of most church folks for sporting events far exceeds gifts to religious and charitable causes.

For the most part, there's little sacrifice or joy in our giving. But Paul lays down the principle that people who give generously out of love for the Lord and His church grow and mature in their faith because they don't count the cost.

Another characteristic peculiar to these Macedonian Christians was that they didn't have to be pressured into giving. On the contrary, Paul says they were *"freely willing, imploring us with much urgency that we would receive the gift"* (vv. 3–4). They evidently felt an inner pressure and concern which compelled their giving. They were not reluctant but joyful in their stewardship.

However, the pattern in most churches is quite different. Our mood is well illustrated by a story I heard many years ago. The setting was at a carnival—the kind that frequented small towns in much of rural Ameria.

Each carnival had its strong man, but the one that came to this little town in Oklahoma featured the "strongest man in the world." To demonstrate the power of his grip the barker would cut a lemon in half and give it to the strong man. With his left hand he would squeeze every drop of moisture out of it. The barker would then work the crowd to sell tickets for the rest of the performance inside the tent. And as an additional come-on, he said the carnival would pay anyone from the audience twenty-five dollars for every drop of juice that person could squeeze from the lemon. This attention-getter attracted the usual run of local talent, but none of them was successful. Then a small nondescript man asked if he might try. Using only his thumb and two fingers of one hand he squeezed three additional drops of juice from the lemon half.

As the amazed carnival barker paid him his seventy-five dollars, he asked for the secret to his ability. He replied, "I've been the treasurer in our church for twenty-five years, and compared to trying to squeeze money out of reluctant members for the budget, that lemon was easy." But meeting a church budget that way only produces guilt, anxiety, and resentment. Joy and Christian growth come to those who assume the responsibility for the Lord's work gladly.

And finally, Paul tells us that joyful giving flows from the gift of self. His statement that they *"first gave themselves to the Lord, and then to us by the will of God"* (v. 5) gives us the clue to their generosity. There is a sense in which the only thing I can really give to God is myself, and this is the gift that needs to come first. Those who give their money but not their hearts have made a lesser gift. As I was sitting in an executive suite high above the city visiting with a very successful businessman, he tried to impress me with his religion by saying, "Reverend, every week I have my secretary mail a check to my church."

This comment reminded me of the missionary who was witnessing to the chief of a very primitive tribe. In response the chief tried to impress the missionary with gifts of horses, blankets, and jewelry. But the missionary said, "My God does not want the chief's horses or blankets or jewelry. My God wants the chief himself." Then the chief smiled and said, "You have very wise God, for when I give Him myself He also gets horses and blankets and jewelry." He showed far more wisdom than my wealthy businessman friend.

MANAGING WELL WHAT IS GIVEN

16 But thanks be to God who put the same earnest care for you into the heart of Titus.

17 For he not only accepted the exhortation, but being more diligent, he went to you of his own accord.

18 And we have sent with him the brother whose praise is in the gospel throughout all the churches,

19 and not only that, but who was also chosen by the churches to travel with us with this gift, which is administered by us to the glory of the Lord Himself and to show your ready mind,

20 avoiding this: that anyone should blame us in this lavish gift which is administered by us—

21 providing honorable things, not only in the sight of the Lord, but also in the sight of men.

22 And we have sent with them our brother whom we have often proved diligent in many things, but now much more diligent, because of the great confidence which we have in you.

23 If anyone inquires about Titus, he is my partner and fellow worker concerning you. Or if our brethren are inquired about, they are messengers of the churches, the glory of Christ.

24 Therefore show to them, and before the churches, the proof of your love and of our boasting on your behalf.

2 Cor. 8:16–24

While these verses may seem like "housekeeping" details, they give us insight into the comprehensive way in which Paul dealt with an issue. And they also model for us the way we should handle money that has been given for the work of the Lord.

One semester while I was in graduate school, I was asked to teach a class in missions. A part of our discussion had to do with the way some of the sending agencies handled the money that had been entrusted to them. We discovered that some of these agencies refused to give any details at all. Then we learned that some of them held out for overhead as much as 60 percent of all they received. Fortunately, the majority of the agencies we studied were responsible and tried in every way possible to keep expenses down so they could send more money for missionary purposes.

We see in these verses that Paul was very wise in insisting that the funds donated be handled so as to avoid criticism of any kind. He asked the church to specify certain persons to be responsible for the money and to deliver it in person to Jerusalem. They chose Titus and two other trusted men.

When Dr. Billy Graham was a young evangelist, his work was financed entirely by a love offering received at the end of the crusade. From this offering he had to take care of his living expenses and those of his team members. As the costs of the crusades grew and the offerings got larger, Dr. Graham became concerned that the way in which the money was handled would become a source of criticism. So, upon the advice of an older mininster, he formed a board of Christian businessmen to handle all the money. Then everyone in the crusade organization was put on salary and the organization's books and Dr. Graham's personal finances were audited and the results made public each year. As a result of his sensitivity and care, his operation has been a model of integrity through the years.

Finally, one of the reasons Paul was able to be so enthusiastic and so convincing about the offering was that he was convinced of its importance. But he was also convinced that their giving was essential to spiritual growth. He made no apologies for asking them to help. I have a friend who is very successful and generous in his own giving. But he also is known for being quite a crusader when it comes to getting other people to give. Once at lunch I teased him about it, and he replied, "It's true that I really work at encouraging my clients and friends to learn that giving can be more fulfilling than getting. But the thing that encourages me is that I have never gotten a single person involved in giving who has not eventually thanked me for introducing him to a new and enjoyable dimension of life."

I was reared in the kind of small rural church where the Sunday school superintendent would say every Sunday, "We're going to take the offering, so all of you boys and girls get out your pennies." I heard that Sunday after Sunday, so when I went to college, I was taken by surprise when the pastor insisted on what he called sacrificial giving. He stressed the importance of tithing, not as a legalistic requirement but in response to God's love as revealed in Christ. He insisted that the real fun in giving was in the "above and beyond" offering.

Now, this went contrary to my "pennies" idea, especially since I was a "hungry student" trying to work my way through school. But slowly my pastor friend got through to me, and I received the gift of "a willing mind" (v. 12) and took the first step toward a lifetime of giving which has been all joy.

CHAPTER NINE

Seeing the Spiritual in the Secular

2 Corinthians 9:1–15

1 Now concerning the ministering to the saints, it is superfluous for me to write to you;

2 for I know your willingness, about which I boast of you to the Macedonians, that Achaia was ready a year ago; and your zeal has stirred up the majority.

3 Yet I have sent the brethren, lest our boasting of you should be in vain in this respect, that, as I said, you may be ready;

4 lest if some Macedonians come with me and find you unprepared, we (not to mention you!) should be ashamed of this confident boasting.

5 Therefore I thought it necessary to exhort the brethren to go to you ahead of time, and prepare your bountiful gift beforehand, which you had previously promised, that it may be ready as a matter of generosity and not as a grudging obligation.

6 But this I say: He who sows sparingly will also reap sparingly, and he who sows bountifully will also reap bountifully.

7 So let each one give as he purposes in his heart, not grudgingly or of necessity; for God loves a cheerful giver.

8 And God is able to make all grace abound toward you, that you, always having all sufficiency in all things, have an abundance for every good work.

9 As it is written:

"He has dispersed abroad;
He has given to the poor;
His righteousness remains forever."

10 Now may He who supplies seed to the sower,

and bread for food, supply and multiply the seed you
have sown and increase the fruits of your
righteousness,

11 while you are enriched in everything for all
liberality, which causes thanksgiving through us to
God.

12 For the administration of this service not only
supplies the needs of the saints, but also is abounding
through many thanksgivings to God,

13 while, through the proof of this ministry, they
glorify God for the obedience of your confession to
the gospel of Christ, and for your liberal sharing with
them and all men,

14 and by their prayer for you, who long for you
because of the exceeding grace of God in you.

15 Thanks be to God for His indescribable gift!

2 Cor. 9:1–15

Anyone who has ever tried to involve other Christians in giving
will be able to identify with everything Paul wrote in this chapter.
There are those who out of naïveté and inexperience actually believe
that all one has to do to raise money for a spiritual cause is to let
the need be known to God's people.

Several years ago I was asked to be the lead pastor in an effort
among the members of churches of our denomination to help raise
money to build one of the buildings for our retreat center. The idea
of the center was supported by all of the churches, and they were
equally excited about using the facility once it was completed.

But in spite of that early excitement, less than twelve of the sixty
churches assigned to me got involved at all. As I sat with the conference center staff and went over the records, I remembered a comment
by Dr. Charles Allen: "If you want to plumb the heights and the
depths of the Christian experience, all you have to do is read the
pledge cards." That Paul was able to overcome so many obstacles
to giving is a testimony to his amazing insight into the human situation and to his wise leadership.

The first verses of this chapter have a very human touch that shows
Paul's understanding of how people think. Because he bragged on
the Macedonians to the Corinthians and on the Corinthians to the
Macedonians, some have accused Paul of trying to manipulate them.

Such criticism seems to overlook the fact that when the offering was first mentioned, the Corinthians had expressed enthusiasm and Paul had shared their feelings with the Macedonian churches. Paul, ever the master-psychologist, had in this case used the enthusiasm and success of one group of Christians to inspire others. Long before Dr. Norman Vincent Peale wrote *The Power of Positive Thinking,* the Apostle used similar techniques to inspire and motivate the young and struggling churches.

Now and then critics of Paul express the idea that he applied pressure by sending advance people on ahead of his visits to encourage more liberal giving. But I don't see anything devious in Paul's method at all. He knew that if the Christians were not prepared to participate it would be embarrassing to them. Paul was a thoughtful master at organization. He knew that the affairs of the church, including the taking of a missionary offering for Jerusalem's needy Christians, needed to be done decently and in order. And he also wanted these young Christians to know that there wasn't anything unspiritual about raising money for God's cause.

After Paul's introductory comments, he then reminds them that there is a spiritual law at work in giving, *"He who sows sparingly will also reap sparingly, and he who sows bountifully will also reap bountifully"* (v. 6). That familiar farm illustration states both the positive and the negative of the same idea. The negative point emphasizes the truth that when a person makes it a habit to give only a little, he or she can expect very little in the way of blessings. On the other hand, though, the personal rewards are great for those who habitually give generously. Paul is applying the "law of the harvest" to the sharing and giving of our material resources.

It is a mistake, I believe, for us to feel that it is unworthy of the Christian to be interested in rewards. While the anticipation of a reward or the fear of loss may not be the highest motivation for doing or not doing something, it is a part of life. It is a fact that those who develop the habit of generosity are blessed of God. But it is a mistake to think of these rewards or blessings as always being material.

In my ministry as a pastor I have known many generous givers and many who were nongivers, and I can bear witness to the truth of Paul's statement. A person who continues to be preoccupied with accumulating material things and does not develop a spirit of generosity always falls short of achieving his or her full potential. In contrast, equally successful people who are generous seem to enjoy a higher quality of life.

Paul then goes on to make an important point in verse 7 when he asks each person to give as *"he purposes in his heart."* This certainly implies that he believes giving comes from making a choice—a purposeful and deliberate decision.

For many years before his death I had a close association with Lowell Berry, who was an active layman in a church in California. Mr. Berry had become wealthy in the commercial fertilizer business and owned plants in several western states. His foundation was the primary funding agency for the Billy Graham Schools of Evangelism. Because of my leadership role in these schools, we were together often.

One evening over dinner I asked him how he got started giving. To my amazement I discovered that when he was twelve years old his pastor had taught him that he ought to give a definite portion of anything he earned to the Lord. After talking it over with his mother and praying about it himself, he committed himself to doing what he believed was right. Lowell smiled as he said, "At the time I decided to give God a portion of all I earned, I didn't earn a thing. It wasn't until I finished college that I earned any money." Our conversation was a reminder to me that it's the decision and not the dollar that creates the giver.

Paul next reminded his readers that it is God who gives us our resources, and it is God who creates the grace of giving in us. In verses 8–10 he gives us a reassuring word about the future. He must have anticipated that someone might argue, "If I give to help the impoverished Christians all it's going to do is create one more impoverished Christian in Corinth." Paul's answer is simply that the God who gave you what you have right now is still *"able to make all grace abound toward you"* (v. 8). Paul then reaches back and picks up on the theme of sowing and reaping, and in what sounds like both a prayer and a blessing, he writes, *"May He who supplies seed to the sower, and bread for food, supply and multiply the seed you have sown and increase the fruits of your righteousness"* (v. 10). Paul is reminding the Corinthians about the provident nature of God very much in the spirit of Jesus who in the Sermon on the Mount told His followers not to be anxious about food or clothing or shelter because "your heavenly Father knows that you need all these things" (Matt. 6:32).

Paul assures his readers here that God would provide them with enough not only to meet their own needs, but to also help others. The *New English Bible's* translation of 2 Corinthians 9:8 reads, "Thus you will have ample means in yourselves to meet each and every situation, with enough to spare for every good cause." The same translation of verse 10 reads, "And you will always be rich enough to be generous." When people insist they are not able to give generously to the cause of Christ, they are contradicting these statements from Scripture.

The first time I read this passage I wondered how rich a person had to be before he or she could be generous. Then I remembered that Paul obviously wasn't talking about generosity as a grace that was developed only after one became financially well-off. It is also something even poor people can experience.

Paul concludes the chapter and ends his discussion of the offering by reminding his readers, and us, that giving has spiritual results. When I was on the staff of my denomination's mission board, I went to a meeting where they were discussing the various budget needs of the board that could be used to motivate church members to give. When the cost for utilities for the various mission facilities was mentioned, a member of the committee stood and said, "I don't think we should emphasize that in our story. No one wants to give money to pay the light bill. They want to do something spiritually."

I'm sure that there were people in Corinth who wondered what was so spiritual about raising money for an offering to buy food for hungry people. But in answer to this question, Paul lists several results of giving that have great spiritual consequences. God is glorified; there are *"many thanksgivings to God"* (v. 12); it proves their love of God (v. 13); the Christians in Jerusalem began to pray for the gentile churches (v. 14). This simply means that what looked like a money-raising project was in reality a kingdom-building event.

One of the things most needed in giving is the ability to look beyond the gift to what God will do with it. Fran was a single woman with a job that didn't pay much, but giving to the church was a part of her commitment even though she had to sacrifice in order to do it. When she read in the church bulletin about an appeal for scholarships to send young people to the church camp for a week, she decided to give an additional seventy-five dollars. Knowing the sacrifice involved in this gift, I asked what made her decide to do it. "Pastor," she replied, "two of the most important decisions I have made in my life about God were made at a youth camp like this one. The thought that through my small gift God might get the attention of one of these bright young people and change their lives was more than I could resist." Giving blesses those who give, those who receive, and the Kingdom of God.

CHAPTER TEN

How to Deal with Critics

2 Corinthians 10:1–18

As a teacher in the classroom, I soon discovered that there was often a difference between what my students thought and what they thought they thought. Consequently, for me one of the real challenges of teaching was to get them to see clearly their real feelings and thoughts.

But this need is not peculiar to students. All of us tend to deceive ourselves on certain issues or subjects. For instance, the average church member thinks that it is always wrong for a person to boast of spiritual achievements, that it is un-Christian to say bad things about your critics, and that Christians who live good lives will have no need of defending themselves. It is quite likely, though, that if these same people were asked to list the outstanding Christians in the New Testament, they would place the Apostle Paul either at the top of the list or near the top. But I wonder what they would think if they were to re-read carefully these concluding four chapters of 2 Corinthians. Here we see Paul defending his character and ministry, exposing and threatening his critics for what they are, boasting of both his credentials and accomplishments, and maintaining his authority as the founder of the Corinthian church.

There are many things about these four chapters that have caused serious Bible scholars to feel they were not originally a part of 2 Corinthians. Instead they believe these chapters are the "severe letter" which Paul referred to in 2 Corinthians 7:8. Their inspiration or authority isn't questioned—only the order. The several different theories about the sequence of Paul's visits and letters to the church at Corinth are discussed in the Introduction to 2 Corinthians in this volume. Whatever the sequence, they were preserved by the church in the form we now have them, and there is no question on the part of anyone as to the situation they addressed and their overall meaning.

There are some Bible students who wonder if these chapters have any real relevance for contemporary Christians other than to provide one or two good texts for sermons on themes such as those often preached on the "thorn in the flesh" (2 Cor. 12:7). But while there is much in these chapters which concern a very specific first-century situation, the way in which Paul responds to his critics gives us some helpful guidelines for our own behavior in similar situations.

AUTHORITY THAT IS REAL

1 Now I, Paul, myself am pleading with you by the meekness and gentleness of Christ—who in presence am lowly among you, but being absent am bold toward you.

2 But I beg you that when I am present I may not be bold with that confidence by which I intend to be bold against some, who think of us as if we walked according to the flesh.

3 For though we walk in the flesh, we do not war according to the flesh.

4 For the weapons of our warfare are not carnal but mighty in God for pulling down strongholds,

5 casting down arguments and every high thing that exalts itself against the knowledge of God, bringing every thought into captivity to the obedience of Christ,

6 and being ready to punish all disobedience when your obedience is fulfilled.

7 Do you look at things according to the outward appearance? If anyone is convinced in himself that he is Christ's, let him consider this in himself, that just as he is Christ's, even so we are Christ's.

8 For even if I should boast somewhat more about our authority, which the Lord gave us for edification and not for your destruction, I shall not be ashamed—

9 lest I seem to terrify you by letters.

10 "For his letters," they say, "are weighty and

powerful, but his bodily presence is weak, and his speech contemptible."

11 Let such a person consider this, that what we are in word by letters when we are absent, such we will also be in deed when we are present.

2 Cor. 10:1–11

As I read these words, I am appalled at the attacks that were apparently leveled at Paul and the pain he must have felt. Because this is a letter, we have only Paul's answer to his critics and are forced to reconstruct from his responses the exact nature of the criticism. A close look at all four chapters seems to reveal the extent and the viciousness of what was being said about him by a very aggressive minority in the church at Corinth. Evidently, they said: (1) that Paul was only brave when he was writing letters but cowardly in face-to-face situations (10:1, 9–10); (2) that his refusal to accept support was a sign that he was inferior (12:13–16); (3) that he did not have the same kind of relationship to Christ that they had (10:7). In addition, (4) they made fun of his appearance and of his speaking ability (11:6); and (5) they said that his boasting was unbecoming of an apostle (10:8). While these five charges do not exhaust the list, we can see from them what Paul was dealing with. His answers are spread out over the last four chapters of the letter.

There are some Bible students who wonder why Paul didn't let his life speak for itself and just ignore his critics. This thought reminds me of an incident in my early college days. A leading Christian composer visited the church I was attending, and during a question-and-answer period someone asked him how he handled criticism of his work. He replied with a condescending air, "A true gentleman never needs to defend himself."

That sounded very "gentlemanly" at the time, but it doesn't seem to follow the pattern Paul gives us here. This is not to say that we should take all criticism seriously. After all, a person who takes every criticism personally and lets responding to the critic become the main agenda of his or her life will soon be controlled by his critics. Although it is not really possible for any person to be totally objective about himself, I don't think that Paul was motivated in his answer by the fact that the criticisms were against him personally. He was far too tough, too secure in his faith, and too preoccupied with the work of sharing Christ to feel the need to stop and defend his own reputation if that was all that was at stake. Instead, I believe, the only possible thing that would prompt such a response from Paul was his feeling that the very future of the church at Corinth hung in the balance. To leave the attack upon himself and his authority unanswered would allow the troublesome but persistent minority to undo all the good that had been done in the church.

Criticism should always be handled in the Spirit of Christ. And because He had been gentle and patient with them they accused Him of being weak. Paul, in turn, confessed to meekness and gentleness, but he claimed it was not the sign of a weak character but of the *"meekness and gentleness of Christ"* (v. 1).

Our picture of meekness makes it more of a vice than a virtue. As Christ used it in the Sermon on the Mount (Matt. 5:5), and as Paul used it here, it is descriptive of controlled anger. I recall a time when we had a beautiful riding horse named Gus. He was large and strong and spirited, but I could put a bridle on him and a small child could control him. Gus was the epitome of an animal under control, but there were times when it was obvious he was responding under duress.

Being meek doesn't imply that we never feel impatience or anger but rather that those feelings are controlled. This attitude of Paul is in stark contrast to the bitterness of the attacks of his critics.

Some restraint needs to be shown in dealing with critics and criticism. Paul told the church that he was not lacking in either spiritual authority or personal strength and that if necessary he would come and show what he could do by punishing *"all disobedience"* (v. 6). The whole picture of Christ when He was being abused is a picture of restraint; after all, he had at his command all the resources of heaven.

I visited one time with a pastor friend who had gone to a great church in which there was an aggressive minority of young adults who challenged his leadership at every turn. It seemed that every meeting of any kind was soured by their complaining and critical spirit. At the very time my friend was wanting to use his energies to lead the church out in evangelism and missions, he was having to expend an inordinate amount of his energies dealing with this recalcitrant element in the church. Sensing the toll it was taking on his spirit and knowing that the great majority of the members didn't agree with the critical group, I asked, "Why don't you use the support you have to remove them all from places of leadership?" He confirmed the fact that he had the power and support to do what I suggested, but he said, "Quite frankly, I think that power ought to be used as a last resort."

BOASTING IN THE LORD

12 For we dare not class ourselves or compare ourselves with those who commend themselves. But they, measuring themselves by themselves, and comparing themselves among themselves, are not wise.

13 We, however, will not boast beyond measure, but within the limits of the sphere which God appointed us—a sphere which especially includes you.

14 For we are not extending ourselves beyond our sphere (thus not reaching you), for it was to you that we came with the gospel of Christ;

15 not boasting of things beyond measure, that is, in other men's labors, but having hope, that as your faith is increased, we shall be greatly enlarged by you in our sphere,

16 to preach the gospel in the regions beyond you, and not to boast in another man's sphere of accomplishment.

17 But *"He who glories, let him glory in the Lord."*

18 For not he who commends himself is approved, but whom the Lord commends.

2 Cor. 10:12–18

Paul's critics came to the church with exaggerated claims for themselves, and since quite a few people were impressed, Paul felt it necessary to expose what was behind their boasting. He accused them of inventing their own criteria for success; they were *"measuring themselves by themselves, and comparing themselves among themselves"* (v. 12). To invent and use a private standard has the effect of having no standard at all. One of the reasons that the work of God is so difficult to evaluate is that it's hard to measure by worldly standards. There is no way we can measure the impact of prayer or the results of a sermon or track inner spiritual growth. It is not easy to know exactly what is being accomplished by faithful Christians who live lives of integrity before their peers and their neighbors. Waiting to judge the impact of teaching the Scripture on the lives of little children seems to take too much patience.

Spiritual work really requires spiritual measurement. But there is always the temptation for us to invent ways of measuring ourselves that focus mainly on the externals—those things which can be seen, measured, and reported. While the amount of offering in the plate, the number present at Bible study, or the numerical growth rate of the church does say something, however, it doesn't say everything. Today's church needs to be very careful with its fascination with standards of success that impress the secular world so that it won't find itself using self-manufactured standards for measuring itself rather than God's measurement.

Paul suggested a standard for boasting that is still applicable for us today: *"He who glories, let him glory in the Lord"* (v. 17). Many of the translations translate the phrase as "let him boast in the Lord." Here Paul is introducing a more valid instrument of measurement. He refuses to use the man-made measuring sticks but insists that boasting not be of mere human accomplishments. The prophet Jeremiah reminded Israel:

> "Let not the wise man
>   glory in his wisdom,
> Let not the mighty man
>   glory in his might,
> Nor let the rich man
>   glory in his riches;
> But let him who glories glory in this,
> That he understands and knows Me,
> That I am the Lord, . . .
> For in these I delight" says the Lord.
> *Jer. 9:23–24*

I don't think that Paul wrote "glory in the Lord" as a spiritual coverup for bragging on ourselves. I think that he actually felt, even when he was forced to speak of his life from the perspective of worldly standards, that the only valid basis for boasting was in what God had done.

Cliff Barrows is one of the best-known musicians in the Christian world, having led great crusade choirs all over the world for more than a third of a century. I have come to know him very well through the years and am constantly amazed at both his ability and his spirit. Through his many years of close association with Dr. Billy Graham in the work of evangelism, in addition to directing the music for the crusades he has produced both the radio and television programs and has carried countless other leadership roles within the team and the association.

Cliff is an excellent speaker, and when I was leading the schools of evangelism for Dr. Graham I made every effort to get him to speak at each of them. The first time he spoke I discovered by his reaction to my introduction a very interesting thing about how he viewed his work. My usual routine was to tell something about what each speaker had done that would be interesting to the audience. Since most of them knew Cliff only as a music director, I took a moment to tell of his other activities and to comment on his great value to the team and its ministry. My introduction so embarrassed him that he had a hard time getting started with his talk. Afterwards I apologized and asked what I had done wrong. He said, "Kenneth, I appreciate your inviting me to speak and I know that you were sincere in your remarks, but it just makes me uncomfortable when someone tries to give me credit for things that God has done." That is boasting in the Lord.

This is not the end of Paul's discussion of his basis for boasting; it continues through chapters 11 and 12. To the casual reader of Scripture, what he writes seems to have a lot of repetition, but a more careful study will reveal that though the theme does not change each time Paul discusses his apostolic authority, he always introduces some new material that contributes to the total.

CHAPTER ELEVEN

The High Cost of Caring

2 Corinthians 11:1–33

There is a part of Paul's experience with the church in Corinth with which every Christian leader can identify. Each of us at some time or another has gotten the word from someone who didn't think we were doing a good job. While it's a very common experience, it is never pleasant. And, to be very honest, it is easy to become so preoccupied with the criticisms of one or two persons that we tend to forget those who appreciate and follow our leadership.

I recall once going to a meeting of the church's long-range study committee. I had attended expecting that I would make a statement about the importance of dreaming a new dream for the church. It was a splendid committee made up primarily of individuals I knew and respected, and I was looking forward to spending time with them. But before I could do more than greet the committee and thank them for the invitation, one of the members of the group whose main focus was on the problems the church must face began to criticize my leadership of the church. He felt that I didn't spend enough time at the church and that my long-range commitment to the church was not clear. He suggested that many of the problems the church faced were due to my failure to give adequate support and encouragement to the staff. Suddenly, in a setting where I had planned to "dream dreams," I found myself very defensive and feeling angry and embarrassed and a bit confused.

But when I read these chapters in which Paul is defending his ministry, I have to admit that my situation was really different from his. The man who gave me the third degree neither disliked me as a person, nor did he question my character, nor was there even the hint of wanting to change the overall direction of the church. Paul was constantly plagued in every church, with individuals who did not agree with him, and he ignored most of them and mentioned very few. But in this case he felt that as a result of the influence of the "false apostles," the church in Corinth was in danger of changing its fundamental beliefs, and it was this fear that motivated him. In this chapter he will produce credentials that his opponents can't match. And, as is true throughout this whole section, he is embarrassed at having been forced to defend his ministry and to appear to be boasting of human accomplishments.

THE PARENTING CONCERN

1 O that you would bear with me in a little folly— and indeed you do bear with me.

2 For I am jealous for you with godly jealousy. For I have betrothed you to one husband, that I may present you as a chaste virgin to Christ.

3 But I fear, lest somehow, as the serpent deceived Eve by his craftiness, so your minds may be corrupted from the simplicity that is in Christ.

4 For if he who comes preaches another Jesus whom we have not preached, or if you receive a different spirit which you have not received, or a different gospel which you have not accepted, you may well put up with it.

5 For I consider that I am not at all inferior to the most eminent apostles.

6 Even though I am untrained in speech, yet I am not in knowledge. But we have been thoroughly made manifest among you in all things.

7 Did I commit sin in abasing myself that you might be exalted, because I preached the gospel of God to you free of charge?

8 I robbed other churches, taking wages from them to minister to you.

9 And when I was present with you, and in need, I was a burden to no one, for what was lacking to me the brethren who came from Macedonia supplied. And in everything I kept myself from being burdensome to you, and so I will keep myself.

10 As the truth of Christ is in me, no one shall stop me from this boasting in the regions of Achaia.

11 Why? Because I do not love you? God knows!

12 But what I do, I will also continue to do, that I may cut off the opportunity from those who desire an opportunity to be regarded just as we are in the things of which they boast.

13 For such are false apostles, deceitful workers, transforming themselves into apostles of Christ.

14 And no wonder! For Satan himself transforms himself into an angel of light.

15 Therefore it is no great thing if his ministers also transform themselves into ministers of righteousness, whose end will be according to their works.

16 I say again, let no one think me a fool. If otherwise, at least receive me as a fool, that I also may boast a little.

17 What I speak, I speak not according to the Lord, but as it were, foolishly, in this confidence of boasting.

18 Seeing that many boast according to the flesh, I also will boast.

19 For you put up with fools gladly, since you yourselves are wise!

20 For you put up with it if one brings you into bondage, if one devours you, if one takes from you, if one exalts himself, if one strikes you on the face.

21 To our shame, I say that we were too weak for that! But in whatever anyone is bold—I speak foolishly—I am bold also.

2 Cor. 11:1–21

It's a little easier to understand the intensity of Paul's feelings for the Corinthian church from the family metaphors he uses in this chapter. His *"I am jealous for you with a godly jealousy"* (v. 2) picks up an analogy that Hosea used in the Old Testament and reminds his readers that their faithfulness to Christ needs to be like that of a husband and wife to each other. But the really strong phrase he uses is his claim, *"I have betrothed you to one husband, that I may present you as a chaste virgin to Christ"* (v. 2).

The first time I read these words in 11:2 the image came to my mind of the "matchmaker" or the marriage broker, because there is a sense in which evangelism is bringing people together with God. Actually, though, it is the picture of the father of the bride who has pledged her in marriage and is anxious that she remain chaste for her future husband. One of Paul's strongest claims to authority over the church—a claim that could not be made by his detractors—was that he had "fathered" the church.

Only once in all the years of my ministry has it been my privilege to be the pastoral leader in the "birthing" of a new church. I was a college student in New Mexico when the church that I attended decided to start a mission in one of the new subdivisions that were being built to provide homes for veterans returning from military service. This was made possible by a member's gift of two lots in the subdivision and a bequest of money designated to be used to begin a new church, and the church's mission committee asked me to be the pastor.

I was single, twenty-one, a junior in the university, and my only means of transportation was a bicycle. Except for the fact that I did not have to raise money to buy the land and build a building, it was a "start from scratch" situation. In the five months it took to plan and build the first small unit I personally visited every family in the entire subdivision. Among the prospects I found enough Christians with experience that I was able to enlist the workers for the Sunday school. I also made the initial contact with a large number of persons who later became Christians and developed into leaders in the church. I watched its birth and its growth, and after several years it was with a real sense of loss that I resigned in order to attend the seminary. On the twenty-fifth anniversary of the church I was invited back as one of the speakers. Though there had been a number of pastors after me who had given excellent leadership, I can still remember having the feeling that my relationship to the church was in a way different because I had participated in the "birthing" process.

Paul was not too subtle in comparing his role in the church with that of his critics. While the image of his role of the father of the bride was fresh on their minds, he suggested that his critics were like the tempter in the Garden of Eden. His great fear was that *"as the serpent deceived Eve by his craftiness, so your minds may be corrupted from the simplicity that is in Christ"* (v. 3).

Then to make sure that there is no misunderstanding of what he is suggesting later in this same chapter, Paul calls his critics false prophets and deceitful workers, comparing them to Satan who corrupted the human race by *"transforming himself into an angel of light"* (v. 14). Paul's rationale for this conclusion was that while they were portraying themselves as "super Christians" they were introducing a different Jesus, a different gospel, and a different spirit into the fellowship (v. 4).

Every generation must deal with its own "false prophets," those who come to the historic church with their own version of Christianity. And what is so confusing to many sincere church members is that propagators of a false gospel can sound so spiritual and so sure of themselves that without even being aware of what's happening they are taken in. A gospel of love and forgiveness and freedom can so subtly be replaced with a gospel of fear and suspicion and guilt and conformity. Instead of being prized and loved and ministered to under this different gospel, the people can be manipulated to meet the ego needs of the leader. What I have described can take place in any church where great care is not taken to preserve the pure gospel of Christ.

After once again defending the fact that he supported himself while he was at Corinth (vv. 7–12), Paul chides the gullibility of some of the Corinthians: *"For you put up with it if one brings you into bondage, if one devours you, if one takes from you, if one exalts himself, if one strikes you on the face"* (v. 20). It's easy to feel Paul's sense of hurt that people whom he had introduced to Christ and whom he had begun to nurture in their faith would so uncritically be taken in by so different an approach. One senses the sarcasm as Paul suggests that he was amazed that the people who couldn't stand him would put up with what they did. With time to reflect upon it and to see the situation duplicated many times, I feel that what Paul was really up against was a kind of man-centered worldliness masquerading as spiritual religion. It will always be possible to get a following if the leader will make all the decisions, thus relieving the members of the responsibility to study, think, or seek God's will; if the leader will make heavy materialistic demands that create a sense of sacrifice; and if the leader beats on the people, at least in a theological sense, creating one big guilt trip. And when I see it happening, I feel the way Paul did about what was happening in Corinth—it is another Jesus, another gospel, and another spirit.

Suffering for the Cause

22 Are they Hebrews? So am I. Are they Israelites? So am I. Are they the seed of Abraham? So am I.

23 Are they ministers of Christ?—I speak as a fool—I am more: in labors more abundant, in stripes above measure, in prisons more frequently, in deaths often.

24 From the Jews five times I received forty stripes minus one.

25 Three times I was beaten with rods; once I was stoned; three times I was shipwrecked, a night and a day I have been in the deep;

26 in journeys often, in perils of waters, in perils of robbers, in perils of my own countrymen, in perils of the Gentiles, in perils in the city, in perils in the wilderness, in perils in the sea, in perils among false brethren;

27 in weariness and toil, in sleeplessness often, in hunger and thirst, in fastings often, in cold and nakedness—

28 besides the other things, what comes upon me daily: my deep concern for all the churches.

29 Who is weak, and I am not weak? Who is made to stumble, and I do not burn with indignation?

30 If I must boast, I will boast in the things which concern my infirmity.

31 The God and Father of our Lord Jesus Christ, who is blessed forever, knows that I am not lying.

32 In Damascus the governor, under Aretas the king, was guarding the city of the Damascenes with a garrison, desiring to apprehend me;

33 but I was let down in a basket through a window in the wall, and escaped from his hands.

2 Cor. 11:22–33

In a move that he confesses makes him feel *"as a fool"* (v. 23), Paul claims that his suffering in behalf of Christ should put him in a totally different category of apostle from that of those who oppose him. He wrote to the Galatians: "Let no one trouble me, for I bear in my body the marks of the Lord Jesus" (Gal. 6:17). As one reads through Paul's account he is immediately aware of the fact that there

283

is information here in 2 Corinthians that is not recorded by Luke in Acts. Had Paul's credentials not been questioned, he probably would never have shared what he wrote here. He was like a doctor who never calls attention to his credentials until someone falsely accuses him of not having either the training, experience, or expertise required in his field. The doctor would then prepare a statement telling every school from which he graduated, every internship served, every seminar attended, every learned article printed, every association participated in, every honor bestowed, every lecture given, and an exhaustive account of all his experience. To a degree this is what Paul did in this passage.

But there was also a sense in which Paul felt that what he had been willing to suffer in behalf of Christ had earned him a right to be heard which those who had not suffered could not claim. I have noticed that I tend to pay closer attention to those who have paid dearly for their faith in Christ. When I was a young professor I met Clarence Jordan, known most widely for his Cotton Patch versions of portions of the New Testament, but whose main ministry in life as a believer in Jesus Christ was to challenge the immorality of a segregated society by establishing the integrated Koinonia Farm near the town of Americus, Georgia. Years before I met him I heard of his work both from those who admired him and those who claimed that he was "nothing but a communist." When my wife and I were visiting her parents, my father-in-law told how many stores had stopped selling supplies to the farm because of the threats of violence against the employees, and that this fear of bombings and other forms of violence had made it necessary for the farm to buy nearly all of its basic supplies somewhere else.

So, when Clarence Jordan came to the seminary campus to speak I went to hear him. I must confess that the things he said carried extra weight with me because I knew of some of the suffering he had borne because of acting upon his understanding of God's will for his life.

There is a phrase in Paul's litany of suffering, written almost as an afterthought, that speaks to all who have known the responsibility for the spiritual life of a congregation. He seems to have been listing the things that had happened to him as they came to his mind with no particular order, when suddenly he momentarily interrupts his train of thought: *"besides the other things, what comes upon me daily [is] my deep concern for all the churches"* (v. 28). I know how very much energy, love, care, prayer, work, worry, study, waiting, meeting, and speaking is involved in the care of one congregation. And Paul had upon him all the churches. This one verse describes the largest burden he carried. If we multiply the cost of caring for the Corinthians as he did by the number of congregations for which he cared, then his statement about the "care of the churches" is a classic understatement.

In chapter 12 Paul concludes his defense of his apostolic authority. This is the chapter in which he opens his heart and tells of a mystical experience (vv. 1–6), of his thorn in the flesh (vv. 7–10), and of his plan to come to the Corinthians for a third time (vv. 14–21). While it continues a now-familiar theme, it does introduce new and helpful material.

CHAPTER TWELVE

The Basis for Glorying

2 Corinthians 12:1–21

The first pastor I recall as a child had a habit of coming to a stopping place in his sermon and then, instead of stopping, he would go on for a few more minutes with a review of everything he had already said. One day in the Sunday school class a boy complained about his irritating habit. Our teacher, Mrs. Mason, replied, "It's true that he goes back and repeats. But if you'll listen carefully, you'll find that almost every time he does that he will mention at least one new thing." I was never quite certain whether it worked out quite that way, but I gave more attention to the sermon each Sunday in an effort to find out.

In this chapter Paul returns to an earlier criticism related to his own support (12:1–17). Today we would call Paul a bi-vocational minister. To me his supporting himself is an example of something good that was twisted by his critics and made to look like something bad. He also mentions that he will be returning to Corinth for the third time and urges the Corinthians to prepare for his visit (v. 14). But the new in this chapter comes as he shares his vision of Paradise (vv. 1–6), as he tells of his "thorn in the flesh" (vv. 7–10), and as he expresses his deep anxiety about what he will find in the church when he does come to visit (12:20).

A VISION OF GOD

1 It is doubtless not profitable for me to boast. I will come to visions and revelations of the Lord:
2 I know a man in Christ who fourteen years ago— whether in the body I do not know, or whether out

of the body I do not know, God knows—such a one
was caught up to the third heaven.

3 And I know such a man—whether in the body
or out of the body I do not know, God knows—

4 how he was caught up into Paradise and heard
inexpressible words, which it is not lawful for a man
to utter.

5 Of such a one I will boast; yet of myself I will
not boast, except in my infirmities.

6 For though I might desire to boast, I will not
be a fool; for I will speak the truth. But I forbear,
lest anyone should think of me above what he sees
me to be or hears from me.

7 And lest I should be exalted above measure by
the abundance of the revelations, a thorn in the flesh
was given to me, a messenger of Satan to buffet me,
lest I be exalted above measure.

8 Concerning this thing I pleaded with the Lord
three times that it might depart from me.

9 And He said to me, "My grace is sufficient for
you, for My strength is made perfect in weakness."
Therefore most gladly I will rather boast in my
infirmities, that the power of Christ may rest upon
me.

10 Therefore I take pleasure in infirmities, in
reproaches, in needs, in persecutions, in distresses, for
Christ's sake. For when I am weak, then I am strong.

2 Cor. 12:1–10

Evidently certain false apostles claimed to have experienced visions
and revelations and had presented this fact to the Corinthian church
as proof that they were superior Christians. The idea of visions as
one of the primary ways in which God revealed Himself and His
word to people was prevalent both in Old Testament and New Testament times. And now Paul's critics were lifting up the importance
of such experiences as a means of discrediting him.

Even as Paul prepares to open up his heart and share a very private
and very personal experience, his reluctance was expressed: *"It is
doubtless not profitable for me to boast"* (v. 1). While God often uses our
sharing of the experiences we have had with Him to inspire others,
we must not become spiritual exhibitionists. We also take the risk

that what is very special and very spiritual to us will be treated by those who hear as something common.

When I started teaching evangelism in the seminary, I began to pray that God would give me a vision for the job. But I wasn't referring to the kind of special revelation such as the one that Isaiah received in the temple (Isa. 6). What I wanted was for the Spirit to help me to see the task through His eyes and from His perspective.

God began to answer my prayer in a very unusual way. For a period of several weeks every experience I had gave me a new vision of the importance of the task I had been called to do. I began seriously to wonder if I would be able to do the job. One day when I was especially aware of my own inadequacy and was asking God to help me as I was reading the Scripture, there came to me a wonderful sense of peace about my teaching. Somehow I knew that God was going to be with me and help me to do what needed to be done.

Almost a year went by and I was really enjoying teaching evangelism. One day, in a class that I felt especially close to, I decided to open my heart and to tell them of this experience through which God had given me reassurance. I had hardly finished when a hand shot up on the back row and a voice asked, "Will we be responsible for this on the final exam?" Before I could assure him that he wouldn't be asked about it on the test, another student asked in a complaining voice, "When will the grader get our term papers back to us?" I felt rebuffed by their insensitivity. It was a painful reminder to me that what is very special to one person may seem very ordinary to another.

I don't know what Paul's motive may have been, but he tells of his vision in the third person as though it had happened to someone else. It may be that it had been so long ago that it was hard to believe that it had really happened to him, or it may have been that the experience was so intense that he was reluctant to speak of it in first person. What everyone does agree on is that Paul is talking about himself. Paul was not sure whether what he saw was the result of his body's being transported to another place or whether God had shown him what He did through the processes of the mind. This is what he meant by *"whether in the body or out of the body I do not know, God knows"* (v. 3). The one thing Paul was sure of was that he had been in the very presence of God.

The origin of the term "Paradise" gives us a picture of a beautifully walled palace garden where, when the king wanted to confer a special honor, he would invite a subject to stroll with him. I think that those who try to draw a picture of heaven from Paul's description have missed the whole point. Paul was saying to those who were too impressed with his critics, "I have had some high moments with God, too," and had proceeded to tell them of one of those experiences.

God used many visions to enlarge Paul's ministry. "And a vision appeared to Paul in the night. A man of Macedonia stood and pleaded with him, saying, 'Come over to Macedonia and help us' " (Acts 16:9). Even while he was in Corinth founding the church, Paul was encouraged in a vision, "Now the Lord spoke to Paul in the night by a vision, 'Do not be afraid, but speak, and do not keep silent; for I am with you, and no one will attack you to hurt you; for I have many people in this city' " (Acts 18:9–10).

That Paul told of the *"thorn in the flesh"* (v. 7) immediately following his account of his vision of God is not accidental, because evidently he felt that the two experiences were related to each other. Paul seemed to believe that the "thorn" was given to him to keep him from being excessively proud of *"the abundance of the revelations"* he had received (v. 7). It wasn't necessary for him to explain what the "thorn" was because either the Corinthians already knew or he felt it was not essential to the point he was making.

Since Paul wrote these words, there has been a lot of speculation as to just what the "thorn in the flesh" was. Most Protestant interpreters tend to think of it as some physical problem such as epilepsy, malaria, tuberculosis, weak eyes, etc. Most Catholics, on the other hand, think it was mental or spiritual in nature—possibly a nagging doubt or a persistent temptation. Still others believe it was his constant exposure to nagging criticism or persecution. But one thing is sure—we don't really know.

Paul does clearly state that he gave himself to earnest and repeated prayer that the thorn might depart (12:8). Instead of removing the "thorn" God gave the reassurance of His grace and reminded Paul that His strength was *"made perfect in weakness"* (v. 9). Paul never came to feel that the thorn in itself was a good thing, believing rather that it was *"a messenger of Satan"* (v. 7). But he did come to that place in his life where he could see how God's grace could transform what was bad into something good in his life.

I think that this is the principle that Paul is stating in Romans

8:28 when he declares that "all things work together for good to those who love God, to those who are the called according to His purpose." He wasn't saying that everything that happened was good. Let's face it—lots of bad things happen to good people. And he wasn't saying that everything that happened was necessarily what God had purposefully willed to happen. But out of experience Paul learned that God could take our weaknesses and use them to demonstrate His power. Paul was affirming that there is nothing that can happen to one of God's children that, if we turn to Him with it, He cannot take us from where we are and begin working some good. God doesn't build a wall around us to isolate us from the risk of harm, but He does surround us with a grace that enables us to transform anything that happens to us.

Learning to Relate to People

11 I have become a fool in boasting; you have compelled me. For I ought to have been commended by you, for in nothing was I behind the most eminent apostles, though I am nothing.

12 Truly the signs of an apostle were accomplished among you with all perseverance, in signs and wonders and mighty deeds.

13 For what is it in which you were inferior to other churches, except that I myself was not burdensome to you? Forgive me this wrong!

14 Now for the third time I am ready to come to you. And I will not be burdensome to you; for I do not seek yours, but you. For the children ought not to lay up for the parents, but the parents for the children.

15 And I will very gladly spend and be spent for your souls; though the more abundantly I love you, the less I am loved.

16 But be that as it may, I did not burden you. Nevertheless, being crafty, I caught you with guile!

17 Did I take advantage of you by any of those whom I sent to you?

18 I urged Titus, and sent our brother with him.

Did Titus take advantage of you? Did we not walk
in the same spirit? Did we not walk in the same steps?
    19 Again, do you think that we excuse ourselves
to you? We speak before God in Christ. But we do
all things, beloved, for your edification.
    20 For I fear lest, when I come, I shall not find you
such as I wish, and that I shall be found by you such
as you do not wish; lest there be contentions,
jealousies, outbursts of wrath, selfish ambitions,
backbitings, whisperings, conceits, tumults;
    21 and lest, when I come again, my God will humble
me among you, and I shall mourn for many who have
sinned before and have not repented of the
uncleanness, fornication, and licentiousness which
they have practiced.
                                  2 Cor. 12:11–21

Almost the only new ground Paul covers here comes as he antici-
pates his third visit and begins to feel anxiety about what he may
find when he arrives. He is genuinely afraid that *"when I come, I shall
not find you such as I wish"* (v. 20), and then he lists eight possible
vices that he hopes not to find. Each of these has to do with personal
relationships, and they represent what will destroy a church. They
stand in stark contrast to the spirit that was characteristic of that
first church described in Acts 2:40–47. They represent a classic statement of the marks of an un-Christian church or of those styles of
relating that will destroy the fellowship of a church. Here I will
merely list each one with a brief explanation and then let the cumula-
tive effect be felt. They are all found in the one verse, 12:20.
(1) Contentions: a synonym for quarreling, from the Greek word
Eris, the goddess of discord. The emphasis was on strife rising out
of a party spirit. (2) Jealousy: the twin word for strife. In the Greek
it literally meant "zeal" and came to mean a zeal only for one's own
side. (3) Outbursts of wrath: not settled, permanent anger but the
anger of a short-fused person who blows up at the slightest provoca-
tion. (4) Selfish ambition: the background of the word describes a
self-seeking political candidate who got into office by unfair means.
(5) Backbiting: speaking against another. (6) Whisperings: gossip.
(7) Conceits: to be swelled up or puffed up. (8) Tumults: disorder;
often used of political disturbances. It is easy to see that the thought

of showing up at the church in Corinth and finding this kind of a spirit would make anyone anxious.

With these words Paul closes his very lengthy defense of his Apostleship in a most effective way. In chapter 13 he will try to get the church ready for his visit.

CHAPTER THIRTEEN

A Warning and a Blessing

2 Corinthians 13:1–14

As we come now to the end of Paul's correspondence with the church at Corinth, I find myself both exhausted and blessed. The weariness comes not from the length of the letters or from the time spent studying them; rather, it comes both from assuming the burden of the church as it struggles to be Christian in a pagan world and from the anxiety of Paul as he attempts to guide them in God's will.

I have read and taught from the Corinthian correspondence for years, but the study connected with this writing has deepened my conviction of the relevance of these letters to individual Christians and to congregations who seek to be God's people in an increasingly secular age. I feel that as I have participated with Paul and the church in their struggle that the words he wrote to them have become God's word to me.

In closing this last chapter of a letter that is often stern and sometimes severe, Paul does not use a "form" ending and just tack it on to this very individualized and personal letter. He reissues the warning about his proposed visit (vv. 1–3), pleads with them to examine themselves and to change (vv. 4–10), and closes with a blessing (vv. 11–14).

> 1 This will be the third time I am coming to you. *"By the mouth of two or three witnesses every word shall be established."*
>
> 2 I have told you before, and foretell as if I were present the second time, and now being absent I write

to those who have sinned before, and to all the rest, that if I come again I will not spare—

3 since you seek a proof of Christ speaking in me, who is not weak toward you, but mighty in you.

4 For though He was crucified in weakness, yet He lives by the power of God. For we also are weak in Him, but we shall live with Him by the power of God toward you.

5 Examine yourselves as to whether you are in the faith. Prove yourselves. Do you not know yourselves, that Jesus Christ is in you?—unless indeed you are disqualified.

6 But I trust that you will know that we are not disqualified.

7 Now I pray to God that you do no evil, not that we should appear approved, but that you should do what is honorable, though we may seem disqualified.

8 For we can do nothing against the truth, but for the truth.

9 For we are glad when we are weak and you are strong. And this also we pray, that you may be made complete.

10 Therefore I write these things being absent, lest being present I should use sharpness, according to the authority which the Lord has given me for edification and not for destruction.

11 Finally, brethren, farewell. Become complete. Be of good comfort, be of one mind, live in peace; and the God of love and peace will be with you.

12 Greet one another with a holy kiss.

13 All the saints greet you.

14 The grace of the Lord Jesus Christ, and the love of God, and the communion of the Holy Spirit be with you all. Amen.

2 Cor. 13:1–14

There is nothing new in what Paul says in this chapter. All of it can be found, sometimes more than once, in the main body of the letter. It is repeated here more as a reminder or a summary, in the same way a parent after a long telephone conversation with a son or daughter who is away in college will close the visit by saying, "Now don't forget that . . ."

These are the things Paul didn't want them to forget: First, he wanted them to remember his coming visit. This he had mentioned earlier (12:14). Second, he reminded them that he was endowed with power—not his own, but God's power working through him. Third, he would not be tolerant toward any who were guilty of sin. And while he doesn't mention who these guilty persons are, he is probably referring to the false apostles and those gullible people who had been taken in by them. He wanted them to know that he had the power to deal with the problem and that when he came he wouldn't be afraid to use it. It was showdown time, and as painful as the thought was, Paul intended to face his foes and deal with the problem.

But we also find in the close Paul's characteristic effort at reconciliation. For him the ministry of reconciliation was more than a message to be preached, it was a style of life. He had no desire to exercise power merely as a show of strength or form. Rather, he makes it clear that he would prefer they examine themselves and handle their own problems (13:5). And there is the hint in Paul's statement that their examination and criticism of him was wrong.

Even today the average congregation feels it can solve most of its problems by getting a new preacher. And the church in Corinth was launching a long tradition by being critical of Paul in order to solve their own problems. Primarily, though, I believe that Paul was expressing his confidence in the fact that people can change, and he was urging them to use his impending visit as an impetus to change. As stern as Paul could be at times, I'm convinced he was always more of a lover than fighter and that his invitation to self-examination and change is his way of saying that he would prefer to come with gentleness rather than sharpness.

Following his custom, Paul closes the letter with a benediction, but this one reflects in its content the gist of the letter (13:11). By using the term *"brethren"* he puts his arms around the entire congregation, and then he makes three requests of them and gives them a promise.

"Become complete" is more than a general call for them to journey toward wholeness. It is also a call for them to mend their ways and to make up their deficiencies.

"Be of good comfort" more literally means "be exhorted" or "heed my appeal." He also urges them to agree with one another, or *"live in peace."* He assures them that even the contentious party spirit will

be overcome if they heed his three requests, for then the *"God of love and peace"* will rule in their hearts.

As a teenage boy who was just discovering girls, I was fascinated with the verse in which Paul called upon the Corinthians to *"greet one another with a holy kiss"* (13:12). I was quite disappointed when I learned that in the synagogue, which is where this custom came from, the men and women sat in different places and the men kissed men and the women kissed women. Paul was not suggesting that this holy kiss be done as an empty gesture but as a sign of agreement, a symbol of the love Christ had given them for each other.

Long before the church developed the formal doctrine of the Trinity, the Apostle Paul was using the three Persons of the Trinity in his benedictions. He said goodbye with a prayer for the presence in the lives of the Corinthians of the grace that finds its source in Christ, and the love that God inspires, and the partnership of life that the Holy Spirit creates (13:14). Even in his final word Paul is issuing a call to a celebration of the life that is "in Christ."

Bibliography

Baird, William. *1 Corinthians, 2 Corinthians.* Knox Preaching Guides. Atlanta: John Knox Press, 1980.

Baird, William. *The Corinthian Church—A Biblical Approach to Urban Culture.* New York: Abingdon Press, 1964.

Barclay, William. *The Letters to the Corinthians.* Philadelphia: Westminster Press, 1956.

Barrett, C. K. *The First Epistle to the Corinthians.* Harper's New Testament Commentaries. New York: Harper & Row, 1968.

_____. *The Second Epistle to the Corinthians.* Harper's New Testament Commentaries. New York: Harper & Row, 1968.

Beazley-Murray, G. R. *2 Corinthians–Philemon.* Broadman Bible Commentary, vol. 11. Nashville: Broadman Press, 1971.

Blair, J. Allen. *1 Corinthians: Devotional Studies on Living Wisely.* Neptune, N.J.: Loizeaux Brothers, 1969.

Brown, Raymond Bryon. *1 Corinthians.* Broadman Bible Commentary, vol. 10. Nashville: Broadman Press, 1970.

_____. *2 Corinthians.* Broadman Bible Commentary, vol. 11. Nashville: Broadman Press, 1970.

Bruce, F. F. *1 and 2 Corinthians.* New Century Bible. Greenwood, S.C.: Attic Press Inc., 1976.

Carson, Donald A. *From Triumphalism to Maturity: An Exposition of 2 Corinthians 10–13.* Grand Rapids: Baker Book House, 1984.

Craig, Clarence T., and Short, John. *First Corinthians.* The Interpreter's Bible, vol. 10. New York: Abingdon-Cokesbury Press, 1953.

Erdman, Charles R. *The First Epistle of Paul to the Corinthians.* Philadelphia: Westminster Press, 1929.

_____. *The Second Epistle of Paul to the Corinthians.* Philadelphia: Westminster Press, 1929.

Fisher, Fred. *Commentary on 1 and 2 Corinthians.* Waco, Texas: Word Books, 1981.

George, David. *2 Corinthians, Galatians, Ephesians.* Layman's Bible Commentary, vol. 21. Nashville: Broadman Press, 1979.

Grosheide, F. W. *Commentary on the First Epistle to the Corinthians.* Grand Rapids: Wm. B. Eerdmans, 1962.

Hering, Jean. *The First Epistle of Saint Paul to the Corinthians.* London: Epworth Press, 1962.

Hodge, Charles. *Commentary on the First Epistle to the Corinthians.* Grand Rapids: Wm. B. Eerdmans, 1976.

Hughes, Philip E. *Commentary on the Second Epistle to the Corinthians.* New International Commentary on the New Testament. Grand Rapids: Wm. B. Eerdmans, 1962.

MacGorman, J. W. *Romans, 1 Corinthians.* Layman's Bible Commentary, vol. 20. Nashville: Broadman Press, 1980.

Martin, Ralph P. *The Spirit and the Congregation: Studies in 1 Corinthians 12–15.* Grand Rapids: Wm. B. Eerdmans, 1984.

Moffatt, James. *The First Epistle of Paul to the Corinthians.* Moffatt New Testament Commentary. New York: Harper and Brothers Publishers, n.d.

Morris, Leon. *The First Epistle of Paul to the Corinthians.* Tyndale New Testament Commentaries. Grand Rapids: Wm. B. Eerdmans, 1958.

Orr, William F., and Wuether, James Arthur. *1 Corinthians.* Anchor Bible. Garden City, N.Y.: Doubleday & Co., 1976.

Redpath, Alan. *Blessings Out of Buffetings: Studies in Second Corinthians.* Old Tappan, N.J.: Fleming H. Revell, 1965.

_____. *The Royal Route to Heaven: Studies in First Corinthians.* Old Tappan, N.J.: Fleming H. Revell, 1960.

Robertson, Archibald, and Plummer, Alfred. *A Critical and Exegetical Commentary on the First Epistle of St. Paul to the Corinthians.* International Critical Commentary. Edinburgh: T. & T. Clark, 1914.

Stedman, Ray C. *Expository Studies in I Corinthians: The Deep Things of God.* Waco, Texas: Word Books, 1981.

Thrall, Margaret E. *The First and Second Letters of Paul to the Corinthians.* Cambridge Bible Commentary. Cambridge: University Press, 1965.

Wagner, Peter C. *A Turned-On Church in an Uptight World.* Grand Rapids: Zondervan Publishing House, 1971.